The Essence of
Mathematics for Business

\WN

The Essence of Management Series

The Essence of Marketing
The Essence of Marketing Research
The Essence of Industrial Marketing
The Essence of International Marketing
The Essence of Services Marketing
The Essence of Financial Accounting
The Essence of Management Accounting
The Essence of Financial Management
The Essence of International Money
The Essence of Mergers and Acquisitions
The Essence of Organizational Behaviour
The Essence of Industrial Relations and Personnel Management
The Essence of Women in Management
The Essence of the Economy
The Essence of International Business
The Essence of Personal Microcomputing
The Essence of Information Systems
The Essence of Operations Management
The Essence of Strategic Management
The Essence of Business Law
The Essence of Entrepreneurship and New Ventures
The Essence of Venture Capital and Buy-outs
The Essence of Small Business
The Essence of Successful Staff Selection
The Essence of Effective Communication
The Essence of Statistics for Business
The Essence of Business Economics
The Essence of Mathematics for Business
The Essence of Total Quality Management
The Essence of Business Taxation

The Essence of Mathematics for Business

H. A. Spooner and D. A. L. Wilson
Aston Business School, Aston University

Prentice Hall

New York   London   Toronto   Sydney   Tokyo   Singapore

First published 1991 by
Prentice Hall Europe
Campus 400, Maylands Avenue, Hemel Hempstead,
Hertfordshire HP2 7EZ
A division of
Simon & Schuster International Group

Typeset in 10/12pt Palatino
by Keyset Composition, Colchester, Essex

Printed and bound in Great Britain by
Redwood Books, Trowbridge, Wiltshire

Library of Congress Cataloging-in-Publication Data

Spooner, H. A. (H. Ann)
    The essence of mathematics for business / by H. A. Spooner and
D. A. L. Wilson.
        p.   cm. — (The Essence of management series)
    Includes index.
    ISBN 0-13-284886-4
    1. Business mathematics.   I. Wilson, D. A. L. (David A. L.)
II. Title.   III. Series.
HF5691.S64   1991
650'.01513 — dc20   91-14996
                                                                         CIP

British Library Cataloguing in Publication Data

Spooner, H. A.
    The essence of mathematics for business.
    — (The essence of management)
    I. Title   II. Wilson, D. A. L.   III. Series
    650.01

    ISBN 0-13-284886-4

---

5   6   7   8   9   00   99   98   97   96

Contents

Contents

Contents

Contents

Preface

Mathematics provides some of the most important tools for modern management – but many managers find mathematics baffling, and so they never come to appreciate its relevance to their problems. Some of them will have closed their minds to the subject while they were still at school, convinced that they could never make any headway with it. Others will have progressed further, but allowed what they had learnt to become rusty through lack of use.

This book is a sympathetic response to the needs of all those who approach mathematics with dread, but realize that they have got to get to grips with it at last. Their objective is usually twofold:

1. to obtain the skills which are needed to achieve their MBA or other qualification;
2. to obtain the confidence to talk sensibly about problems that are formulated in mathematical terms.

It is usually a great morale booster to realize that the second objective can be achieved, but this can only be done by putting aside all preconceived ideas of the inherent difficulty of mathematics and realizing that the great attraction of the subject is that it is logical and consistent, and that quite powerful methods can be developed from simple basic rules. In this respect, mathematics is really no different from any other structured discipline, say music or law or language.

With this readership in mind, we have assumed very few prerequisites – virtually nothing apart from some knowledge of simple arithmetic and the ownership of a good medium-priced scientific calculator. Starting with a firm foundation and slowly building a basic framework of knowledge, the reader will be able to go on to benefit from more advanced texts on the applications of mathematics in management subjects. This book is intended to be an introductory text; we hope that our readers will go on to consult other authors who may develop the ideas which we have introduced in different ways, using different notations, so we have purposely tried to convey the idea of *flexibility in notation but consistency in reasoning*.

The early chapters introduce the basic ideas of algebra, taking the reader through varied examples of algebraic reasoning and numerical work to be done on the calculator. Simple applications of these ideas to management problems are introduced from Chapter 1 and the range of applications expands as the book progresses. We feel that it is important for the reader to develop a feel for problem formulation as well as a facility for manipulating numbers and formulae. Numerous fully worked examples are included in the text and additional examples are given at the end of each chapter (with answers at the end of the book). Some applications run on from chapter to chapter, being developed further as more advanced techniques are introduced.

In the final chapter we discuss general matters concerning the application of mathematics in a business context, including some advice on how to formulate and solve real-life problems. We emphasize that a manager cannot avoid the need to understand something about mathematics by thinking that mathematical problems can simply be entrusted to an expert. Such experts need to be briefed and their findings need to be interpreted, so all parties must be able to communicate in the common language of mathematics.

This text is designed either to be used for individual study or as the basis of a course with lectures and tutorials. Our experience is that classes requiring this sort of course include people with widely different perceptions of the difficulties of each of the topics that we have included. Because of this, we do not recommend how long should be spent on each topic. We simply say: 'Take it at your own pace, and don't panic!'

Ann Spooner
David Wilson

1

Elementary algebra

Introduction

The main aim in any application of mathematics is to formulate and solve problems. To do this it is essential to have the correct tools. Basic algebra is one such tool. A proficiency in manipulating algebraic expressions makes the understanding and solution of mathematically expressed problems much easier. This chapter starts from 'square one' and no prior knowledge is assumed. Readers already proficient in the use of algebra should skip to Chapter 3. The examples at the end of the chapter have been graded in order of difficulty. Working through them should provide a reasonable level of familiarity with algebraic notation and the ability to use an algebraic approach to the formulation and solution of problems.

1.1 Algebraic expressions and equations

The definitions of algebraic expressions and equations are best illustrated by means of examples. Simple examples have been used in this section; more complicated examples will appear in the later chapters.

Example 1.1
If a profit of £5 is made on every unit of a certain product that is sold, the profit (in £) on two units is 5×2, the profit on three units is 5×3,

and so on. If we wish to generalize this kind of statement, we introduce a letter to denote the number of units sold. Any letter may be used; in this case we shall call the number of units sold n.

The profit on n units sold will then be $5 \times n$. The n is called a *variable* and the constant 5 is its *coefficient*.

The expression $5 \times n$ could also have been written as $5.n$. The dot between the 5 and n signifies multiplication. Where there is no ambiguity the multiplication sign is omitted altogether. In this case the expression would be written as $5n$. (In computer programming the asterisk symbol * is used to denote multiplication. Similarly the symbol / is used instead of ÷ to denote division.)

The gross profit on sales depends upon the number of units sold, which we called the variable n, and is said to be a *function* of the variable n. We may write this as

$f(n) = 5n.$

A function can be denoted by any letter; in this case the letter f has been chosen. The variable(s) upon which the value of the function depends are listed within brackets after the letter.

In Example 1.1 above, if no units are sold ($n = 0$) there is no loss to the company. However, in practice there are usually some fixed overhead costs such as rates and rent to be covered. Let us suppose that the overheads are £50, so that £50 has to be deducted from the value of any sales in order to calculate the profit. Working in pounds sterling, the new relationship between profit and number of units sold is

net profit $= 5 \times$ (no. of units sold) $- 50$

or.

$F(n) = 5n - 50.$

The notation $f(n)$ was used for the gross profit, so the slightly different notation, $F(n)$, is used for the net profit.

In order to break even (make zero net profit), we must have a value of n which satisfies the *equation*

$0 = 5n - 50$ or $50 = 5n.$

The *solution* to this is $n = 50/5 = 10$. In other words, with a profit of £5 on each unit ten units must be sold in order to cover the cost of the overheads; more than ten units sold will result in an actual net profit.

Terms such as $5n - 50$ are referred to as *algebraic expressions*. When the expression is set equal to a particular value it is called an *algebraic equation* or simply an equation.

The use of symbols such as n, $f(n)$ and $F(n)$ to represent quantities that may take various values enables us to simplify and manipulate relationships such as those between profit and numbers of units sold in our examples above. This becomes especially useful when the relationships are more complicated.

In the same way as firms are distinguished by using distinct trading names, algebraic functions which differ even to the smallest extent must have different names because they represent different expressions. Thus gross profit and net profit have different meanings in practice which are reflected by their different algebraic 'names', $f(n)$ and $F(n)$.

1.2 The addition and subtraction of algebraic forms

Example 1.2
If a pencil costs x pence and two pencils are purchased they cost $2x$ pence. If a further three pencils are purchased they cost an additional $3x$ pence. In all, five pencils have been bought at a total cost of $5x$ pence. The total cost could have been obtained as the sum

$2x + 3x = 5x$ pence.

Example 1.3
If ten pencils are bought at a cost of x pence each and then four pencils are returned and their cost refunded, the total expenditure on pencils is the cost of six pencils which is $6x$ pence. This could be written as the difference between the cost of the initial purchase and the refund, that is

$10x - 4x = 6x$ pence.

Rule 1.1: Collecting up identical terms

Terms where the letters are *exactly* the same may be simplified or 'collected up' by adding and subtracting the coefficients as specified.

Example 1.4
Simplify the expression

$12x + 6x - 3x + 4x - 2x.$

Solution
First check that all of the terms in the expression contain only the variable x. Since this is true, Rule 1.1 applies.

The sum of the coefficients of x is $12 + 6 - 3 + 4 - 2 = 17$. Therefore the answer is

$$12x + 6x - 3x + 4x - 2x = 17x.$$

Example 1.5
If five pencils were bought at a cost of x pence each and three pens were bought at a cost of y pence each, the total purchase cost would be $5x + 3y$. This cannot be simplified further since the costs x and y are different variables relating to different items.

Rule 1.2: Collecting up different terms

Algebraic terms in an equation may only be added or subtracted if they have *exactly* the same configuration of variables.

Example 1.6
Simplify the expression

$$5y + 3z + 6y + 4z.$$

Solution
First collect up the terms involving y to give $5y + 6y = 11y$.
Next collect up the terms in z to give $3z + 4z = 7z$.
The answer is

$$5y + 3z + 6y + 4z = 11y + 7z.$$

Example 1.7
Simplify the expression

$$11a + 7b - 6a - 4b.$$

Solution
Collect up the terms in a and then the terms in b to give the answer

$$11a + 7b - 6a - 4b = 5a + 3b.$$

Rule 1.3: Multiplication of variables

The term xy means 'variable x times variable y'. Terms containing xy must be collected up separately from the 'x' terms and the 'y' terms.

Example 1.8
In a particular transaction, n items are sold. The profit on each item varies with currency fluctuations. The profit in pounds sterling per item might be called p. The total profit per transaction is then £np. The individual variables, n, the number of items sold per transaction, and p, the profit per item at that date, clearly have a different meaning from the term np, which expresses the total profit per transaction in pounds sterling.

Example 1.9
Simplify the expression

$$2d + 5w + 4wd + 4w + 2h - 6d + 7wd.$$

Solution
Collect up the terms in d; these are

$$2d - 6d = -4d.$$

Next collect up the terms in w; these are

$$5w + 4w = 9w.$$

Next collect up the terms in wd; these are

$$4wd + 7wd = 11wd.$$

The answer is then

$$-4d + 9w + 11wd + 2h.$$

Note the result

$$2d - 6d = -4d.$$

Rule 1.4: Positive and negative terms

The general rule for combining positive and negative terms is to subtract the smallest term from the largest term and give the result the sign of the largest term.

Thus $120 - 200 = -80$.

If your revenue was £120 and your expenses £200 you would be in debt to the tune of £80. In other words, your balance would be −£80.

Note
In mathematics a loss or negative quantity is indicated by the use of the minus sign and *never* by the use of brackets as in accounting.

1.3 Products of positive and negative real numbers

Let a and b denote any positive real numbers. Then:

$$(+a) \times (+b) = +ab; \qquad (+a) \times (-b) = -ab;$$
$$(-a) \times (-b) = +ab; \qquad (-a) \times (+b) = -ab.$$

It is usually easier to remember these rules in terms of words as follows:

Plus times plus   = plus

Plus times minus = minus

Minus times plus = minus

Minus times minus= plus.

If there is no sign attached to a particular term it is understood to be positive.

In some cases it helps to clarify where the signs should go if brackets are used to indicate precisely the term to which the sign is attached.

Example 1.10

$$2 \times 3 = (+2) \times (+3) = 6 \qquad\qquad (-2) \times (-3) = 6$$
$$2 \times (-3) = -6 \qquad\qquad\qquad (-2) \times 3 = -6.$$

Example 1.11

$$2 \times 3 \times 4 = 24 \qquad\qquad (-2) \times 3 \times 4 = -24$$
$$(-2)(-3) \times 4 = 24 \qquad\qquad (-2)(-3)(-4) = -24.$$

Note the use of the brackets to define the negative numbers. When several quantities are multiplied together mistakes with the signs can often be avoided by using brackets in this way. An odd number of minus signs multiplied together give a negative result, while an even number of terms with minus signs multiplied together give a positive result. If an incorrect solution to a problem is obtained it is always worth checking the signs of the constituent terms since this is one of the most common sources of error.

Rule 1.5: The balancing of equations

If numbers or algebraic terms are transferred from one side of an equals sign to the other then their signs are changed. For example, $5 - 3 = 2$, hence $5 = 2 + 3$ or $5 - 3 - 2 = 0$.

This is analogous to 'balancing the books' in accounting. Any operation or change to one side of an equation must be balanced by an equivalent operation to the other side of the equation. The idea of maintaining the balance of an equation continues in more complicated circumstances. In general if an operation is carried out on one side of an equation the same operation must be carried out on the other side. For instance, if one side is multiplied by the factor 10 to convert decimal coefficients to whole numbers the other side would also be multiplied by 10.

Example 1.12
Solve the equation

$$7x - 20 = 2x.$$

Solution
Collect up the terms in x on one side of the equals sign and the constant terms (those with numbers only) on the other side of the equals sign.

$$7x - 2x = 20$$
$$5x = 20 \quad \text{(using Rule 1.1)}$$
$$x = 20/5 \quad \text{(dividing both sides by 5)}$$
$$x = 4 \quad \text{(simplifying the right-hand side).}$$

Check the result by substituting 4 for x in the original equation:

$$7 \times 4 - 20 = 2 \times 4, \quad \text{i.e. } 28 - 20 = 8,$$

which is correct.

1.4 Expansion of bracketed terms

To expand a bracket, each term inside the bracket is operated on in turn by the term outside the bracket. For every simple algebraic operation there is an arithmetic equivalent. When in doubt, try the operation with easy numbers for which you know the answer and then use the same method for the algebraic example.

Example 1.13

We could write $2 \times 10 = 20$ as

$$2 \times (7 + 3) = 2 \times 7 + 2 \times 3 = 14 + 6$$
$$= 20.$$

If we write x instead of 7 then $7 + 3$ becomes $x + 3$ and 2×7 becomes $2x$ as in Example 1.14.

Example 1.14

$$2(x + 3) = 2x + 2 \times 3 = 2x + 6.$$

Example 1.15

$$a(a + 3) = a \times a + 3a = a^2 + 3a.$$

The term a^2 means $a \times a$.

Example 1.16

$$\frac{a + 3}{2} = \frac{1}{2} \times (a + 3) = \frac{a}{2} + \frac{3}{2}.$$

This type of function is one where newcomers to algebra sometimes make mistakes. Remember that every term in the numerator (top line) is divided by the term in the denominator (bottom line).

Example 1.17

$$\frac{a + 3}{a + 2} = \frac{a}{a + 2} + \frac{3}{a + 2}.$$

Example 1.18

Expand the brackets

$$(20 + 1)(30 - 2).$$

Solution

Multiply each term in the second bracket by 20 and then each term in the second bracket by 1 to give:

$$(20 + 1)(30 - 2) = 20(30 - 2) + 1(30 - 2)$$
$$= 20 \times 30 + 20 \times (-2) + 1 \times 30 + 1 \times (-2)$$
$$= 600 - 40 + 30 - 2$$
$$= 588.$$

Check the result by multiplying 21 by 28 on your calculator.

Example 1.19

Expand the brackets in the expression

$$(a + 2)(a + 3).$$

Solution

$$(a + 2)(a + 3) = a(a + 3) + 2(a + 3)$$
$$= a \times a + 3a + 2a + 2 \times 3$$
$$= a^2 + 5a + 6,$$

using Rule 1.2 in the last step to collect up the terms $3a$ and $2a$. Remember that $a \times a$ is written as a^2.

The answer can be checked by substituting an easy numerical value for the variable a. For example, let $a = 4$, since this is small and differs from the constant value in the expression.

Then the left-hand side of the equation is

$$(a + 3)(a + 2) = (4 + 3)(4 + 2)$$
$$= \quad 7 \times 6$$
$$= 42.$$

The right-hand side of the equation is then

$$a^2 + 5a + 6 = 4 \times 4 + 5 \times 4 + 6$$
$$= 42,$$

which equals the left-hand side.

These algebraic principles can be useful for performing multiplication when a calculator is not available. For example:

$$98 \times 4 = (100 - 2) \times 4 = 400 - 8 = 392;$$

$$19 \times 21 = (20 - 1)(20 + 1) = 400 - 20 + 20 - 1 = 399.$$

The following general forms are useful.

$$a(b + c) = ab + ac$$

$$\frac{(a + b)}{c} = \frac{a}{c} + \frac{b}{c}$$

$$(a + b)(c + d) = ac + ad + bc + bd$$

$$(a + b)(c - d) = ac - ad + bc - bd.$$

Exercise
Try out each one of these forms by substituting $a = 2, b = 3, c = 4$ and $d = 5$. In each of the given equations, substitute the numbers for each letter and show that the expressions on each side of the equals sign give the same value. Repeat the procedure with values of a, b, c and d of your own choice.

1.5 Fractions

Dealing with algebraic fractions is the same as dealing with arithmetic fractions. The terminology is the same in both cases.

For the fraction $\dfrac{a}{b}$, the quantity a is the *numerator*,
the quantity b is the *denominator*.

The methods used in the following examples can be extended to the addition or subtraction of more than two fractions.

Example 1.20
Evaluate

$$\frac{2}{3} + \frac{5}{4}.$$

Elementary algebra

Solution
The first step is to find the *lowest common denominator* between the denominators 3 and 4. This is the smallest number into which both denominators can be divided. In this example the lowest common denominator (LCD) is 12, since 3 is a factor of 12 and 4 is a factor of 12.

$$\frac{2}{3}+\frac{5}{4}=\frac{2\times4}{3\times4}+\frac{5\times3}{3\times4}$$

$$=\frac{2\times4+5\times3}{3\times4}$$

$$=\frac{23}{12}.$$

It is more usual to go directly to the second line of the answer, but if in doubt write out the answer in full as specified above.

Example 1.21
Simplify

$$\frac{2}{(x+3)}+\frac{5}{(x+4)}.$$

Solution

$$\frac{2}{(x+3)}+\frac{5}{(x+4)}=\frac{2(x+4)}{(x+3)(x+4)}+\frac{5(x+3)}{(x+3)(x+4)}$$

$$=\frac{2(x+4)+5(x+3)}{(x+3)(x+4)}.$$

It is customary to simplify the numerator of the right-hand side of the equation but leave the denominator in brackets. In this example the answer may be written as

$$\frac{2}{(x+3)}+\frac{5}{(x+4)}=\frac{2x+8+5x+15}{(x+3)(x+4)}=\frac{7x+23}{(x+3)(x+4)}.$$

Example 1.22
Evaluate 2/3 + 5/9. (Note the oblique strokes to indicate division.)

Solution

$$\frac{2}{3}+\frac{5}{9}=\frac{2\times3+5\times1}{3\times3}=\frac{11}{9}.$$

Example 1.23
Simplify

$$\frac{2}{(x+3)}+\frac{5}{(x+3)^2}, \text{ where } (x+3)^2 \text{ means } (x+3)(x+3).$$

Solution

$$\frac{2}{(x+3)}+\frac{5}{(x+3)^2}=\frac{2(x+3)+5\times1}{(x+3)(x+3)}=\frac{2x+6+5}{(x+3)^2}=\frac{2x+11}{(x+3)^2}.$$

Example 1.24
Simplify

$$\frac{2x}{(x+3)}-\frac{5y}{(x+y)}.$$

Solution

$$\frac{2x}{(x+3)}-\frac{5y}{(x+y)}=\frac{2x(x+y)-5y(x+3)}{(x+3)(x+y)}$$

$$=\frac{2xx+2xy-5xy-15y}{(x+3)(8x+y)}$$

$$=\frac{2x^2-3xy-15y}{(x+3)(x+y)}.$$

Remember that $x^2 = xx$ means 'x times x'.

Example 1.25
Simplify

$$\frac{3a}{(a+1)}+\frac{2}{(a-3)}-\frac{5}{a}.$$

Solution

$$\frac{3a}{(a+1)} + \frac{2}{(a-3)} - \frac{5}{a} = \frac{3a(a-3)a + 2(a+1)a - 5(a+1)(a-3)}{(a+1)(a-3)a}$$

$$= \frac{3aaa - 9aa + 2aa + 2a - 5(aa + a - 3a - 3)}{(a+1)(a-3)a}$$

$$= \frac{3aaa - 9aa + 2aa + 2a - 5aa - 5a + 15a + 15}{(a+1)(a-3)a}$$

$$= \frac{3aaa - 12aa + 12a + 15}{(a+1)(a-3)a}.$$

Clearly, writing *aaa* for '*a* times *a* times *a*' is cumbersome. If the variable *a* were multiplied by itself many more times it would be impossible to see easily how many multiples were involved. It is necessary, therefore, to have some notation for dealing with such situations. This is done by extending the notation we have already used in writing a^2 for $a \times a$. The numbers used as superscripts are called either *exponents* or *powers*.

1.6 Exponents

Instead of writing $a \times a$ we normally use the notation a^2, which is read as '*a* squared' or '*a* to the power of two'. Similarly $a \times a \times a$ is written a^3, which is read as '*a* cubed' or '*a* to the power of three'.

For any positive integer n, a^n, read as '*a* to the power of n', denotes the product of n terms, each equal to a. In this expression, a is called the *base* and n is called the *exponent* or *power* of a. We may also use fractional or negative exponents.

Note the following two special cases which are frequently used and should be remembered:

1. that $a^1 = a$; the exponent or power 1 is rarely written explicitly but is understood;
2. for any variable a, $a^0 = 1$, no matter what value a takes. (See Rule 1.9 below.)

Quantities involving powers (exponents) can be evaluated using a calculator. It is a good idea to work through some simple examples where the results can be found by using mental arithmetic and then to apply the same method to more complicated examples.

On most calculators the keys used are marked x^y which is read as 'the value x raised to the power y' or $x^{1/y}$ which is read as 'x to the power $1/y$' or the 'yth root of x'.

The general procedure for raising any value x to the power y is as follows.

Enter x on the display

Press x^y

Enter y

Press =

The result will then appear in the display.

The exponent, y, can be expressed either as an integer (whole number), a decimal or a fraction. There are two ways of dealing with fractions. The method chosen depends upon the type of calculator available. (See Examples 1.32 and 1.33.) Negative values of y (Example 1.36) are dealt with in a similar fashion.

Example 1.26
Evaluate 2^3.

Enter 2 on the display

Press x^y

Enter 3

Press =

The result 8 will then appear in the display.
Since $2^3 = 2 \times 2 \times 2 = 8$ we know that the answer is correct.

Example 1.27
Use the procedure described above to confirm that $3^4 = 81$.
Using mental arithmetic, $3^4 = 3 \times 3 \times 3 \times 3 = 9 \times 9 = 81$.

Example 1.28
Simplify $2^2 \times 2^3$.

Solution

$$2^2 = 2 \times 2 \qquad 2^3 = 2 \times 2 \times 2$$

$$2^2 \times 2^3 = (2 \times 2) \times (2 \times 2 \times 2) = 2^5.$$

Check: $2^2 \times 2^3 = 4 \times 8 = 32$.

If the base 2 is replaced by a, the exponent 2 is replaced by m and the exponent 3 by n, then the example above can be expressed as a general rule.

Rule 1.6

To multiply quantities represented by the same base with different exponents, simply add the exponents.

$a^m \times a^n = a^{m+n}$.

Example 1.29

$a^2 \times a^3 = a^{2+3} = a^5$.

Putting $a = 2$ in Example 1.28 gives an answer of 2^5. Thus Example 1.28 is a special case of this more general example.

Example 1.30
Simplify $(2^3)^2$.

Solution

$$(2^3)^2 \text{ means } (2^3) \times (2^3) = (2 \times 2 \times 2) \times (2 \times 2 \times 2)$$
$$= 2^6.$$

The example above can be translated into a general rule by replacing the base 2 by a, the exponent 3 by m and the exponent 2 by n.

Rule 1.7

To raise a term involving an exponent to a power, multiply the exponent by the power.

$(a^m)^n = a^{mn}$.

Example 1.31

$(a^2)^3 = a^{2\times3} = a^6$.

Example 1.30 is a special case, with $a = 2$, of this more general example.

Evaluating the *n*th root

In Example 1.27 the value of $3^4 = 81$ was found. If we had wanted to reverse this process and find the fourth root of 81 we would have written this as $81^{1/4}$.

In general the *n*th root of some quantity, *a*, is written as $a^{1/n}$.

The *square root* of *a* is denoted by $a^{1/2}$ or $\sqrt[2]{a}$ or simply $\sqrt{}$. This is the number which, when squared, equals *a*.

The *cube root* of *a* is denoted by $a^{1/3}$ or $\sqrt[3]{a}$. This is the number which, when cubed, equals *a*.

The *fourth root* of *a* is written as $a^{1/4}$ or $\sqrt[4]{a}$. This is the number which, when multiplied together four times, equals *a*.

Since the power 1/2 or the square root is commonly used, on most calculators there is a square root key marked $\sqrt{}$. For exponents of 1/2 it is easier to use this key; for other fractional exponents the method illustrated below must be used.

There are two easy ways of finding the fourth root of 81 using a calculator.

Example 1.32

Evaluate $\sqrt[4]{81}$ which may also be written as $81^{1/4}$.

Method 1   If your calculator has an $x^{1/y}$ key this is the easiest method.

Enter 81

Press $x^{1/y}$

Enter 4

Press =

The answer 3 is shown in the display.

Method 2   Convert the fraction 1/4 to the decimal 0.25 and use the x^y key.

Enter 81

Press x^y

Enter 0.25

Press =

The answer 3 is shown in the display.

Thus 3 is the fourth root of 81. This means that if 3 is multiplied by itself four times the value 81 is obtained. This can be explained by using Rule 1.7.

Start with $3^4 = 81$. Remembering that any operation on one side of an equation must also be carried out on the other side in order to maintain the balance of the equation, we take the fourth root of both sides:

$$(3^4)^{1/4} = (81)^{1/4},$$

$$3^{4 \times 1/4} = 3^1 = 3 = 81^{1/4}.$$

Example 1.33
Evaluate $(3^2)^{1/2}$.

Solution
Use Rule 1.7:

$$(3^2)^{1/2} = 3^{2 \times 1/2} = 3^1 = 3.$$

Rule 1.8

For different bases with the same exponent, note the following:

$$a^n b^n = (ab)^n; \qquad a^n/b^n = (a/b)^n.$$

Example 1.34
Use a calculator to confirm that

$$(0.7)^2 \times (1.5)^2 = (1.05)^2.$$

Solution
Evaluate the left-hand side first: $(0.7)^2 = 0.49$ and $(1.5)^2 = 2.25$. The product of these two is $0.49 \times 2.25 = 1.1025$ and this gives the value of the left-hand side.

Next evaluate the right-hand side: $1.05^2 = 1.1025$. Thus

$$(0.7)^2 \times (1.5)^2 = (1.05)^2.$$

Example 1.35
Use a calculator to confirm that

$$\frac{2^4}{8^4} = \left(\frac{2}{8}\right)^4.$$

Solution
Evaluate 2^4 and 8^4; then divide the one by the other to obtain the value of the left-hand side of the equation. Evaluate 2/8 and raise the answer to the power 4 to obtain the right-hand side of the equation.

Rule 1.9

Any quantity raised to the power 0 takes the value 1. It is most important to remember this rule since it is frequently used.

1.7 Negative exponents

A negative exponent indicates division. The term

$$a^{-1} \text{ means } \frac{1}{a}; \quad a^{-2} \text{ means } \frac{1}{a^2}; \quad a^{-3} \text{ means } \frac{1}{a^3}; \quad a^{-n} \text{ means } \frac{1}{a^n}.$$

Thus, using Rule 1.6 with $m = 1$ and $n = -1$,

$$a \times \frac{1}{a} = a^1 \times a^{-1} = a^{1-1} = a^0$$

and, using Rule 1.9,

$$a^0 = 1.$$

Example 1.36
Use a calculator to show that

$$\frac{1}{2^3} = 2^{-3}.$$

Solution
Evaluate the left-hand side first: $2^3 = 8$ and $1/8 = 0.125$. Next evaluate the right-hand side. Quantities involving negative powers can be evaluated using the following procedure:

Enter 2

Press x^y

Enter 3

Press the $+/-$ key to change the sign to minus

Press $=$

Then $2^{-3} = 0.125$ appears in the display, proving the equality.

All of the rules stated for positive exponents apply equally to negative exponents.

Example 1.37

$$\frac{a^2}{a} = \frac{a \times a}{a} = a^2 \times a^{-1} = a.$$

Example 1.38

$$\frac{a^6}{a^2} = a^6 \times \frac{1}{a^2} = a^6 \times a^{-2} = a^4.$$

1.8 Cancelling out terms

Consider the ratio

$$\frac{12}{4}.$$

The numerator can be written as the multiple of the factors 4 and 3. Thus the ratio can be written as

$$\frac{4 \times 3}{4} = 3,$$

since the factor of 4 in the numerator cancels out the factor of 4 in the denominator.

The same process of cancelling out terms can be used in algebraic expressions. Thus

$$\frac{a \cdot b}{a} = b.$$

Example 1.39
Simplify the expressions

(i) $\frac{a^2 b}{a}$ and (ii) $\frac{a^4}{a^3}.$

Solution

(i) $\dfrac{a^2b}{a} = \dfrac{a.a.b}{a} = a.b.$

(ii) Use Rule 1.6 here to write $a^4 = a^3 \times a^1$, then

$$\dfrac{a^4}{a^3} = \dfrac{a^3.a}{a^3} = a.$$

The common factors can be cancelled out in more complicated expressions.

Example 1.40
Simplify the expression $(ab + a^2b)/a$.

Solution

$$(ab + a^2b)/a = \dfrac{ab + a^2b}{a} = \dfrac{ab}{a} + \dfrac{a^2b}{a} = b + ab.$$

This result could be further simplified by factorization to give $b(1 + a)$.

1.9   The order and hierarchy of operations

Where ordinary numbers or variables are multiplied together, the order in which this is carried out is immaterial to the answer. Thus

$$2 \times 4 = 4 \times 2$$

and

$$a \times b = b \times a$$

and

$$b \times (1 + a) = (1 + a) \times b, \text{ etc.}$$

The only commonly used instance where the order in which the variables are written affects the result is that where *matrices* are multiplied together. This is explained in Chapter 6.

There is a universally accepted order for carrying out the operations of addition, subtraction, multiplication and division. The mnemonic BODMAS for Brackets, Of, Divide, Multiply, Add, Subtract is useful for remembering the order of operations; the meaning is indicated below:

1. Brackets: Evaluate the contents of any brackets first.
2. Of: Calculate any proportions (or percentages) such as a quarter (or 25%) of any amount.
3. Divide: Carry out division next.
4. Multiply: Carry out multiplication next.
5. Add: Add next.
6. Subtract: Subtract next.

Example 1.41
Evaluate

$$\frac{1}{4} \times (2 + 6 \times 4) + \frac{126}{5} - 12.4.$$

Solution
Using the BODMAS mnemonic, evaluate the contents of the bracket first:

$$(2 + 6 \times 4).$$

Within the bracket the hierarchy is applied: multiply first, then add to give the bracket contents as

$$2 + 24 = 26.$$

The problem is now

$$\frac{1}{4} \times 26 + \frac{126}{5} - 12.4.$$

Now work out 1/4 of 26, then divide 126 by 5 to give

$$6.5 + 25.2 - 12.4.$$

Then add

$$31.7 - 12.4$$

and subtract to give the answer

$$19.3.$$

Hence

$$\frac{1}{4} \times (2 + 6 \times 4) + \frac{126}{5} - 12.4 = 19.3.$$

1.10 Factorization

If an algebraic expression can be written as a product of other (smaller) expressions, then these are called its *factors*. Examples are given at the end of this chapter which illustrate the usefulness of factorization; it is also used in the next chapter in solving equations. The principle of factorization can be demonstrated numerically.

Example 1.42
Consider the sum $3 + 12 = 3 + 3 \times 4 = 3(1 + 4)$.

The 3 is a factor of both the first term and the second term. Since it is a factor of both terms, it can be taken as a factor outside the bracket. Numerically $3(1 + 4) = 15$ which is the same as $3 + 12$.

Factorizing in this way sometimes makes mental arithmetic calculations easier. If, for example, we wished to calculate 3×39 this could be done by taking $3 \times 40 - 3$ which is $3(40 - 1)$.

The factorizing of algebraic expressions is carried out in a similar fashion.

Example 1.43
Factorize the expression $b + ab$.

Solution
There is a common factor of b which can be taken outside the bracket. Thus

$$b + ab = 1 \times b + ab = (1 + a)b.$$

This could have been written as $b(1 + a)$. Try substituting $b = 2$ and $a = 3$ in $(1 + a)b$ and in $b(1 + a)$ to convince yourself that this is true.

Example 1.44
Factorize the expression $6a + 3ab$.

Solution
Newcomers to algebra will find it is best to work systematically, considering the numerical coefficients first and then each variable in turn.

There is a common factor of 3 to be taken outside the bracket:

$$6a + 3ab = 3 \times 2a + 3ab = 3(2a + ab).$$

Inside the bracket there is a common factor of *a* which can be taken outside the bracket:

$$6a + 3ab = 3a(2 + b).$$

Always check the answer by multiplying out the bracket to confirm that you get the same expression as that given initially.

Example 1.45
Factorize the expression $x^2y + xy^2$.

Solution
There is a common factor of *x* which can be taken outside the bracket:

$$x^2y + xy^2 = x.x.y + x.y.y = x(x.y + y.y).$$

There is a common factor of *y* which can be taken outside the bracket:

$$x^2y + xy^2 = x(xy + yy) = xy(x + y).$$

Example 1.46
Factorize the expression $ac + bc + ad + bd$.

Solution
In this case there are no factors common to all four terms in the expression. Try factorizing the terms in pairs:

$$(ac + bc) + (ad + bd).$$

The first pair of terms has a common factor of *c*; the second pair has a common factor of *d*:

$$(ac + bc) + (ad + bd) = c(a + b) + d(a + b).$$

There is now a common factor of $(a + b)$ in both terms; this common factor can be taken outside the bracket:

$$ac + bc + ad + bd = (a + b)(c + d).$$

The same result could have been obtained by pairing the first with the third term and the second with the fourth term:

$$(ac + ad) + (bc + bd) = a(c + d) + b(c + d)$$
$$= (c + d)(a + b) = (a + b)(c + d).$$

Example 1.47
Factorize the expression $ac - bc - ad + bd$.

Solution
Either: Pair the terms in c and d as indicated:

$$(ac - bc) - ad + bd = c(a - b) - d(a - b) = (a - b)(c - d).$$

Or: Pair the terms in a and b as indicated:

$$(ac - ad) - bc + bd = a(c - d) - b(c - d) = (a - b)(c - d).$$

Note that

$$-(a - b) = -a + b \quad \text{and} \quad -(c - d) = -c + d$$
$$= b - a \qquad\qquad = d - c.$$

Thus $(a - b)(c - d)$ is the same as $(b - a)(d - c)$, since $[-(a - c)][-(c - d)] = +(a - b)(c - d)$.

The terms in a summation may be written in any order, but it is usual to write positive terms first in a final result. Thus $a + b = b + a$ and $a - b = -b + a$. Remember that if there is no sign attached to a term then that term is assumed to be positive.

Example 1.48
Factorize the expression $ax - 3 + a - 3x$.

Solution

$$a(x + 1) - 3(x + 1) = (x + 1)(a - 3).$$

Some expressions can be factorized by grouping terms and then noticing common factors, as demonstrated in Examples 1.46, 1.47 and 1.48. Other expressions may be factorized by trial and error, but there are some which cannot be factorized at all.

Useful standard forms are as follows.

STANDARD FORM 1.1
$$(x + a)(x - b) = x^2 + (a + b)x + ab$$

and

STANDARD FORM 1.2
$$(rx + a)(sx + b) = rsx^2 + (as + br)x + ab.$$

If the coefficient of x^2 is 1 then Standard Form 1.1 is used; if the coefficient of $x^2 \neq 1$ then Standard Form 1.2 is used. (The symbol $\neq$ means 'not equal to'.) These standard forms can be used to help factorize expressions of the type given on the right-hand sides of the equations.

Example 1.49
Factorize the expression

$$f(x) = x^2 + 7x + 10.$$

Solution
Since the coefficient of x^2 is 1, compare the expression above with Standard Form 1.1.

Compare $x^2 + (a + b)x + ab = (x + a)(x + b)$

with $x^2 +$ $7x + 10.$

Comparing the coefficients in both expressions it can be seen that

   $ab = 10$ and $a + b = 7.$

The integer factors of 10 are 5×2 and 10×1. The most obvious possible pairs of values for a and b are

   $a = 2, b = 5,$ or $a = 10, b = 1.$

Try each pair in turn in the equation $a + b = 7$. It can be seen that the only pair of values which satisfies this equation is $a = 2, b = 5$.
   The expression therefore factorizes to

   $x^2 + 7x + 10 = (x + 2)(x + 5).$

Note
In this case it does not matter if the values are reversed and $a = 5, b = 2$ are used since the coefficient of x^2 is 1. In Example 1.51 where the coefficient of $x^2 \neq 1$ the values of a and b cannot be interchanged.

Example 1.50
Factorize the expression

$$f(x) = x^2 + x - 12.$$

Solution
Compare the expression with Standard Form 1.1.

Compare x^2 $+$ $(a + b)x + ab$

with x^2 $+ 1x - 12.$

Thus $ab = -12$ and $a + b = 1$.

Since ab is negative and we know from Section 1.3 that 'minus times a plus = minus' either a or b must be negative. The possible pairs of integer values for a and b are

$a = 6, b = -2$ or $a = -6, b = 2$

or $a = 3, b = -4$ or $a = -3, b = 4$

or $a = 1, b = -12$ or $a = -1, b = 12$.

Try each of the pairs in turn in the equation $a + b = 1$.
For the first two pairs

$6 - 2 \neq 1$ and $-6 + 2 \neq 1$.

For the second two pairs

$3 - 4 \neq 1$ but $4 - 3 = 1$.

Thus the correct values are $a = 4, b = -3$ and the expression factorizes as

$x^2 + x - 12 = (x + 4)(x - 3)$.

Always check the result by reversing the process and multiplying out the brackets to confirm that you arrive back at the initial expression.

Example 1.51
Factorize the expression

$f(x) = 3x^2 + 10x + 8$.

Solution
Since the coefficient of x^2 is not equal to 1, use Standard Form 1.2.

Compare $\quad rsx^2 + (as + br)x + ab = (rx + a)(sx + b)$

with $\quad\quad\quad 3x^2 + \quad\quad 10x + \quad 8$.

Thus $\quad\quad rs = 3, \quad as + br = 10, \quad ab = 8$.

Possible integer values are

$(r = 3, s = 1);\quad (a = 2, b = 4);$
$(r = 1, s = 3);\quad (a = 4, b = 2);$
$\quad\quad\quad\quad\quad\quad (a = 8, b = 1);$
$\quad\quad\quad\quad\quad\quad (a = 1, b = 8)$.

The problem now is to find pairs of values for r and s with a and b which satisfy the equation $as + br = 10$.

Try $(r = 3, s = 1)$ with $(a = 2, b = 4)$:

$$as + br = 2 \times 1 + 4 \times 3 \neq 10.$$

Try $(r = 1, s = 3)$ with $(a = 2, b = 4)$:

$$as + br = 2 \times 3 + 4 \times 1 = 10$$

which is correct.
The expression factorizes as

$$3x^2 + 10x + 8 = (x + 2)(3x + 4).$$

Check the result by multiplying out the brackets on the right-hand side of the equation.

1.11 Degree of an expression

Taking x as a typical variable, an expression involving only a constant and x (possibly with a constant coefficient) is said to be 'of first degree' or 'linear' in x.

An expression involving x^2 and lower powers of x is said to be 'of second degree' or 'quadratic' in x.

An expression involving x^3 is said to be 'of third degree' or 'cubic', and so on.

Example 1.52
The expression $f(x) = 3x + 2$ is of degree 1 or *linear*.

Example 1.53
The expression $f(x) = 2x^2 + 3x - 2$ is of degree 2. An expression of degree 2 is called a *quadratic* expression.

Example 1.54
The expression $f(x) = x^3 + x^2 + 4x - 1$ is of degree 3 and referred to as a *cubic* expression.

Example 1.55
The expression $f(x) = 2x^5 + x^4 + x - 9$ is of degree 5.

The difference of two squares

If the expression to be factorized is the difference between two perfect squares it can be written as in Standard Form 1.3 given below.

> STANDARD FORM 1.3 $a^2 - b^2 = (a - b)(a + b)$.

The factors in this case are always of the form given on the right-hand side of Standard Form 1.3.

Example 1.56

Factorize the expression

$$f(x) = 9x^2 - 49.$$

Solution

Compare the expression with Standard Form 1.3 for the difference between two squares.

Compare $a^2 - b^2 = (a - b)(a + b)$

with $9x^2 - 49$.

It can be seen that $a^2 = 9x^2$,   so that $a = 3x$,

and $b^2 = 49$,   so that $b = 7$.

The expression factorizes as

$$9x^2 - 49 = (3x - 7)(3x + 7).$$

Check the result by multiplying out the brackets on the right-hand side of the equation.

1.12   Perfect squares

If a quadratic expression can be expressed as the product of two identical linear factors then it is said to be 'a perfect square'. The standard form used for factorizing a quadratic expression into a perfect square is as follows.

> STANDARD FORM 1.4 $a^2 + 2ab + b^2 = (a + b)^2$.

It is therefore the perfect square of the factor $(a + b)$.

Example 1.57
Factorize the expression

$$9x^2 + 12x + 4.$$

Solution
The first and last terms in the expression are the squares of $3x$ and 2 respectively. The middle term is twice the product of $3x$ times 2. Compare the expression with the general form of the perfect square.

Compare $\qquad a^2 + 2ab + b^2 = (a + b)^2$

with $\qquad\qquad 9x^2 + 12x + 4.$

Thus $a = 3x$ and $b = 2$; $2ab = 2 \times 3x \times 2 = 12x.$

The expression factorizes into

$$9x^2 + 12x + 4 = (3x + 2)^2$$

and so it is a perfect square.

1.13 Applications

Compound interest
The value, S_n, at the end of n time periods of an initial sum or 'principal', P, is found by using the formula

$$S_n = P(1 + i)^n,$$

where i is the rate of interest per time period and the interest is compounded over the n time periods (see Chapter 4 for the explanation of this formula). In Example 1.58 to 1.60 we show how this general formula may be used in different ways according to what information we are given and what we are required to find.

Example 1.58
If Mr Brown invests £1000 in a savings account at a rate of 8% per annum compound interest what will be the value of the investment if he leaves it untouched for a period of:

(i) 1 year,
(ii) 5 years?

Solution

The value after n years can be found by applying the formula

$$S_n = P(1+i)^n.$$

In this example $P = £1000$ and $i = 0.08$, thus

$$S_n = 1000(1+0.08)^n = 1000(1.08)^n.$$

(i) To find the value after 1 year put $n = 1$ in the formula above:

$$S_1 = 1000 \times 1.08 = 1080.$$

After 1 year the value of the investment will have risen to £1080.
(ii) To find the value after 5 years put $n = 5$ in the formula:

$$S_5 = 1000(1.08)^5 = 1000 \times 1.4693 = 1469.33.$$

After 5 years the value of the original investment of £1000 will have risen to £1469.33.

Example 1.59

In 1975 Mrs Smith invested £350 in the shares of a retail company. Twelve years later she sold the shares for £1500. Ignoring the dealing costs for buying and selling the shares, what has been the annual compound rate of increase of the capital value of the shares over this 12 year period?

Solution

In this example we have $n = 12$ years, $P = £350$, $S_{12} = £1500$. Putting these values into the formula gives

$$1500 = 350(1+i)^{12}.$$

The problem now is to solve the equation for i. The first step is to divide both sides of the equation by 350 to give

$$\frac{1500}{350} = (1+i)^{12}.$$

Thus

$$(1+i)^{12} = 4.2857.$$

Remember that $(1+i) = (1+i)^1$ and evaluate this using Rule 1.7. Starting with

$$(1+i)^{12} = 4.2857,$$

if we operate with the exponent 1/12 on the left-hand side of the equation we must do the same with the right-hand side in order to retain the balance of the equation. Thus

$$[(1 + i)^{12}]^{1/12} = [4.2857]^{1/12} = 4.2857^{0.0833}.$$

Hence $\quad (1 + i) = 1.1289$

and $\quad\quad\quad i = 0.1289.$

There has been an annual rise of 12.89% in the capital value of the shares over the 12 year period.

This value of i could have been obtained by using *logarithms*; this method is explained in Chapter 5.

The compound interest formula can be rearranged to read

$$P = S_n/(1 + i)^n.$$

In this form it can be used to determine P for given values of n, i and S_n, in other words to determine the amount of money which must be invested now in order to realize a sum of S_n pounds in n years' time, given that the interest rate is $100 \times i\%$ per annum.

Example 1.60
Mr Jones plans to retire in 10 years' time. He has calculated that he needs a capital sum of £50 000 when he retires. If the rate of interest offered on a particular investment remains at 9% per annum over the next 10 years and the interest is reinvested in the same investment each year, what sum must Mr Jones invest now in order to realize the capital sum of £50 000 in 10 years' time?

Solution
The compound interest formula is

$$S_n = P(1 + i)^n.$$

In this case we have $n = 10$, $S_{10} = £50\,000$ and $i = 0.09$. Putting these values into the formula gives

$$50\,000 = P(1 + 0.09)^{10}$$

$$50\,000 = P(1.09)^{10}.$$

Evaluate $(1.09)^{10} = 2.3674$ using the x^y key.

Thus $\quad 50\,000 = P \times 2.3674$

and $\quad\quad\quad P = 50\,000/2.3674 = 21\,120.54.$

If Mr Jones invests £21 120.54 now at 9% per annum interest he will have £50 000 in 10 years' time.

ADDITIONAL EXAMPLES

A1.1 Simplify the following expressions by collecting like terms.

(i) $7x - 3x + 10x - 5x$
(ii) $18a + 13 - 9a + 5a - 3$
(iii) $5u - 6v + 8u - 2uv + 4v + uv.$

A1.2 Expand the following expressions by multiplying out the terms in brackets; then simplify by collecting like terms.

(i) $(3a + 2b)(a - 7b)$
(ii) $(x + 2y)(x^2 + 3xy + y^2).$

A1.3 Solve the following equations.

(i) $7x + 5 - 3x = 20x + 15$

(ii) $\dfrac{(x + 3)(2x - 7)}{(x + 3)} = 5.$

A1.4 Find the lowest common denominator and simplify the following expression.

$$\frac{5}{x - 7} + \frac{8}{x + 3}.$$

A1.5 Evaluate the following quantities, using a calculator where necessary.

(i) $2^2 \times 2^6$ (ii) $2^8/2^2$ (iii) $2^8 \times 2^{-2}$
(iv) $3^2 \times 3^{1/2}$ (v) $5^{1/3}$ (vi) $3^2 \times 3^{1/2} \times 5^{1/3}.$

A1.6 Use a calculator to evaluate the following (correct to four decimal places).

(i) 2^7 (ii) $(-4)^3$ (iii) $(2/7)^{-2}$
(iv) $2^{1/6}$ (v) $\sqrt{(7^3)}$ (vi) $81^{-0.5}.$

A1.7 Simplify the following expressions

(i) $\dfrac{a^8}{a^6}$ (ii) $a^8 . a^{-2}$

(iii) $b^{1/2} . b^2$ (iv) $\dfrac{c^2}{c^{1/2}}$

(v) $\left(\dfrac{c^2}{c^{1/2}}\right)^2$ (vi) $c^2 . c^{1/2} . d^{1/3}.$

A1.8 Simplify the following expressions and factorize them (where applicable).

(i) $7x + 5x + 12$

(ii) $7x + 5x + 12x^2$

(iii) $3xy + 6y$

(iv) $3x^2 y + 6xy$

(v) $7xy + 5xy + 12x^2 y$

(vi) $\dfrac{7xy + 5x^2 y^2 + 2x^2 y}{xy}$.

A1.9 Reduce the following expressions to their simplest forms.

(i) $3a + b + 2a - 4b$

(ii) $2a + 4ab + 3a^2 + ab$

(iii) $a^2(3a + 4b + 2a)$

(iv) $\dfrac{(3a^3 + 4a^2 + a)}{a}$.

(v) $(b^3)^{1/2}$

(vi) $2a^2 + 2a + 3a^2 + 4a^4$.

A1.10 Evaluate the expressions in Question A1.9 for $a = 2$ and $b = 3$.

A1.11 Expand the brackets in the expressions given below.

(i) $(x + 2)(x + 4)$

(ii) $(x + 2)^2$

(iii) $(x + 1)(x - 1)$

(iv) $(x + a)(x + b)(x + c)$

(v) $(x + a)^2(x + b)$

(vi) $(x - 2)^3$.

A1.12 Factorize the following expressions.

(i) $12a^2 b - 24ab^2$

(ii) $8x^2 y^3 + 16x^3 y^2 + 4x^2 y^2$

(iii) $a^2 + ab + ac + bc$

(iv) $2cx + dx - 2x^2 - cd$

(v) $x^2 - 8x + 15$

(vi) $6x^2 + x - 5$

(vii) $5 - 23x - 10x^2$

(viii) $5a^2 - 4ab - 9b^2$

(ix) $49x^2 - 9$

(x) $8x^2 - 32y^2$

(xi) $x^2 + 8x + 16$

(xii) $4x^2 + 4x + 1$.

A1.13 Electric light switches are manufactured in batches that each contain q switches. The cost (in £) of producing a batch is a function of q, denoted by $C(q)$, which is defined by

$$C(q) = 150 + 3.5q.$$

Find the quantity of switches that will result in a batch manufacturing cost of £500.

A1.14 The net profit (in £) from selling *N* garden sheds is reckoned to be

$P(N) = 25N - 60.$

How many sheds must be sold in order to break even at least (i.e. not make a loss)?

A1.15 Suppose that your house is now worth £100 000 and that its value will rise according to the compound interest formula (Examples 1.58 and 1.59) at an annual rate of 7%. What would be the value of the house after 3 years?

2

Solving equations

Introduction

Many problems can be described in the form of a *mathematical model* or *formula*. Once the physical problem has been formulated in algebraic terms, the attention of the analyst is turned to specific aspects of the more general problem. For example, if the model relating profit to sales revenue has been formulated, one point of interest is the level of sales required to break even, that is the exact point where the profit changes from being negative to being positive. This level is found by setting the revenue value equal to zero and solving the resulting equation. In most cases, algebraic operations of the type described in Chapter 1 are carried out in order to arrive at the simplest form of the relevant model, and then the equation is solved.

The type of solution sought depends to a large extent upon the nature of the problem. If the input data available is imprecise, there is no point in calculating a solution correct to several decimal places, since the accuracy of the solution cannot be greater than the accuracy of the input data. In many such cases, a graphical solution is adequate and has the advantage of being easier to obtain than an analytical or algebraic solution. In some 'real-life' problems, the equations to be solved are so complex that a solution can be found only by using a computer and the techniques of computational mathematics. In such cases, special computer packages are often available to provide solutions to particular types of problem.

2.1   Drawing graphs

There are several ways of defining coordinates: the most frequently used are called *cartesian coordinates*. Two axes are drawn at right angles to each other and the location of each point is defined by reference to its position relative to each axis, in much the same way as longitude and latitude locate a geographical point. If the variable y is expressed as a function of the variable x, that is $y = f(x)$, then it is usual to use the horizontal axis as the x-axis and the vertical axis as the y-axis. The axes cross at the point where $x = 0$ and $y = 0$; this point is called the *origin*. By convention, when we list the coordinates of a point, the value relating to the horizontal axis is always written first and that relating to the vertical axis is written second, so the origin is the point ($x = 0$, $y = 0$) – usually written simply as (0, 0). We shall restrict ourselves to problems involving only two axes, although more axes can be used.

2.2   Straight-line or linear functions

If y is a *straight-line* or *linear* function of x, then the function of x contains only values of x and constants. To draw any graph of y against x, the value of y for each value of x must be found and then the points plotted on the graph. To draw a straight line, only two points need be calculated; these points are then joined using a ruler and the line can then be extended in either direction in order to draw the graph for all the values of x and y which are of interest. For other curves which are not straight lines (non-linear in mathematical jargon), many more points are needed in order to draw the graph accurately.

Consider the linear function

$y = x.$

Putting $x = 0$ in the expression gives $y = 0$, so this line passes through the origin. Remember that the origin is the point ($x = 0$, $y = 0$). When $x = 6$, putting this value into the equation gives $y = 6$. Since y is a linear function of x, we only need to join the two points ($x = 0$, $y = 0$) and ($x = 6$, $y = 6$) with the aid of a ruler in order to draw the graph. The graph of the function is given in Figure 2.1(a). It can be seen that an increase of one unit in the value of x produces an increase of one unit in the value of y. Any two points on the line could have been used to draw the graph. Try substituting other values of x into the function to convince yourself that all of the points lie on the same straight line.

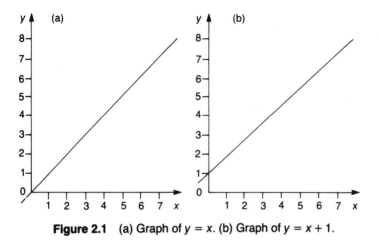

Figure 2.1   (a) Graph of y = x. (b) Graph of y = x + 1.

Now consider the function

$$y = 2x.$$

Since there is no constant term in the expression, this line also passes through the origin because when $x = 0$ we find that $y = 2 \times 0 = 0$. When $x = 5$, then $y = 2 \times 5 = 10$; using the convention x-value first and y-value second, this point is written as (5, 10). The points (0, 0) and

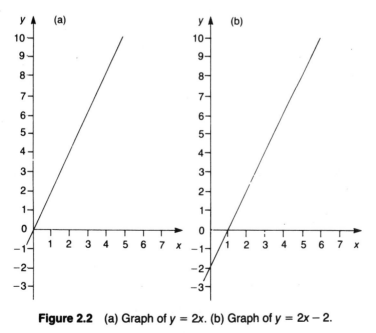

Figure 2.2   (a) Graph of y = 2x. (b) Graph of y = 2x − 2.

37

(5, 10) are joined to produce the graph in Figure 2.2(a). It can be seen that an increase of one unit in x produces an increase of two units in y, which is the slope of the line. The *slope of the line* for a straight-line equation is the coefficient of x.

The introduction of a constant into the equation has no effect upon the slope; it simply moves the curve up if the constant is positive or down if the constant is negative.

Consider the function

$$y = x + 1.$$

The graph of y against x is given in Figure 2.1(b). Compare this with the graph of the function $y = x$ in Figure 2.1(a). The slope is the same as before since the coefficient of x is 1 in both graphs, but in Figure 2.1(b) each value of y is one unit higher than the values in Figure 2.1(a). When $x = 0$, then $y = 1$ and the line does not pass through the origin. The point where the line crosses the y-axis is called the *intercept*, that is the value of y when $x = 0$. In this case the slope is 1 and the intercept is 1. In the case when $x = 6$, we find that $y = 6 + 1 = 7$, one unit greater than the corresponding value for the function $y = x$ which we considered above.

Consider now the function

$$y = 2x - 2.$$

Substituting $x = 0$ into the equation gives the value $y = -2$ when $x = 0$. Substituting $x = 5$ into the equation, we find $y = 2 \times 5 - 2 = 8$. The slope is the same as that in Figure 2.2(a) but the whole line has been moved two units down the graph. The intercept is -2 and the slope is $+2$.

A *negative coefficient of x* means that y decreases as x increases.

Consider the function

$$y = -2x + 8.$$

When $x = 0$ then $y = 8$. When $x = 4$ then $y = -2 \times 4 + 8 = 0$.

An increase of one unit in x produces a decrease of two units in y. The graph is given in Figure 2.3. The slope is -2 and the intercept is $+8$.

The general form of the linear equation can be written in various ways. The most usual are:

$$y = ax + b, \quad \text{where } a \text{ and } b \text{ are constants};$$

$$y = mx + c, \quad \text{where } m \text{ and } c \text{ are constants};$$

$$\text{and } y = \beta_0 + \beta_1 x, \quad \text{as used in regression analysis.}$$

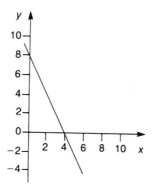

Figure 2.3 Graph of $y = -2x + 8$.

We shall use Standard Form 2.1,

> STANDARD FORM 2.1 $\quad y = ax + b$

where a and b may be positive or negative.

Here a is the slope of the line and b is the intercept (the value of y where $x = 0$ and the line crosses the y-axis). A positive value of the coefficient of x means that an increase in x causes an increase in y; a negative value of the coefficient of x means that an increase in x causes a decrease in y.

2.3 Quadratic functions

Quadratic functions contain only terms in x^2, x and constants. The corresponding curves are always ∪ shaped or ∩ shaped. This type of curve is known as a *parabola* and is symmetric. Nearly every commonly used curve has a standard form. In the case of the quadratic curve this is

> STANDARD FORM 2.2 $\quad y = ax^2 + bx + c$

where it is understood that each of the coefficients a, b and c may be either positive or negative.

Example 2.1
Consider the function

$$y = x^2 - 6x + 8.$$

To plot the graph the value of y is calculated for various values of x. If you are not very sure about using a calculator then work out each term on the right-hand side separately and then add the terms to obtain the value of y. The graph is shown in Figure 2.4.

The curve in Figure 2.4 is symmetric about the line $x = 3$ and crosses the x-axis twice at the points ($x = 2$, $y = 0$) and ($x = 4$, $y = 0$). The values $x = 2$ and $x = 4$ are solutions to the equation

$$x^2 - 6x + 8 = 0,$$

since $y = 0$ when $x = 2$, and $y = 0$ when $x = 4$.

If the characteristic of interest for this function was the smallest value of y, it would be advisable to draw a more detailed graph on a larger scale, with more points calculated and plotted between, say, $x = 1.5$ and $x = 4.5$. The curve changes direction from y decreasing as x increases to y increasing as x increases; that is, the slope of the curve changes from being negative to positive when x is equal to some value near 3. The precise point where this change in direction takes place is called the *minimum value* of y or simply the *minimum*.

x	x^2	$-6x$	$+8$	y
0	0	0	+8	8.0
0.5	0.25	-3.0	+8	5.25
1.0	1.0	-6.0	+8	3.0
1.5	2.25	-9.0	+8	1.25
2.0	4.0	-12.0	+8	0.0
2.5	6.25	-15.0	+8	-0.75
3.0	9.0	-18.0	+8	-1.0
3.5	12.25	-21.0	+8	-0.75
4.0	16.0	-24.0	+8	0.0
4.5	20.25	-27.0	+8	1.25
5.0	25.0	-30.0	+8	3.0

Figure 2.4 Graph of $y = x^2 - 6x + 8$.

2.4 Cubic functions

The standard form of the cubic function is usually written as

STANDARD FORM 2.3 $\quad y = ax^3 + bx^2 + cx + d.$

As with the quadratic curve, each of the coefficients a, b, c and d may be either positive or negative.

A cubic function may have two turning points or have a point of inflexion. A turning point, as the name suggests, is a point on the graph where the value of y reaches a peak (*maximum*) or trough (*minimum*). A *point of inflexion* is a point on the graph where the curve flattens out and then continues in the same upward (or downward) direction as before.

Example 2.2
Consider the cubic function

$$y = x^3 + x^2 - 0.25x - 0.25.$$

First draw the graph of y against x. Since this function is fairly complicated it is easier to calculate the value of y for each x-value in stages. The components of y are given in the column headings and then summed across each row to give y for that value of x.

	Column number				
x	(1) x^3	(2) x^2	(3) $-0.25x$	(4) -0.25	y
−1.5	−3.375	2.25	+0.375	−0.25	−1.00
−1.25	−1.9531	1.5625	+0.3125	−0.25	−0.3281
−1.0	−1.0	1.0	+0.25	−0.25	0.00
−0.75	−0.4219	0.5625	+0.1875	−0.25	0.0781
−0.5	−0.125	0.25	+0.125	−0.25	0.00
−0.25	−0.0156	0.0625	+0.0625	−0.25	−0.1406
0.0	0.0	0.0	0.0	−0.25	−0.25
0.25	0.0156	0.0625	−0.0625	−0.25	−0.2344
0.5	0.125	0.25	−0.125	−0.25	0.00
0.75	0.4219	0.5625	−0.1875	−0.25	0.5469
1.0	1.0	1.0	−0.25	−0.25	1.50

The values in the y column are the sum of columns (1) to (4).

Wherever the curve crosses the x-axis (Figure 2.5), the value of y is zero. In this case, the curve crosses the x-axis in three places: at $x = -1.0$, $x = -0.5$, $x = +0.5$.

Since $y = 0$ at these points, these three values of x are the solutions to the equation

$$x^3 + x^2 - 0.25x - 0.25 = 0.$$

These solutions are also referred to as the *roots* of the equation. There is a maximum at approximately $x = -0.75$, $y = 0.0781$ and a minimum at approximately $x = 0$, $y = -0.25$. These points are also known as *stationary points*, since the slope of the curve is zero at these points. If the graph had been drawn on a larger scale, the values of the stationary points could have been found more precisely. An alternative would have been to use the methods of *calculus*, as explained later, or a numerical procedure to achieve greater accuracy.

Example 2.3

Consider the function

$$y = \tfrac{1}{2}x^3 - 3x^2 + 6x + 5.$$

The same method as that used in Example 2.2 was employed to calculate the y-values. The curve crosses the x-axis in only one place, at about $x = -0.625$. The value of y increases steadily from $y = -23.0$, when $x = -2.0$, to approximately ($x = 2.0$, $y = 9.0$) when the curve is horizontal; then y continues to increase as x increases. The point ($x = 2.0$, $y = 9.0$), where the curve is horizontal, is a point of inflexion.

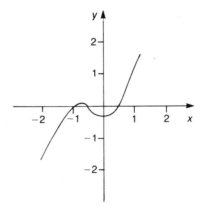

Figure 2.5   Graph of $y = x^3 + x^2 - 0.25x - 0.25$.

Since there is only one point where the curve crosses the *x*-axis it follows that there is only one real solution to the equation

$\frac{1}{2}x^3 - 3x^2 + 6x + 5 = 0.$

The graph is plotted in Figure 2.6.

2.5 Algebraic solution of equations

The algebraic solution of equations utilizes the methods of algebraic manipulation explained in Chapter 1. In every instance the answer can

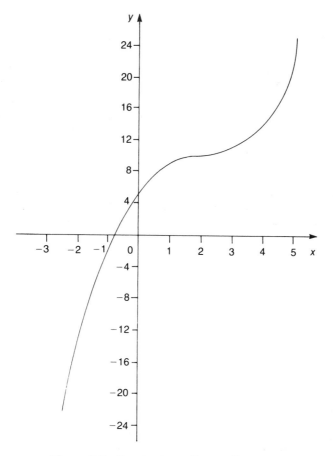

Figure 2.6 Graph of $y = x^3/2 - 3x^2 + 6x + 5$.

and should be checked by substituting the solution(s) obtained back into the *original* equation. If you substitute back into any equation obtained after a process of simplification, then any mistakes made during that simplification process will not be discovered.

Work carefully through the following examples, and then the exercises at the end of the chapter. Remember, also, that there are many ways of simplifying and solving an equation; if you use a different method which gives a correct solution, that will always be acceptable.

It is quite common to obtain a term in an expression which is some value multiplied by zero. In such cases the following rule applies.

Rule 2.1

Multiplying any value by zero gives a result of zero.

Think of receiving a tax rebate of exactly £0 each month for 3 months. At the end of 3 months the taxman will have given you £3 × 0, which is precisely zero. The same principle applies even if the term multiplied by zero is very complicated. It is used frequently in the following examples, where the result of multiplying a bracketed term by zero is zero.

2.6 Equations involving fractions

The solution of equations involving fractions utilizes the algebra of Section 1.5.

Example 2.4
Solve the equation

$$\frac{3}{(x+4)} + \frac{5}{(x+7)} = 0.$$

Solution
First simplify

$$\frac{3}{(x+4)} + \frac{5}{(x+7)}.$$

That is,

$$\frac{3}{(x+4)} + \frac{5}{(x+7)} = \frac{3(x+7)+5(x+4)}{(x+4)(x+7)}$$

$$= \frac{3x+21+5x+20}{(x+4)(x+7)}$$

$$= \frac{8x+41}{(x+4)(x+7)}.$$

Now solve the simplified equation

$$\frac{8x+41}{(x+4)(x+7)} = 0.$$

Multiply both sides of the equation by $(x+4)(x+7)$ to remove the fraction. The equation then becomes

$8x + 41 = 0 \times (x+4)(x+7)$

$8x + 41 = 0$ using Rule 2.1

$8x = -41$

$x = -5.125$ is the required solution.

If more than two fractions are involved, the method is the same as that illustrated above but with more cumbersome algebra.

2.7   Quadratic equations

Quadratic equations can sometimes be solved by factorizing the equation and then equating each bracketed term to zero.

Example 2.5
Solve the equation $x^2 - 6x + 8 = 0$.

Solution
Factorize the left-hand side of the equation into

$x^2 - 6x + 8 = (x-2)(x-4).$

then $(x-2)(x-4) = 0.$

This means that $(x - 2) = 0$ or $(x - 4) = 0.$

Thus $x = +2$ or $x = +4.$

The solution is $x = 2$ and $x = 4$.

The values $x = 2$ and $x = 4$ are also called the *roots* of the equation $x^2 - 6x + 8 = 0$. These roots were obtained graphically in Figure 2.3. Clearly in this example it is quicker to find the algebraic solution to the equation than to draw the graph of x against y and find the points where the curve crosses the x-axis. For cubic and higher-order equations it is usually easier to draw the curve unless a very precise solution is needed.

2.8   Formula for solving quadratic equations

The factors of quadratic expressions are not always obvious. When this is so, a standard formula is used to find the roots of the corresponding quadratic equation.

The standard form of the quadratic equation is written as

STANDARD FORM 2.4 $ax^2 + bx + c = 0$

where the coefficients a, b and c may be positive or negative.

The quadratic equation to be solved is compared with this standard form. The coefficients a, b and c are found by inspection and substituted into the equation given below to obtain the solution, or roots, of the equation.

The roots of this standard equation are

STANDARD FORM 2.5 $x = \dfrac{-b \pm \sqrt{b^2 - 4ac}}{2a}.$

That is, one root is obtained by using the plus sign before the square root term and the other by using the minus sign before the square root term. Written separately the roots would be

$$x = \frac{-b + \sqrt{b^2 - 4ac}}{2a} \quad \text{and} \quad x = \frac{-b - \sqrt{b^2 - 4ac}}{2a}$$

Example 2.6
Solve the equation $x^2 - 6x + 8 = 0$ using the standard formula defined above.

Solution
Compare $x^2 - 6x + 8 = 0$ with the standard form

$$ax^2 + bx + c = 0.$$

It can be seen by comparing the coefficients in both equations that $a = 1$, $b = -6$, $c = 8$. Substitute these values into the standard formula:

$$x = \frac{-(-6) \pm \sqrt{(-6)^2 - 4 \times 1 \times 8}}{2 \times 1},$$

$$x = \frac{+6 \pm \sqrt{4}}{2}.$$

The roots of the equation are

$$x = \frac{6+2}{2} = 4 \quad \text{and} \quad x = \frac{6-2}{2} = 2.$$

The solution should be checked by substituting back into the original equation, $x^2 - 6x + 8 = 0$.
Here:

check the first answer,
put $x = 4$: $\quad 4^2 - 6 \times 4 + 8 = 0 \quad$ correct,

and the second answer,
put $x = 2$: $\quad 2^2 - 6 \times 2 + 8 = 0 \quad$ correct.

Example 2.7
Solve the equation $x^2 + 1.1x - 3 = 0$.

Solution
Compare $x^2 + 1.1x - 3 = 0$ with the standard form

$$ax^2 + bx + c = 0.$$

It can be seen that $a = 1$, $b = 1.1$, $c = -3$. Substitute these values into the standard form,

$$x = \frac{-b \pm \sqrt{b^2 - 4ac}}{2a}.$$

This gives

$$x = \frac{-1.1 \pm \sqrt{1.1^2 - 4 \times 1 \times (-3)}}{2 \times 1}$$

$$= \frac{-1.1 \pm \sqrt{1.21 + 12}}{2} = \frac{-1.1 \pm \sqrt{13.21}}{2}$$

and finally

$$x = \frac{-1.1 \pm 3.634\,556}{2}.$$

The roots are then

$$x = \frac{-1.1 + 3.634\,556}{2} \quad \text{and} \quad x = \frac{-1.1 - 3.634\,556}{2},$$

i.e. $x = 1.267\,278$ and $x = -2.367\,278.$

The results can be checked by substituting these values of x in the equation

$$x^2 + 1.1x - 3 = 0.$$

It should now be clear that there is often more than one way of solving mathematical problems.

Note
Since the square root of a negative number involves imaginary values, real solutions will only exist if the term $b^2 - 4ac$ under the square root sign is positive, that is if $b^2 \geq 4ac$, where the symbol $\geq$ means 'greater than or equal to'. If the value of $b^2 - 4ac$ is negative this often indicates that a mistake has been made in formulating the problem.

2.9   Solution of cubic equations

Cubic equations formulated from most practical management applications have three solutions. Such an equation can be written as the multiple of three brackets. It is sometimes possible, if there are simple coefficients, to solve a cubic equation by factorizing directly into three bracketed terms. In other cases it may be possible to find one factor and then use the method shown below in Example 2.8 to reduce the cubic equation to that factor times a quadratic equation, which can then be solved using Standard Form 2.5 for the solution of quadratic equations. If you are defeated by these algebraic methods you can always fall back on the graphical method of solution. As long as the required degree of accuracy is obtained, it is of little consequence what method of solution is employed.

Example 2.8
Solve the equation $x^3 + 2x^2 - 5x - 6 = 0$.

Solution
Try the solution $x = -1$. Check that this is a solution by substituting $x = -1$ into the equation in the usual way:

$$(-1)^3 + 2(-1)^2 - 5(-1) - 6 = 0,$$

thus $x = -1$ is a root of the equation and $(x + 1)$ is a factor of the equation. The expression

$$f(x) = x^3 + 2x^2 - 5x - 6$$

can therefore be factorized into the form

$$f(x) = (x + 1) \times \text{(a quadratic expression)}.$$

By using the standard form of a quadratic equation, expanding the brackets and equating the coefficients, we can then find the quadratic factor:

$$f(x) = (x + 1)(ax^2 + bx + c) = x^3 + 2x^2 - 5x - 6$$
$$ax^3 + (a + b)x^2 + (b + c)x + c = x^3 + 2x^2 - 5x - 6.$$

Equating the coefficients of x^3, x^2 and the constant gives

$$a = 1, \quad c = -6, \quad a + b = 2.$$

Since $a = 1$ this gives $\quad b = 2 - a = 1.$

Substitute $a = 1$, $b = 1$ and $c = -6$ into the quadratic expression to give

$$(x + 1)(x^2 + x - 6) = 0,$$

where either $(x + 1) = 0$ or $(x^2 + x - 6) = 0.$
Consider now the quadratic equation

$$x^2 + x - 6 = 0.$$

This factorizes to $(x - 2)(x + 3) = 0$.

Thus $x - 2 = 0$ or $x + 3 = 0$

and $x = 2$ and $x = -3$.

The equation can now be written as

$(x + 1)(x - 2)(x + 3) = 0$.

The three roots of the cubic equation are

$x = -1, \quad x = 2, \quad x = -3$.

The solutions should be checked in the usual way.

Exercise
Draw the graph of the function

$$y = x^3 + 2x^2 - 5x - 6$$

and use it to confirm the solution obtained in Example 2.8 above.

2.10   Applications

Fixed and variable costs
Many mathematical models used in production planning involve the assumption that the total cost of producing a quantity q of some product is made up of two parts:

1. A *fixed cost*, sometimes called a set-up cost, which we may denote by s. This fixed cost is independent of the quantity q produced and includes items such as overheads, loan interest and rents which have to be paid even if nothing is produced.
2. A *variable cost*, which we may write as cq, where c is the unit cost, that is the cost per unit produced. The unit cost will include such items as the cost of material, the cost of manpower, etc.

Ignoring any other types of cost, the total cost of production, TC, may then be written as a straight-line or linear function of q:

$TC = s + cq$.

Example 2.9
Consider a product where the fixed cost is £28.00 and the unit cost is
£0.80. Find what quantity of production would correspond to a total
cost of £60.00.

Solution
Working in units of £1, we write

$$TC = 28 + 0.80q.$$

When $TC = 60$, we have $\qquad 60 = 28 + 0.80q.$

Rearranging gives $\qquad 0.8q = 60 - 28 = 32,$

and so $\qquad q = 32/0.8 = 40.$

Thus forty items will cost a total of £60 to produce.

Rates of demand and stock levels
The demand for any product controls the level of stock needed at any
particular time. Below are some simple models explaining how the
stock level might vary with time.

Let q denote the number of units of some product which are in stock
at time t, where t is measured in days. Suppose we start at time $t = 0$
with an initial stock level of q_0 units. If the rate of demand for the
product is r units per day, then after t days the total demand, D, will be
$D = rt$, that is the number of days times the rate of demand per day. If
all of this demand is to be met from existing stock, then after t days the
remaining stock will be the difference between the initial stock, q_0, and
the total demand, D, to date.

In mathematical terms this may be written as

$$q = q_0 - D$$

or $\quad q = q_0 - rt.$ $\hfill$ (2.1)

Equation (2.1) above is the mathematical model which describes this
particular stock situation.

We are usually interested in finding values of t which correspond to
given values of q. The values q_0 and r in this model are constant; such
constants in a model are referred to as *parameters of the model* or simply
parameters. Given the parameter values we can determine q for any
value of t using equation (2.1). To find t for any value of q we simply
need to rearrange equation (2.1).

Thus: $\qquad rt = q_0 - q,$

hence $\qquad t = (q_0 - q)/r.$

Example 2.10
Suppose that the initial stock is 500 units and the rate of demand is 30 units per day. If there is no replenishment of stocks, find how long the initial stock will last.

Solution
We are told that $q_0 = 500$ and $r = 30$.
We want to find the time t when the remaining stock q is zero. We already know that

$t = (q_0 - q)/r$.

Put $q_0 = 500$, $q = 0$ and $r = 30$ in the above equation:

$t = (500 - 0)/30 = 500/30 = 16.67$.

Hence the 500 units of stock will last for just under 17 days.

Example 2.11
Using the model in Example 2.10 above, a decision is made to reorder when the stock level is reduced to 50% of the initial stock. Find how many days will pass before it is necessary to reorder.

Solution
We have the same parameter values of $q_0 = 500$ and $r = 30$.
   We need to reorder when q is 50% of the initial value q_0, that is when $q = 250$ units. Put $q_0 = 500$, $q = 250$ and $r = 30$ in the model:

$t = (q_0 - q)/r$

$\quad = (500 - 250)/30$

$\quad = 250/30 = 8.33$.

Hence it is necessary to reorder in just over 8 days. Since the rate of demand is constant we could have obtained this value by realizing that we would reach a level of half the initial stock at a time which was half the time taken to reduce the stock to zero.

What happens if the demand is not constant?
It is likely that the rate of demand for a product will vary with time. For example, the rate might increase steadily with time, so that

$r = k + st,$ (2.2)

where s and k are both positive constants. When $t = 0$ the rate of demand is k. Thus k is the initial rate of demand and s is the daily increase in the rate of demand.

We started out with the model in equation (2.1)

$q = q_0 - rt.$

Now substitute for r in the above equation

$q = q_0 - (k + st)t$

and simplify the right-hand side.

$q = q_0 - kt - st^2.$

This is now a *quadratic* equation in the variable t.

Example 2.12
Suppose that the initial stock is still 500 units, as in Example 2.10 above, but that the rate of demand is now

$r = 30 + 5t,$

that is, we have $k = 30$ and $s = 5$.

Find how long it will take for the initial stock to be used up, assuming that there is no replenishment.

Solution
We need to find the value of t corresponding to a stock level of $q = 0$ in the model

$q = q_0 - kt - st^2.$

Substitute $k = 30$, $s = 5$, $q_0 = 500$ and $q = 0$ in the above equation:

$0 = 500 - 30t - 5t^2.$

Rearranging:

$5t^2 + 30t - 500 = 0.$

Compare this with Standard Form 2.4,

$at^2 + bt + c = 0.$

A comparison of the coefficients of the t terms gives $a = 5$, $b = 30$ and $c = -500$.

The formula for the solution of a quadratic equation is

$$t = \frac{-b \pm \sqrt{[b^2 - 4ac]}}{2a}$$

Substitute for a, b and c.

$$t = \frac{-30 \pm \sqrt{[30^2 - 4 \times 5(-500)]}}{2 \times 5}$$

$$= \frac{-30 \pm \sqrt{[900 + 10\,000]}}{10}$$

$$= \frac{-30 \pm \sqrt{10\,900}}{10}$$

$$= \frac{-30 \pm 104.4}{10}.$$

This gives the solutions $t = 7.44$ and $t = -13.44$.

The negative value of t has no meaning in the context of this problem, since we cannot go back to a time before the initial stock was defined. The only feasible solution is that the initial stock of 500 units will last for about $7\frac{1}{2}$ days.

Decreasing rate of demand

We might equally well have supposed that the rate of demand r decreased with time. In which case, the model for the rate of demand would be written as

$r = k - st,$

where s is now the rate of decrease in demand per unit of time.

This type of model might be appropriate when a product is reaching the end of its life cycle.

Note

Some care is needed in choosing a sensible value for the negative s in such cases because the total demand, $D = rt$, should continue to rise over the whole time span covered by the model. If D were to fall, this would imply that customers were sending stock back – not a desirable situation.

ADDITIONAL EXAMPLES

A2.1   Simplify the following expressions.

(i) $\dfrac{x+y}{3} + \dfrac{(x^2+y)}{4}$ (ii) $\dfrac{x}{(x+a)} - \dfrac{y}{(x+b)}$

Solving equations

(iii) $\dfrac{(x^2 + 6x + 8)}{(x + 2)}$ (iv) $\dfrac{a^4 + a^2 b}{a^2}$

(v) $\dfrac{x^3 + 6x^2 + 11x + 6}{(x + 1)}$.

A2.2 (i) Factorize the expression $x^2 + 6x + 8$ and hence obtain the roots of the equation

$$x^2 + 6x + 8 = 0.$$

Plot the graph of $y = x^2 + 6x + 8$ and confirm the results obtained by factorizing the expression. Plot the graph for values of x between $x = -7$ and $x = +1$.

(ii) Plot the graph of the function $y = 3x^2 + 7x - 5$ and use the graph to confirm that the roots of the equation $3x^2 + 7x - 5 = 0$ are $x = 0.57$ and $x = -2.90$. Plot the graph for values of x between $x = -5$ and $x = +3$.

(iii) Plot the graph for the function

$$y = x^3 - 1.5x^2 - x + 1.5$$

between the values $x = -2$ and $x = +3$. Determine the roots of the equation

$$x^3 - 1.5x^2 - x + 1.5 = 0.$$

A2.3 Use the standard formula for solving the following quadratic equations. Substitute back into each original equation in order to check your results.

(i) $(x + 3)(x - 5) = 20$

(ii) $x(10x - 21) = 10$

(iii) $x^2(4x^2 - 1) = 72(x^2 - 2)$

Hint: Let $x^2 = y$ and solve for y; hence obtain the four roots for x.

(iv) $\dfrac{5}{(x - 5)} - \dfrac{3}{(x - 3)} = \dfrac{2}{(x + 2)}$.

A2.4 (i) Show that $x = -1$ is a root of the equation

$$2x^3 + 7x^2 + 8x + 3 = 0.$$

(ii) If $x = -1$ is a root of the cubic equation in part (i) above, then $(x + 1)$ is a factor of the left-hand side. Use this result to find the other factors and hence find the other two roots of the equation.

55

The Essence of Mathematics for Business

A2.5 Simplify the algebra and then solve for x in each of the equations below.

(i) $\dfrac{3x^3 - 5x^2 - 12x}{x} = 0$

(ii) $10x^2 + 5x = 6x + 3$

(iii) $18x^2 - 30x = 72$

(iv) $3x^3 - 2x^2 - 17x - 12 = 0.$

3

Simultaneous equations and inequalities

Introduction

The examples of equations which we have considered in Chapters 1 and 2 all dealt with single equations, each with just one unknown variable (which we have usually called x). However, real-life problems usually involve more than one variable and the simultaneous solution of a number of equations. A set of equations with several variables, which requires us to find values of each variable so that all the equations are satisfied at the same time, is referred to as a set of simultaneous equations.

In the following Examples 3.4 to 3.10, use a calculator to perform the calculations indicated at each stage in the procedure. The examples are arranged in increasing order of difficulty and are intended to build up an understanding of the methodology of solving simultaneous equations. Readers who have already met simultaneous equations can start at Example 3.4. Start working at your chosen point and follow through each step of the workings on your own calculator. The solution of simultaneous equations is straightforward once a few examples have been completed. Work slowly and carefully if you are not yet confident with the procedure.

3.1   Simple equations with one variable

In Section 2.5 we showed how an equation with only one variable may be solved. This method is illustrated again in Examples 3.1 and 3.2.

Example 3.1
Solve $2x = 4$.

Solution
Divide both sides of the equation by 2, thus making the coefficient of x equal to 1.

$$\frac{2x}{2} = \frac{4}{2} = 2.$$

Simplifying both sides gives the solution

$x = 2$.

Example 3.2
Solve $3y/2 = 12$.

Solution
Divide both sides of the equation by 3/2 to obtain the solution:

$$\frac{3y/2}{3/2} = \frac{12}{3/2} = \frac{2}{3} \times 12 = 8.$$

The solution is $y = 8$.

3.2   Pairs of equations

Consider a situation where a manufacturer makes two products X and Y which require labour and material resources. Each unit of product X requires 1 hour of labour and 3 kg of material for its production. Each unit of product Y requires 2 hours of labour and 4 kg of material for its production. There are 20 hours of labour and 50 kg of material allocated each week to the production of these two products. Knowing the amount of resources available and the resource requirements for each product it is possible to determine how many of each type of product should be manufactured in order to utilize fully the available resources. The solution is obtained by setting up and solving a pair of simultaneous equations. This is done in Example 3.3 below.

Example 3.3
Determine the number of units of product X and product Y which should be produced each week in order to utilize fully all of the resources given above.

Solution
The first step is to allocate a variable to the number of each product. Call the number of product X produced per week x and the number of product Y produced y. Then consider each resource in turn.

For labour each unit of product X takes 1 hour and each unit of product Y takes 2 hours. A total of 20 hours is available. The labour equation is

$$1x + 2y = 20.$$

For material each unit of product X takes 3 kg and each unit of product Y takes 4 kg. A total of 50 kg is available. The material equation is

$$3x + 4y = 50.$$

The problem is now reduced to solving the pair of equations

$$x + 2y = 20$$
$$3x + 4y = 50.$$

It is usually easier to keep track of the procedure by labelling the equations. In this and subsequent examples the equations are labelled A, B, C as appropriate.

A $\quad x + 2y = 20$

B $\quad 3x + 4y = 50.$

The solution is found by eliminating one of the two variables from an equation, solving for the remaining variable and then determining the value of the other variable by 'back substitution'. We can change the value of any coefficient in an equation by either multiplication or division by a constant, provided that *all* other terms in that equation are operated on in exactly the same manner. The balance of the equation must be maintained.

Looking at the pair of equations we can see that if the coefficient of x in equation A were 3, like the coefficient of x in equation B, we could subtract equation A from equation B and eliminate x. To make the coefficient of x into 3 in equation A we simply multiply every term in A by 3 to obtain a new equation, which we label A' in order to distinguish it from the original version. The operations which are carried out on each equation are recorded on the left-hand side so that we can keep track of what is going on.

A × 3 = A' $3x + 6y = 60$. Write equation B underneath A':

B $\qquad 3x + 4y = 50$.

Now subtract equation A' from equation B.

B − A' $0 + 4y - 6y = 50 - 60$

$\qquad\qquad -2y = -10$.

Now we have an equation with only one variable which can easily be solved.

Solving for y gives $y = -10/-2 = +5$.

Knowing that $y = 5$ enables us to return to equation B which contains terms in x and y.

B $\qquad 3x + 4y = 50$. Put $y = 5$ in this equation.

$\qquad 3x + 4 \times 5 = 50$. Now the only unknown variable is x.

$\qquad 3x + 20 = 50$

$\qquad\qquad 3x = 50 - 20 = 30$

$$x = \frac{30}{3} = 10.$$

Always check the solution. Substitute for x and y in the unused equation A and make sure that the left-hand side equals the right-hand side.

In $\qquad x + 2y = 20$, put $x = 10$ and $y = 5$:

$\qquad 10 + 2 \times 5 = 20$ which is correct.

The solution is to make ten units of product X and five units of product Y each week in order to utilize fully the labour and material resources.

Note

It makes no difference to the solution whether equation B is subtracted from equation A or vice versa. The value of $(-10)/(-2) = +5$ is the same as the value obtained by subtracting equation B from equation A.

3.3   Using a set of equations as a model

It is sometimes possible to use sets of algebraic equations to represent 'real-life' situations as we have shown in Example 3.3 above. Such sets of equations are referred to as models. Modelling is the name given to the technique of producing the equations. Some more simple examples of models of resource allocation problems are given later in this chapter. The advantage of using a mathematical model is that a situation can be simulated, usually with the help of a computer, and the effect of changing constraints such as economic factors or resource availability can be investigated at very little cost.

Example 3.4
The firm Makit and Sons are considering the production of two wooden toys, the Whatsit and the Thingummy. It takes 2 hours to produce a batch of Whatsits and 3 hours to produce a batch of Thingummys. There are 7 hours in the working day. Each batch of Whatsits takes 3 tonnes of material and each batch of Thingummys takes 7 tonnes of material. Each working day 13 tonnes of material are available. How many batches of each product should Makit and Sons produce each day in order to utilize exactly all of the available labour and material resources?

Solution
First represent the number of batches of Whatsits per day by the variable x. Next represent the number of batches of Thingummys per day by the variable y. Now consider each resource in turn.

Labour:
One batch of Whatsits uses 2 hours, thus x batches use $2x$ hours.
One batch of Thingummys uses 3 hours, thus y batches use $3y$ hours.
The total hours used on both products is $2x + 3y$, which must equal the 7 hours available each day.
   Hence we have $2x + 3y = 7$ for labour.

Material:
One batch of Whatsits uses 3 tonnes, x batches use $3x$ tonnes.
One batch of Thingummys uses 7 tonnes, y batches use $7y$ tonnes.
The total material used on both products is $3x + 7y$ tonnes which must equal the 13 tonnes available each day.
   Hence we have $3x + 7y = 13$ for material.

The problem now reduces to finding the values of x and y which simultaneously satisfy the pair of equations

A $\hspace{3cm}$ $2x + 3y = 7$

B $\hspace{3cm}$ $3x + 7y = 13.$

We need to eliminate x and then solve for y. In Example 3.3 the coefficient of x in equation A was 1. If we divide every term in equation A above by 2 we can make the coefficient of x unity in this equation and then proceed as we did in Example 3.3. This process of making the coefficient of the leading variable unity is generally referred to as *normalizing* the equation.

A' = A/2 $\hspace{1cm}$ $x + 1.5y = 3.5.$ $\hspace{0.5cm}$ Write equation B below A'.

B $\hspace{2.4cm}$ $3x + 7y = 13.$

Multiply A' by 3 to obtain the same coefficient of x in both equations A' and B.

A' × 3 = A" $\hspace{0.5cm}$ $3x + 4.5y = 10.5.$ $\hspace{0.5cm}$ Write B below A".

B $\hspace{2.2cm}$ $3x + 7y = 13.$ $\hspace{0.8cm}$ Subtract equation A" from B,

B – A" $\hspace{2cm}$ $2.5y = 2.5$

$$y = \frac{2.5}{2.5} = 1.0.$$

Now that we have the value $y = 1.0$, the value of x can be determined from any equation containing terms in x and y. Use equation B.

B $\hspace{2.2cm}$ $3x + 7y = 13.$ $\hspace{0.5cm}$ Put $y = 1$ in this equation.

$$3x + 7 \times 1 = 13$$

$$3x = 13 - 7 = 6$$

$$x = 2.$$

The solution to the pair of equations is $x = 2.0$, $y = 1.0$.

Check the solution using equation A which was not used to obtain x. Put $x = 2$ and $y = 1$ in A. If the solution is correct then

$$2x + 3y = 7.$$

We have $\hspace{0.5cm}$ $2 \times 2 + 3 \times 1 = 7$ which is correct.

Thus in order to use exactly all of the labour and material each day two batches of Whatsits and one batch of Thingummys should be produced.

Simultaneous equations and inequalities

There are many other methods of solving simultaneous equations with simple integer coefficients. The advantage of using this elimination procedure is that it can easily be applied to examples with large coefficients or where several decimal places are involved. The pair of equations to be solved in Example 3.5 below may look more difficult to solve than those in Example 3.4 because the coefficients are given to three decimal places but the steps to be followed in obtaining the solution are exactly the same in both examples. It will take longer to key the figures into the calculator in Example 3.5, but mathematically speaking both solutions follow exactly the same procedure.

Example 3.5
Solve the equations

A $\quad 1.732x + 1.501y = 10.643$

B $\quad 2.549x + 7.323y = 6.127.$

Solution
The general procedure is to eliminate the leading variable, x, solve for y and then substitute back in order to find x.

The steps taken in obtaining the solution are as follows:

Step 1: Normalize equation A by making the coefficient of x in equation A unity.
Step 2: Multiply A′ by the coefficient of x in equation B to produce equation A″.
Step 3: Subtract A″ from B and eliminate x.
Step 4: Solve for y.
Step 5: Use equation B to evaluate x.
Step 6: Check the solution in equation A.

Step 1 Normalize equation A by dividing every term by 1.732.

A′ = A/1.732 $\qquad x + 0.866\,63y = 6.144\,92.$

Step 2 Multiply equation A′ by 2.549.

A″ = A′ × 2.549 $\quad 2.549x + 2.209\,04y = 15.663\,40$

B $\qquad\qquad\qquad 2.549x + \quad 7.323y = 6.127.$

Step 3 Eliminate x.

B′ = B − A″ $\qquad\qquad 5.113\,96y = -9.536\,40.$

Step 4 Solve for y.

$$y = \frac{-9.536\,40}{5.113\,96} = -1.864\,78.$$

Step 5 Evaluate x.
Substitute $y = -1.864\,78$ in B to find x.

$$2.549x + 7.323 \times (-1.864\,78) = 6.127$$

$$2.549x = 19.782\,78$$

$$x = \frac{19.782\,78}{2.549} = 7.761\,00.$$

The solution is $x = 7.761\,00$, $y = -1.864\,78$ to five decimal places.

Step 6 *Check* the solution using the other unused equation A.

$$1.732 \times 7.761\,00 + 1.501 \times (-1.864\,78) = 10.643\,02.$$

This is correct to three decimal places.

Note that in order to be accurate to three decimal places it is necessary to work to at least five decimal places (two more significant places than the data given in the coefficients).

Although this method of solution may, at first sight, appear more difficult than some other elementary methods, it forms the basis of a widely used algorithm for solving more complicated sets of simultaneous equations. An algorithm is a set of arithmetic procedures which is repeated as necessary to obtain a solution to an algebraic problem.

3.4 Sets of three or more equations

The general procedure for solving sets of simultaneous equations is always the same. The variables are eliminated one at a time until a single equation in one variable remains. This equation is solved and the solution used to obtain the value of the next variable. The process of 'back substitution' is continued until the complete solution is obtained.

Simultaneous equations and inequalities

Example 3.6
Solve the set of simultaneous equations

A $\quad x + 4y + 3z = 10$

B $\quad 5x + 7y - 4z = 12$

C $\quad 2x + 3y - 2z = 5.$

Solution
Steps 1 to 4 below are followed to eliminate x:

    Step 1: Multiply A by the coefficient of x in B to obtain A′.
    Step 2: Subtract A′ from B and eliminate x in B.
    Step 3: Multiply A by the coefficient of x in C to obtain A″.
    Step 4: Subtract A″ from C to eliminate x from C.

We now have a pair of simultaneous equations, B′ and C′ in y and z, to be solved. This is done by repeating the elimination procedure for a two-variable problem which we used in Example 3.4:

    Step 5: Normalize equation B′ to obtain equation B″.
    Step 6: Multiply B″ by the coefficient of y in equation C′.
    Step 7: Subtract B‴ from equation C′ to eliminate y from C′.
    Step 8: Solve for z.
    Step 9: Substitute for z in equation C′ to evaluate y.
    Step 10: Substitute for y and z in equation C to evaluate x.
    Step 11: Check the solution in equations A and B.

Steps 1 and 2   Eliminate x from equation B.
    Multiply equation A by 5 and then subtract the result from B.

A′ = A × 5 $\quad 5x + 20y + 15z = 50$

B $\qquad\qquad\quad 5x + 7y - 4z = 12.$

B′ = B − A′ $\quad 0 - 13y - 19z = -38.$

Steps 3 and 4   Eliminate x from equation C.
    Multiply equation A by 2 and then subtract the result from C.

A × 2 = A″ $\qquad 2x + 8y + 6z = 20$

C $\qquad\qquad\quad 2x + 3y - 2z = 5.$

C′ = C − A″ $\qquad 0 - 5y - 8z = -15.$

We now have the pair of equations

B' $-13y - 19z = -38$

C' $-5y - 8z = -15.$

Step 5 Normalize B' by dividing through by -13. Remember that dividing a negative term by a negative term gives a positive term.

B″ = B'/(−13) $y + 1.462z = 2.923.$

Steps 6 and 7 Multiply equation B″ by 5 and add the result to equation C' to eliminate y from C'.

B‴ = B″ × 5 $5y + 7.310z = 14.615$

C' $-5y - 8z = -15.$

Add B‴ to C' to eliminate y.

C″ = C' + B‴ $0 - 0.690z = -0.385$

$$z = \frac{-0.385}{-0.690} = 0.558.$$

To find y, substitute $z = 0.558$ into C'.

$$-5y - 8 \times 0.558 = -15$$
$$-5y = -10.536$$
$$y = 2.107.$$

To find x, substitute $y = 2.107$ and $z = 0.558$ into C.

$$2x + 3 \times 2.107 - 2 \times 0.558 = 5$$
$$2x = 5 - 3 \times 2.107 + 2 \times 0.558 = -0.205$$
$$x = -0.103.$$

The solution is $x = -0.103$, $y = 2.107$, $z = 0.558$.

Check the solution using equations A and B which were unused in the back substitution to find x and y.

A $-0.103 + 4 \times 2.107 + 3 \times 0.558 = 9.999$

correct to two decimal places.

B $5 \times (-0.103) + 7 \times 2.107 - 4 \times 0.558 = 12.002$

correct to two decimal places.

Example 3.7
Solve the set of equations

A $\quad 3x + 4y + 3z = 10$

B $\quad 5x + 7y - 4z = 12$

C $\quad 2x + 3y - 2z = 5.$

Solution
The difference between this set of equations and those in Example 3.6 is that here the coefficient of x in equation A is not unity. The first step is, therefore, to normalize equation A and then proceed exactly as we did in Example 3.6. The coefficients are given to the nearest whole number. In order to ensure that the solution obtained achieves the same accuracy it is necessary to carry at least two decimal places. For the reasons given in Example 3.5 it is common to carry more decimal places in order to 'be on the safe side'. When the solution is checked any inaccuracy will show up. If you are sure that any errors are not due to arithmetic mistakes, then go back and work through the problem carrying more decimal places.

Step 1 Normalize equation A by dividing through by 3.

A' = A/3 $\qquad x + 1.333y + z = 3.333$

B $\qquad 5x + 7y - 4z = 12$

C $\qquad 2x + 3y - 2z = 5.$

Now the set of equations are of the same form as those in Example 3.6 and the solution follows the same steps.

Step 2 Eliminate x between equations A' and B.

A" = A' × 5 $\qquad 5x + 6.665y + 5z = 16.665$

B $\qquad 5x + 7.000y - 4z = 12.$

B' = B - A" $\qquad 0.335y - 9z = -4.665.$

Step 3 Eliminate x between equations A' and C.

A''' = A' × 2 $\qquad 2x + 2.666y + 2z = 6.666$

C $\qquad 2x + 3.000y - 2z = 5.$

C' = C - A''' $\qquad 0.334y - 4z = -1.666.$

We now have to solve the pair of equations

B' $0.335y - 9z = -4.665$

C' $0.334y - 4z = -1.666.$

Step 4   Normalize B'.

B" = B'/0.335 $y - 26.866z = -13.925.$

Step 5   Multiply B" by 0.334 and eliminate y between B" and C'

B"' = B" × 0.334 $0.334y - 8.973z = -4.651$

C' $0.334y - 4.000z = -1.666.$

C' − B"' $4.973z = 2.985$

so $z = 0.600$

to three decimal places.

Step 6   Substitute $z = 0.6$ into C' and find y.

C' $0.334y - 4 \times 0.6 = -1.666$

$0.334y = 0.734$

$y = 2.198.$

Step 7   Substitute $z = 0.6$ and $y = 2.198$ into C and find x.

C $2x + 3 \times 2.198 - 2 \times 0.600 = 5$

$2x = 5 - 5.394 = -0.394$

$x = -0.197.$

Step 8   Check the solution $x = -0.197$, $y = 2.198$, $z = 0.600$ in the unused equations A and B.

A $3 \times (-0.197) + 4 \times 2.198 + 3 \times 0.600 = 10.001$

B $5 \times (-0.197) + 7 \times 2.198 - 4 \times 0.600 = 12.001.$

The right-hand side of each equation is accurate to two decimal places.

Note that throughout the calculations the solution $z = 0.6$ has been written as 0.600, retaining the two final zeros, in order to remind us that we have worked with three decimal places and not rounded to only one.

It usually does not matter greatly which particular method is used to solve simultaneous equations, provided that it gives the correct answer without too much algebraic or arithmetic effort. The elimination method that we have described meets these requirements, is reasonably easy to check, and can readily be extended for use in solving larger sets of equations. For sets of two, three or even four equations with simple coefficients, this method of hand calculation is usually quicker than setting up a special computer package. However, for larger sets of equations a computer would normally be used.

3.5   Independent and dependent equations

A solution to a set of simultaneous equations can only be found where all of the equations are independent of one another. The concept of dependency is best illustrated by means of examples.

Consider the set of equations

A $\quad$ $3x + 4y + 3z = 10$

B $\quad$ $5x + 7y - 4z = 12$

C $\quad$ $6x + 8y + 6z = 20.$

If you examine the coefficients of the terms in equation C, you will see that each coefficient is twice the corresponding coefficient in equation A. Thus equations A and C are not independent of one another. Whenever one of the equations is dependent upon one or more of the other equations in the set, it is not possible to find a unique solution to the set of equations.

Consider the set of equations

A $\quad$ $3x + 4y + 3z = 10$

B $\quad$ $5x + 7y - 4z = 12$

C $\quad$ $11x + 15y + 2z = 32.$

In this case each coefficient in equation C can be obtained by using the relationship.

C coefficient $= 2 \times$ A coefficient $+$ B coefficient.

The first coefficient is $\quad 2 \times 3 + 5 = 11.$

The second coefficient is $\quad 2 \times 5 + 7 = 15$, etc.

Once again, no solution exists for this set of equations because all of the equations are not independent. Even if a dependent relationship is not obvious it will show up in the course of finding the solution.

Example 3.8
Solve the set of equations

A		$3x + 4y + 3z = 10$
B		$5x + 7y - 4z = 12$
C		$11x + 15y + 2z = 32.$

Solution
Eliminate x between equations A and B, and between A and C.

$B' = B - A \times 5/3$ $\quad$ $0.3333y - 9z = -4.6667$

$C' = C - A \times 11/3$ $\quad$ $0.3333y - 9z = -4.6667.$

Since equations B' and C' are identical, there is no unique solution for y or z and hence no solution for x.

If a computer is being used to obtain the solution to a set of equations where a dependency exists between one or more equations an error message will be output. If several equations are very close to being dependent on one another a warning message will be output. If a set of equations is close to being dependent and hence close to being impossible to solve uniquely it is said to be *ill-conditioned*. This term will be explained further in Chapter 6 on matrices. The general rule for a unique solution to exist for a set of simultaneous equations is that there must be the same number of independent equations as there are variables in the set of equations.

3.6   Linear and non-linear equations

In the examples used so far in this chapter, all of the equations have involved only the addition or subtraction of multiples of the variables. Such sets of equations are described as *linear*. Any equation which uses powers of the variables, logarithms or exponentials is referred to as *non-linear*.
    The pair of equations

$$y + 6x - x^2 = 8$$

and $\quad$ $2x + y = 6$

is non-linear since it involves a term in x^2. The algebraic method of solution is the same as for sets of linear equations. If possible eliminate each variable in turn until only one variable remains and then use the method of back substitution to obtain the value of the other variables. For some very complicated sets of equations algebraic solutions cannot be found. In such cases 'numerical methods', which are numerical approximations to exact solutions, are usually employed to solve the equations. For sets of non-linear equations involving only two variables an approximate solution may also be found by using graphical methods. The solution to the pair of equations given above is found by both algebraic and graphical methods in Examples 3.9 and 3.10.

Example 3.9
Use an algebraic method to solve the pair of non-linear equations

A $\quad y + 6x - x^2 = 8$

B $\qquad 2x + y = 6.$

Solution
We need to eliminate either the variable x or the variable y, leaving an equation containing only one variable. From equation B it is possible to find y in terms of x; this is then substituted into equation A so that x can be found.
    From equation B:

$$y = 6 - 2x.$$

Substitute for y in equation A:

$$6 - 2x + 6x - x^2 = 8.$$

Collect up the terms:

$$6 + 4x - x^2 = 8$$
$$-8 + 6 + 4x - x^2 = 0$$
$$-2 + 4x - x^2 = 0.$$

This is a quadratic equation. Rearrange it into the standard order and compare it with Standard Form 2.4:

$$-x^2 + 4x - 2 = 0.$$

Standard Form 2.4 $\qquad ax^2 + bx + c = 0.$

We have $a = -1, b = 4, c = -2$; put these values into the formula for the solution of a quadratic equation

$$x = \frac{-b \pm \sqrt{b^2 - 4ac}}{2a}.$$

Hence

$$x = \frac{-4 \pm \sqrt{16 - 4 \times (-1) \times (-2)}}{2 \times (-1)} = \frac{-4 \pm \sqrt{16 - 8}}{-2}.$$

This gives the solutions $x = 3.4142$ and $x = 0.5858$.

Use equation B, $y = 6 - 2x$, to evaluate y.

When $x = 3.4142$, then $y = 6 - 2 \times 3.4142 = -0.8284$.

When $x = 0.5858$, then $y = 6 - 2 \times 0.5858 = 4.8284$.

The solution may be checked by substituting $x = 3.4142$, $y = -0.8284$ into the left-hand side of equation A to obtain the value 8.

The same check is done for the other solution $x = 0.5858$, $y = 4.8284$.

Example 3.10

Use a graphical method to obtain the solutions to the pair of equations

A $\quad y + 6x - x^2 = 8.$

B $\quad\quad 2x + y = 6.$

Solution

Rearrange the equations to give y as a function of x.

A $\quad y = 8 - 6x + x^2$

B $\quad y = 6 - 2x.$

Now plot the curves for equation A and equation B on the same graph using the methods of Chapter 2. This graph is shown in Figure 3.1. The solutions to the pair of equations are the values of x and y which simultaneously satisfy both equations, that is the points which are simultaneously on both curves where they cross. It can be seen by inspection that the solutions are approximately $x = 0.6$, $y = 4.8$ and $x = 3.4$, $y = -0.8$, agreeing with our solution in Example 3.9.

Clearly it is not possible to be very accurate with a graphical solution to a pair of equations but such solutions are useful on occasions. If it is not necessary to obtain a solution to an accuracy of several decimal places then it is often much quicker to solve a pair of non-linear simultaneous equations using a graphical method rather than to

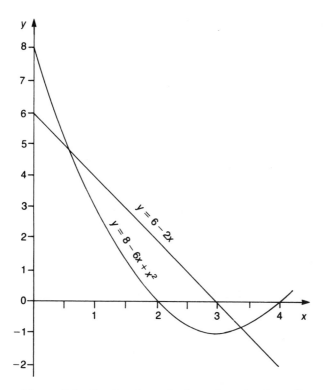

Figure 3.1   Graphs of $y = 6 - 2x$ and $y = 8 - 6x + x^2$.

struggle with complicated algebra in order to find the solution to an accuracy which is not required.

3.7   Inequalities

In Examples 3.3 and 3.4 the resources available were used completely. In practice this rarely happens and some quantity less than the total resource available is utilized.

Consider the labour resource in Example 3.4. Here $2x$ hours are used on batches of Whatsits and $3y$ used on Thingummys, taking up a total of $2x + 3y$ hours of labour per day. There is up to 7 hours of labour available each day. This may be written in words as

$2x + 3y$ is less than or equal to 7 hours.

Such a relationship is referred to as an *inequality*.

73

Clearly it is necessary to have symbols to replace phrases such as 'less than or equal to'. These are listed below:

The symbol > means 'greater than'.

The symbol < means 'less than'.

The symbol ≥ means 'greater than or equal to'.

The symbol ≤ means 'less than or equal to'.

It is essential to learn the precise definitions of the symbols used in inequalities. Generally speaking the algebraic rules concerning inequalities are very similar to those for equalities.

Rules for the use of inequalities

Rule 3.1

An inequality is unaltered by the addition, subtraction, multiplication or division by a *positive* quantity.

Consider, first, a numerical example to illustrate the rule.

Example 3.11
Let $a = 7, b = 4, c = 2$. We now have

$7 > 4$	or	7 is greater than 4,
$7 + 2 > 4 + 2$	or	9 is greater than 6,
$7 - 2 > 4 - 2$	or	5 is greater than 2,
$7 \times 2 > 4 \times 2$	or	14 is greater than 8,
$\dfrac{7}{2} > \dfrac{4}{2}$	or	3.5 is greater than 2.

Now consider the general case.

If $\quad a > b \quad$ and $c > 0$, that is c is positive

then $\quad a + c > b + c,$

$\qquad a - c > b - c,$

$\qquad\quad ac > bc,$

$\qquad\quad \dfrac{a}{c} > \dfrac{b}{c}.$

Rule 3.2

If numbers or algebraic terms are transferred from one side of an inequality sign to the other then their signs are changed.

Consider a numerical example

Example 3.12
Let $a = 7, b = 4, c = 2$.

If

$$7 + 2 > 4,$$

then changing the sign of the $+2$ term when changing sides gives

$$7 > 4 - 2.$$

If

$$7 - 2 > 4,$$

then changing the sign of the -2 term when changing sides gives

$$7 > 4 + 2.$$

Now let us use Example 3.12 to help us formulate the general case. Put a, b and c instead of 7, 4 and 2 respectively.

If $\quad a + c > b$

then $\quad a > b - c.$

If $\quad a - c > b$

then $\quad a > b + c.$

Rule 3.3

If both sides of an inequality are multiplied or divided by a *negative* quantity, then the direction of the inequality is reversed.

Consider the numerical example below.

Example 3.13
Let $a = 7, b = 4, c = -2$.

We know that $\qquad 7 > 4;$ $\qquad$ multiply both sides by -2,

then $\qquad 7 \times (-2) < 4 \times (-2)$ $\qquad$ and the inequality sign is reversed.

In words this is read as ' − 14 is less (more negative) than −8'.
   Divide both sides of the inequality by −2. Then

$$\frac{7}{(-2)} < \frac{4}{(-2)}$$

and the inequality sign is reversed. That is, '−3.5 is less (more negative) than −2'.

For the general case,

if $a > b$ and $c < 0$, that is c is negative,

then $ac < bc$

and $\dfrac{a}{c} < \dfrac{b}{c}$.

Rule 3.4

When the terms on each side of an inequality need to be inverted, the direction of the inequality sign is reversed.

Consider a numerical example first and then the general case.

Example 3.14
Simplify the inequality

$$\frac{3}{4} < \frac{12}{x} .$$

Invert both sides. Remember that any operation on one side of an inequality must be balanced by the same operation on the other side. Reverse the direction of the inequality.

$$\frac{4}{3} > \frac{x}{12} .$$

Once the x term is above the fraction line the inequality can be rearranged.

$$\frac{4 \times 12}{3} > x,$$

giving the inequality $16 > x$. That is, 'x is less than 16' which is the same as saying '16 is greater than x'.

Now consider the general case.

If

$$\frac{a}{c} > \frac{b}{d}$$

then

$$\frac{c}{a} < \frac{d}{b}.$$

If

$$b < a$$

then

$$\frac{1}{b} > \frac{1}{a}.$$

Example 3.15
Substitute the values $a = 7$, $b = 4$, $c = 2$, $d = 3$ into the general case above used to illustrate Rule 3.4.

Since $\frac{7}{2} > \frac{4}{3}$ then $\frac{3}{7} < \frac{3}{4}$.

That is, '7/2 is greater than 4/3' and '3/4 is greater than 2/7'.
Since $4 < 7$ then $\frac{1}{4} > \frac{1}{7}$.

That is, '4 is less than 7' and '1/7 is less than 1/4'.

Graphical methods can sometimes be used to illustrate the regions which satisfy inequalities.

Example 3.16
Shade the area on the graph which satisfies the inequality

$$2x_1 + 5x_2 \leq 20.$$

Method
First consider the equation $2x_1 + 5x_2 = 20$ and rearrange the terms to read $x_2 = -\frac{2}{5}x_1 + \frac{20}{5}$ or $x_2 = -0.4x_1 + 4$.

This is the equation of a straight line. Draw the line as shown in Figure 3.2.

Every point on this line satisfies the equality above. We now need to determine on which side of the line are those values of x_1 and x_2 which satisfy the inequality and on which side are those values which do not satisfy the inequality.

Consider the point $(x_1 = 1, \ x_2 = 1)$ below the line. This point satisfies the inequality, since putting these values into the left-hand side gives

$$2 \times 1 + 5 \times 1 = 7,$$

which is less than 20 and therefore satisfies the inequality.

Now consider the point $x_1 = 1$, $x_2 = 5$ above the line. These values do not satisfy the inequality since

$$2 \times 1 + 5 \times 5 = 27,$$

which is greater than 20 and therefore does not satisfy the inequality.

Putting this information on to the graph gives the area below the line, including the points on the line

$$x_2 = -0.4x_1 + 4 \quad \text{or} \quad 2x_1 + 5x_2 = 20$$

as the area containing those values of x_1 and x_2 which satisfy the inequality $2x_1 + 5x_2 \leq 20$.

Example 3.17

Shade the area of the graph which satisfies the inequality

$$2x_1 + x_2 \leq 12.$$

Method

First consider the equation

$$2x_1 + x_2 = 12$$

and plot the corresponding line

$$x_2 = -2x_1 + 12$$

as shown in Figure 3.3.

The point $(x_1 = 1, \ x_2 = 1)$ below the line satisfies the inequality.

The point $(x_1 = 7, \ x_2 = 1)$ above the line does not satisfy the inequality. The shaded area, including the line

$$2x_1 + x_2 = 12,$$

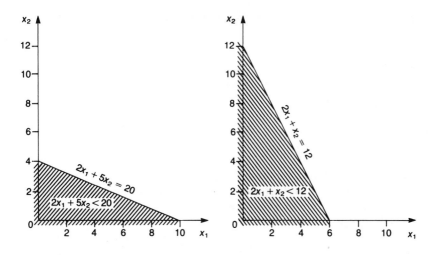

Figure 3.2 Shaded region satisfies the inequality $2x_1 + 5x_2 \leq 20$.

Figure 3.3 Shaded region satisfies the inequality $2x_1 + x_2 \leq 12$.

is the area containing the values of x_1 and x_2 which satisfy the inequality

$$2x_1 + x_2 \leq 12.$$

3.8   Simultaneous inequalities

Sets of inequalities can be used to model an actual situation in much the same way as sets of equations. Consider Example 3.4 again; if the requirement here was to use any amount of the resources, up to the limit of those available, the set of inequalities would be

$$2x + 3y \leq 7$$

$$3x + 7y \leq 13.$$

It is usual to consider such allocations of resources in conjunction with a strategic requirement such as the maximization of profit or the minimization of total costs. Problems formulated in such a manner are referred to as *linear programming* problems. We shall deal here only with problems involving two variables, which can be explained graphically. An example of a pair of inequalities is given in Example 3.18 below.

Example 3.18

Shade on a graph the area which jointly satisfies the inequalities

$$2x_1 + 5x_2 \leq 20$$

$$2x_1 + x_2 \leq 12.$$

Method

We have considered these two inequalities separately in Examples 3.16 and 3.17 above. To obtain the graph which applies when they operate simultaneously, we simply superimpose Figure 3.3 on to Figure 3.2 to obtain Figure 3.4.

The area with double shading on Figure 3.4 then represents the overlap between the single-shaded areas containing points which satisfy the individual inequalities. Hence the double-shaded area satisfies both inequalities,

$$2x_1 + 5x_2 \leq 20$$

$$2x_1 + x_2 \leq 12.$$

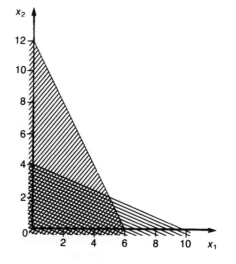

Figure 3.4 Double-shaded region satisfies the inequalities $2x_1 + 5x_2 \leq 20$ and $2x_1 + x_2 \leq 12$.

3.9 Applications of inequalities

Example 3.19
A firm produces products A and B. Each week, x_1 thousand A items and x_2 thousand B items are to be produced. There are 20 tonnes of raw material available each week for making the products. There are also 12 hours per week of machine time available for the production. Product A requires 2 tonnes of material per thousand items and product B requires 5 tonnes of material per thousand items. Product A takes 2 hours of machine time per thousand items and product B takes 1 hour of machine time per thousand items. What are the feasible values for x_1 and x_2, the quantity of products A and B made each week?

Solution

Material   The total amount of material used cannot exceed 20 tonnes per week. The inequality

$$2x_1 + 5x_2 \le 20$$

must be satisfied.

Machine time   The amount of machine time available is 12 hours per week. The inequality

$$2x_1 + x_2 \le 12$$

must be satisfied.

A general condition   It is impossible to produce a negative number of items, thus there are the additional constraints on the variables x_1 and x_2,

$$x_1 \ge 0 \quad \text{and} \quad x_2 \ge 0,$$

which must also be satisfied.
  The region of feasible values for x_1 and x_2 is the shaded area in Figure 3.5, including the lines bounding the region. This region is similar to that in Figure 3.4 but the additional constraints $x_1 \ge 0$ and $x_2 \ge 0$ mean that it is bounded by the horizontal and vertical axes.

Example 3.20
Two projects are being considered for approval.
  Project 1 requires an initial outlay of £450 of capital and has a net present value (NPV) of £200.

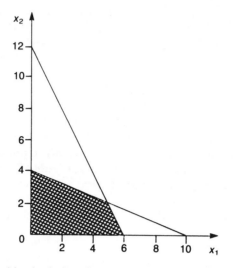

Figure 3.5 Double-shaded region satisfies the inequalities $2x_1 + 5x_2 \le 20$, $2x_1 + x_2 \le 12$, $x_1 \ge 0$, $x_2 \ge 0$.

Project 2 requires an initial outlay of £500 of capital and has an NPV of £220.

There is only £600 of capital available for initial investment in the projects. Determine by graphical means the best apportionment of capital to these projects such that the total combined NPV of the two projects is maximized.

Solution
It is not possible to fund both projects fully since this would require an outlay of £950 and only £600 is available. This means that only a proportion of each project can be carried out.

Call the proportion of project 1 to be carried out x_1. The amount invested in project 1 is then £450x_1.

Call the proportion of project 2 to be carried out x_2. The amount invested in project 2 is then £500x_2.

Now consider the constraints upon the project parameters. The constraint that the initial outlay must not exceed £600 is written as

$450x_1 + 500x_2 \le 600.$

In addition, the proportion of each project carried out must be somewhere between 0 and 1. This is written as

$0 \le x_1 \le 1,$

$0 \le x_2 \le 1.$

The object is to maximize the total net present value which we shall write as TNPV.

The NPV for project 1 is £200. If a proportion, x_1, of project 1 is carried out, then the NPV attributable to this proportion will be $200x_1$. Similarly, the NPV for project 2 is £220. If a proportion, x_2, of project 2 is carried out, then the NPV will be $220x_2$.

The TNPV is given as

$$\text{TNPV} = 200x_1 + 220x_2.$$

The constraints are:

$$450x_1 + 500x_2 \leq 600,$$

$$0 \leq x_1 \leq 1,$$

$$0 \leq x_2 \leq 1.$$

We now need to maximize the function TNPV subject to the set of constraints listed. It can be shown that the maximum will occur at one of the corners of the feasible region. The next step, then, is to draw a graph showing the feasible region and to determine the coordinates of the corners.

Consider first the inequality

$$450x_1 + 500x_2 \leq 600$$

and the equality

$$450x_1 + 500x_2 = 600.$$

Rearrange the equality to give

$$x_1 = \frac{600}{500} - \frac{450x_1}{500}$$

hence,

$$x_2 = 1.20 - 0.90x_1.$$

Draw this line on the graph. The points which satisfy the inequality lie on or below this line.

Next consider the inequalities $0 \leq x_1 \leq 1$ and the associated equalities

$$x_1 = 0 \quad \text{and} \quad x_1 = 1.$$

Draw these on the graph. The points which jointly satisfy these inequalities lie on or between the parallel lines $x_1 = 0$ and $x_1 = 1$.

Lastly consider the inequalities $0 \leq x_2 \leq 1$. The points which jointly satisfy these inequalities lie on or between the parallel lines $x_2 = 0$ and $x_2 = 1$.

The shaded area in Figure 3.6 is the area which jointly satisfies all of the inequalities.

Having determined the feasible region we can now find out which point in that region maximizes TNPV. This point will be at one of the corners of the region. The corners have been labelled A, B, C, D and E. We need to determine the values of x_1 and x_2 at each of these points, and then substitute these values into the function

$$\text{TNPV} = 200x_1 + 220x_2$$

in order to see which point maximizes TNPV.

At point A: $x_1 = 1$ and $x_2 = 0$; TNPV is given as

$$\text{TNPV} = 200 \times 1 + 220 \times 0 = 200.$$

At point D: $x_1 = 0$ and $x_2 = 1$; TNPV is given as

$$\text{TNPV} = 200 \times 0 + 220 \times 1 = 220.$$

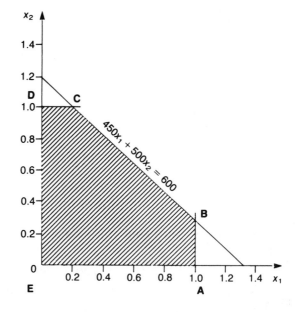

Figure 3.6 Shaded region satisfies the inequalities $450x_1 + 500x_2 \leq 600$, $0 \leq x_1 \leq 1, 0 \leq x_2 \leq 1$.

Point B is the point where the lines $x_1 = 1$ and $x_1 = 1.333 - 1.111x_2$ cross. Putting $x_1 = 1$ into the equation $x_1 = 1.333 - 1.111x_2$ gives the solution $x_2 = 0.3$. Substitute $x_1 = 1$ and $x_2 = 0.3$ into the function TNPV to find the TNPV at point B,

$$TNPV = 200 \times 1 + 220 \times 0.3 = 266.$$

Point C is the point where the lines $x_2 = 1$ and $x_1 = 1.333 - 1.111x_2$ cross. This occurs at the point $(x_1 = 0.222, x_2 = 1)$. At point C the TNPV is

$$TNPV = 200 \times 0.222 + 220 \times 1 = 264.444.$$

Table 3.1 shows a summary of these calculations.

It can be seen that the maximum TNPV is £266.00 at point B where $x_1 = 1.0$ and $x_2 = 0.3$. This means that the optimum strategy is to carry out all of project 1 and 0.3 or 30% of project 2.

The method used in Example 3.20 is a simple illustration of a technique generally referred to as *linear programming*. This technique is widely used for solving practical problems involving decisions about resource allocation. If only two resources are involved, then it is possible to use the graphical approach illustrated. If the problem requires the allocation of more than two resources, then a linear programming computer package is usually used. The approach to a larger problem is the same as that used in Example 3.20. The constraints must be defined together with the function to be optimized; the only difference is that the problem will involve more constraints. If a computer package is to be used then obtaining the solution is relatively easy.

Table 3.1

Point	x_1	x_2	TNPV
A	1.0	0	200.00
B	1.0	0.3	266.00
C	0.222	1.0	264.44
D	0	1.0	220.00
E	0	0	0

The Essence of Mathematics for Business

ADDITIONAL EXAMPLES

A3.1 Solve the following sets of simultaneous equations.

(i) $x + y = 6$
$x - y = 2$

(ii) $3x + 4y = 9$
$5x + 2y = 10$

(iii) $2x + 3y + z = 6$
$3x + 5y - 4z = 2$
$5x - 2y + 3z = 7$

(iv) $3x + 2y - 3z = 33$
$5x - 4y + 10z = 27$
$8x + 2y - 7z = 52$

(v) $2.0x + 0.5y + 1.4z = 8.0$
$1.5x + 2.0y + 0.6z = 5.6$
$1.9x - 1.7y + 0.3z = 4.3$

(vi) $2.1x + 3.0y + 1.5z = 6.3$
$3.2x + 1.7y + 3.0z = 7.3$
$1.6x + 1.9y - 2.3z = 4.2.$

A3.2 Solve the simultaneous equations

$x^2 + y^2 = 4x + 3$
$x - 3y = 1.$

A3.3 (i) Plot the graph of

$y = 3x/(2x^2 + 5)$

between $x = 0$ and $x = 3$.

(ii) By superimposing the graph of

$80y = 6x + 17$

on that plotted in (i) find all the values of x and y which satisfy the pair of equations

$y = 3x/(2x^2 + 5)$ and $80y = 6x + 17$.

A3.4 The Makit Manufacturing Company produces three main types of product. Each product passes through three manufacturing stages with a separate labour force assigned to each stage. The table below shows the time that an item of each type requires for each stage in the manufacturing process and the total labour in man hours available for each stage.

	Type A	Type B	Type C	Total labour available
Stage 1	5	7	8	695
Stage 2	3	4	7	510
Stage 3	2	3	4	320

How many items of each type must be produced in order to use completely the man hours of labour available at each stage of the production process?

Simultaneous equations and inequalities

A3.5   A boatyard produces three types of glass-fibre boat, each of which has to pass through three stages of manufacture. The numbers of man days required at each stage for one boat of each type are shown in the table below, together with the corresponding total man days of labour available.

	Type A	Type B	Type C	Total labour available
Stage 1	4	10	10	162
Stage 2	1	7	12	110
Stage 3	4	8	8	140

You are required to find the quantities of each type of boat that should be produced so that all available labour is fully utilized. Also find the total cost of producing these quantities of boats, given that all labour is costed at £50 per man day, materials cost £400 for each type A boat, £1100 for each type B boat and £2000 for each type C boat.

A3.6   The Fabrikant Company manufactures three products of type A, B, and C. The resources available for a 1 month work period are 55 units of machine time, 139 units of manpower and 108 units of material. It takes 2 units of machine time, 9 units of manpower and 7 units of material to produce 1 batch of 1000 items of type A. It takes 3 units of machine time, 5 units of manpower and 6 units of material to produce a batch of 1000 items of type B. It takes 4.5 units of machine time, 12 units of manpower and 8 units of material to produce a batch of 1000 items of type C.

   In order to use exactly all of the available resources, x batches of product A, y batches of product B and z batches of product C are to be manufactured. Use the information given above to determine the values of x, y and z.

A3.7   The Lukatme Clothing Company produces three types of garment. Each garment must pass through a cutting stage, a machining stage and a finishing stage. Each garment of type A requires 0.5 hours in cutting, 2 hours in machining and 1 hour in finishing. Each garment of type B requires 1 hour in cutting, 3 hours in machining and 1.5 hours in finishing. Each garment of type C requires 2 hours in cutting, 5 hours in machining and 1.5 hours in finishing. With the present staffing levels there are 96 hours per day available for cutting, 268 hours for machining and 104 hours for finishing. Calculate the *exact* number of garments of each type which must be made in a day in order to utilize exactly all of the work hours available per day.

A3.8   A maintenance department employs fitters, electricians and carpenters. Amongst other jobs, they are required to service three types of machine: X, Y and Z. After allowing for time that has been allocated to other jobs, the

87

number of hours in a particular week which they have available for servicing these machines are: fitters 196, electricians 177, carpenters 107.

The number of hours required to service each type of machine is shown in the table below.

	Type X	Type Y	Type Z
Fitter	5.3	2.1	4.7
Electrician	7.2	8.3	0.6
Carpenter	0	3.5	4.5

(i) Assuming that fitters, electricians and carpenters can work on the machines in any order without interfering with each other, find the number of each type of machine (correct to two decimal places) which could be serviced in the week if all the available workers' time is used.

(ii) Supposing that the solutions to (i) must be rounded down to give integer numbers of machines serviced, find the corresponding amounts of unused time ('slack') for each type of worker.

4

Series

Introduction

All managers are faced with data in the form of *sequences* or *series*. These may relate to costs or profits associated with particular discrete quantities produced or sold, so the first term in the sequence might be the cost of one unit, the second the cost of two units, and so on. In other cases the terms may consist of totals accumulated over fixed periods such as days, weeks, months, quarters or years; typical examples would be weekly numbers of items sold, monthly numbers of breakdowns in a machine shop, or quarterly repayments of a debt.

When the terms in the sequence contain irregular or random elements, so that even when we know several terms there is no way of predicting exactly what the next term will be, statistical methods are needed to describe the behaviour of the sequence. However, in this chapter we shall concentrate on methods of describing particular kinds of completely regular sequences and find ways of simplifying some of the arithmetic associated with them.

4.1 Arithmetic progression (AP)

Example 4.1
Suppose that we keep a record of the number of units of product A sold in five successive weeks, as shown in the table on p. 90.

Week	1	2	3	4	5
Sales	6	10	14	18	22

Clearly the sales are increasing from week to week. Further inspection shows that each week they increase by the same amount – four units. Another way of expressing this would be to say that the *difference* between sales in any two successive weeks is constant and equal to 4.

In this example we have data for 5 weeks only, but if we had weekly sales figures following the same pattern and extending over many months, or even over several years, it would clearly be very convenient if we could find a suitable mathematical notation to express this pattern in a compact form and so enable us to carry out further analysis without having to write out a long list of weekly figures at each stage of the analysis.

Let us use j to denote the week number and a to denote the number of units of product A, so that a_j (a with subscript j) denotes the number of units sold in week j. Thus $a_1 = 6$ denotes sales in week 1, $a_2 = 10$ denotes sales in week 2 and so on.

The fact that the difference is constant can then be written as follows.

For the first 2 weeks $\quad a_2 - a_1 = 4,$

for the second 2 weeks $\quad a_3 - a_2 = 4,$

for the third 2 weeks $\quad a_4 - a_3 = 4,$

for the fourth 2 weeks $\quad a_5 - a_4 = 4,$

and in general $a_{j+1} - a_j = 4$ for $j = 1, 2, 3, 4$.

This last statement, 'for $j = 1, 2, 3, 4$', is the usual way of indicating that some relationship (in this case the relationship between a_j and a_{j+1}) is true for any of the values of j that are listed, that is for $j = 1, j = 2, j = 3$ or $j = 4$.

The fact that the sales rise by four units each week can be used to obtain a formula for expressing the value of a_j in terms of this difference and the value of a_1:

$a_2 = a_1 + 4$

$a_3 = a_2 + 4 = (a_1 + 4) + 4 = a_1 + 4 \times 2$

$a_4 = a_3 + 4 = (a_1 + 4 \times 2) + 4 = a_1 + 4 \times 3$

$a_5 = a_4 + 4 = (a_1 + 4 \times 3) + 4 = a_1 + 4 \times 4.$

From this we can see that in each of the weeks numbered from 2 to 5 the sales can be found by taking sales for week 1 (a_1) and adding some multiple of the difference (4). The appropriate multiple is the week number minus one. In general, we may therefore write the sales in week j as

$$a_j = a_1 + 4(j-1) \quad \text{for} \quad j = 1, 2, 3, 4, 5.$$

Notice that when $j = 1$ this equation reduces to $a_1 = a_1 + 0$.

We can generalize further by writing the common difference between the weekly sales as d (which happens to equal 4 in this particular case) and supposing that we have n terms (where $n = 5$ in this case). The typical term in the sequence, representing the sales in week j, can then be expressed as the first term plus $(j-1)$ times the common difference, which is now d:

$$a_j = a_1 + (j-1)d \quad \text{for} \quad j = 1, 2, \ldots, n. \tag{4.1}$$

Any sequence in which there is a *common constant difference* between successive terms, so that the typical term can be written in the form of equation (4.1), is called an *arithmetic progression* (with the stress on the e of *arithmetic*), usually abbreviated to AP.

Note that if we have an AP with its typical term given by equation (4.1) and we plot a_j against j, as in Figure 4.1, we get a set of points lying on a straight line with slope d. The intercept on the vertical axis will be $a_1 - d$, which can be denoted by a_0 since it too obeys equation (4.1) when $j = 0$ and so forms part of the same sequence as the other a_j terms.

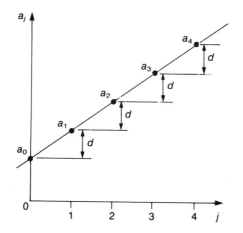

Figure 4.1 The terms of an arithmetic progression.

Example 4.2
Suppose that a warehouse starts week 1 with a stock of 100 units of product B; call this stock b_1. Then let b_j be the stock at the start of any subsequent week ($j = 2$ to 6), taking values as shown in the table below. Check that these stock levels form an arithmetic progression (AP) and find an expression for the typical term.

Week, j	1	2	3	4	5	6
Stock, b_j	100	93	86	79	72	65

Solution
Here we find that $b_2 - b_1 = -7$, $b_3 - b_2 = -7$, etc., so that $b_{j+1} - b_j = -7$ for all $j = 1$ to 5. Hence this sequence has a common difference, $d = -6$ (notice the *negative* sign, which indicates a *decrease* in b as we increase j), so the sequence of stock levels is an AP and, by analogy with equation (4.1), we may write the typical term as

$$b_j = b_1 + (j-1)d = b_1 - 7(j-1) = 100 - 7(j-1).$$

This shows that the stock level is being reduced by 7 units each week. Having obtained this general expression, we could go on to solve other problems. For example, if demand continued to be 7 units per week, we could proceed as follows to find how many weeks it would take to use up all of the original 100 units of stock.

Suppose that b_j is the last positive term in the sequence. We already know that

$$b_j = 100 - 7(j-1) \quad \text{and also that} \quad 0 \le b_j.$$

Hence $0 \le 100 - 7(j-1)$.

We are looking for the largest value of j that satisfies this last inequality. Using the methods which we developed in Chapter 3, we can expand the bracket on the right-hand side and rearrange the terms to give $0 \le 100 - 7j + 7$; hence

$$7j \le 107 \quad \text{so} \quad j \le 107/7$$

and the largest j to satisfy this is 15. We can check this by noting that our general formula for b_j tells us that the stock level at the beginning of week 15 is

$$b_{15} = 100 - 7(14) = 100 - 98 = 2.$$

Assuming that 7 units are demanded during the week, the original stock will therefore be exhausted and, unless more stock is delivered to the warehouse, the stock level will reach zero at some time during week 15.

Example 4.3
In the following table, c_j denotes the stock of product C at the start of week j. Find whether these stock levels form an AP.

Week, j	1	2	3	4	5	6
Stock, c_j	150	144	140	135	130	123
Difference, $c_{j+1} - c_j$	−6	−4	−5	−5	−7	

Solution
Because the differences, $c_{j+1} - c_j$, are not constant, this sequence of stock levels does not form an AP.

4.2 The sigma notation for summation

In Example 4.1, we had a record of the weekly sales of product A. We might wish to add together the sales in several weeks in order to find cumulative sales, and then perhaps go on to use the cumulative total to calculate when to reorder product A or how much profit this product will yield over a certain period. As a first step in solving this type of problem, we introduce some standard notation for the sum of a number of terms in a sequence.

One convention is to use S_n to denote the sum of the first n terms of a sequence. Using this, the cumulative sales of product A would be:

$S_1 = a_1$ after 1 week,

$S_2 = a_1 + a_2$ after 2 weeks,

$S_3 = a_1 + a_2 + a_3$ after 3 weeks

and in general

$S_n = a_1 + a_2 + a_3 + \ldots + a_n$ after n weeks.   **(4.2)**

For a whole year of 52 weeks there would be 52 terms, but if we are concerned with their algebraic representation (as opposed to their numerical values) there is very little point in explicitly listing each one of them.

One standard way of representing this kind of sum of many terms is to follow the convention that we have used in equation (4.2), which is to list two or three initial terms, follow these by dots (usually three of these) to represent terms that are to be included but are not written out in full, and finish with the last term to be included (e.g. a_n, or a_{52}). However, even this convention is often felt to involve too much repetition.

The essential ideas are:

1. that we are adding terms of the type a_j and
2. the subscript j on a_j is to run from 1 to n.

Introducing the symbol Σ, 'capital sigma' (which is the Greek equivalent of S), for *summation* we can write a very compact general expression for the sum of the first n terms of any sequence (not necessarily an AP) in which the typical term is a_j:

$$S_n = \sum_{j=1}^{n} a_j \ . \tag{4.3}$$

The right-hand side of equation (4.3) is read 'the sum of the a_j terms for j equals 1 to n'. We call $j = 1$ the *lower limit* and $j = n$ the *upper limit* for summation; it is conventional to write '$j = $' only against the lower limit. Limits are normally placed above and below the sigma (Σ) but to avoid printing difficulties they may be placed after the sigma, so that (4.3) might be printed $S_n = \Sigma_{j=1}^{n} a_j$.

One advantage of using the sigma notation instead of S_n is that we are not restricted to only considering the first n terms of a sequence. By adjusting the limits, we can start and stop at any terms.

If there is no ambiguity, the limits may be omitted, but it is good practice to include them wherever possible. Almost any letter may be used as the subscript representing the label on the typical term over which we are summing; however, the most common choice is j or i or r unless these letters have been allocated some other meaning in a particular problem.

Example 4.4
Evaluate

$$\sum_{i=1}^{3} x_i \quad \text{and} \quad \sum_{i=2}^{4} x_i$$

given that $x_1 = 6, x_2 = 9, x_3 = 17, x_4 = 30$. Notice that our typical term is now denoted by x_i with i running from 1 to 4.

Solution
In the first case, the fact that the lower limit is 1 and the upper limit is 3 tells us that we need to add terms labelled from 1 to 3 inclusive, so

$$\sum_{i=1}^{3} x_i = [x_1 + x_2 + x_3] = 6 + 9 + 17 = 32.$$

In the second case, the limits tell us to omit the first term but add terms labelled 2 to 4 inclusive, so

$$\sum_{i=2}^{4} x_i = [x_2 + x_3 + x_4] = 9 + 17 + 30 = 56.$$

In practice we would omit the stage shown in square brackets and proceed directly to the numerical values.

Example 4.5
Given that $t_1 = 7$, $t_2 = 3$ and $t_3 = 5$, evaluate

$$\sum_{r=1}^{3} t_r^2.$$

Solution
Since the typical term is t_r^2, we are being asked to square the t terms and then add the squares, so the required answer is

$$7^2 + 3^2 + 5^2 = 49 + 9 + 25 = 83.$$

It is most important to distinguish this problem from that of evaluating

$$\left(\sum_{r=1}^{3} t_r\right)^2,$$

which involves first adding the t values and *then* squaring the total, so the answer to this second problem would be

$$(7 + 3 + 5)^2 = 15^2 = 225.$$

The distinction between (1) squaring and then adding and (2) adding and then squaring is crucial for understanding many formulas that are used in statistics. To avoid mistakes, just remember the BODMAS rule from Chapter 1; this tells us to *evaluate the contents of any brackets first*.

Example 4.6
In statistics, if we have a sample of size n consisting of the observed values $x_1, x_2, \ldots, x_n$, a quantity called the *sample variance* is given by the formula

$$\text{sample variance} = \frac{1}{n-1}\left[\sum x^2 - \frac{1}{n}\left(\sum x\right)^2\right],$$

where the limits for summation are $i = 1$ to n in each case and we have omitted the label i on the x-values. Use this formula to find the sample variance when the observed values are: 4, 7, 3, 6, 8.

Solution
There are five values, so $n = 5$ and $n - 1 = 4$.
   The sum of the x-values is

$$\sum x = 4 + 7 + 3 + 6 + 8 = 28$$

and the sum of the squared x-values is

$$\sum x^2 = 4^2 + 7^2 + 3^2 + 6^2 + 8^2$$

$$= 16 + 49 + 9 + 36 + 64 = 174.$$

Substituting these values into the formula gives

$$\text{sample variance} = \tfrac{1}{4}[174 - \tfrac{1}{5}(28)^2]$$

$$= 17.2/4$$

$$= 4.3.$$

4.3   Sum of terms of an AP

We now return to the specific problem of summing the terms of an AP, which led us to look for suitable notation at the start of Section 4.2. We need to recall that formula (4.1) enabled us to define the jth term of an AP as being the first term plus $(j - 1)$ times the common difference:

$$a_j = a_1 + (j - 1)d.$$

Now let us see how we can use this to evaluate S_n, the sum of n terms which we defined in formula (4.2), for any value of n.
   In column A of Table 4.1, we have listed each of the n terms which together add up to S_n, starting with a_1 at the top and a_n at the bottom. In

Series

Table 4.1 The sum of n terms of an AP.

Row	Column A	Column B	Col. A + Col. B = Column C
1	a_1	$a_1 + (n-1)d$	$2a_1 + (n-1)d$
2	$a_1 + d$	$a_1 + (n-2)d$	$2a_1 + (n-1)d$
3	$a_1 + 2d$	$a_1 + (n-3)d$	$2a_1 + (n-1)d$
.	.	.	.
.	.	.	.
.		.	
$n-2$	$a_1 + (n-3)d$	$a_1 + 2d$	$2a_1 + (n-1)d$
$n-1$	$a_1 + (n-2)d$	$a_1 + d$	$2a_1 + (n-1)d$
n	$a_1 + (n-1)d$	a_1	$2a_1 + (n-1)d$
Total	S_n	S_n	$n[2a_1 + (n-1)d] = 2S_n$

column B we have listed the same n terms but in the reverse order, so that a_n appears at the top and a_1 at the bottom; obviously though, they still add up to S_n since they are exactly the same terms as those in column A.

Now consider adding terms which occur on the same row of column A and column B. On row 1, we have $a_1 + [a_1 + (n-1)d]$ which equals $2a_1 + (n-1)d$; we put this into column C. On row 2, we have $[a_1 + d] + [a_1 + (n-2)d]$ which also equals $2a_1 + (n-1)d$ and goes into column C. In fact each of the n rows gives a total of $2a_1 + (n-1)d$ when we add the entry in column A to that in column B and put the result into column C.

Since column C consists of n terms, each equal to $2a_1 + (n-1)d$, the total of all the terms in this column will be $n[2a_1 + (n-1)d]$. However, it must also equal the total of column A, which is S_n, plus the total of column B, which is also S_n.

Hence

$$2S_n = n[2a_1 + (n-1)d]$$

and so

$$S_n = \frac{n}{2}[2a_1 + (n-1)d]. \tag{4.4}$$

Dividing by 2 inside the square bracket, we obtain the general formula for the sum of n terms of an AP:

$$S_n = \sum_{j=1}^{n} a_j = n\left[a_1 + \frac{(n-1)}{2}d\right]. \qquad (4.5)$$

There are several equivalent ways of writing this result but formula (4.5) is the most convenient to use if we know the first term (a_1), the common difference (d) and the number of terms (n).

Example 4.7
With the data of Example 4.1, we have the first term $a_1 = 6$, the common difference $d = 4$ and the number of terms $n = 5$. Hence

$$S_5 = 5[6 + \tfrac{1}{2}(5-1) \times 4] = 5 \times 14 = 70.$$

As only five terms are involved in this case, we can check the answer by simply adding them all together:

$$S_5 = 6 + 10 + 14 + 18 + 22 = 70.$$

If we know that the sequence is an AP and know the values of the first and last terms (a_1 and a_n) and the number of terms (n), it is generally more convenient to rewrite formula (4.4) in terms of a_1 and a_n as

$$S_n = \frac{n}{2}[a_1 + a_1 + (n-1)d]$$

$$= \frac{n}{2}[a_1 + a_n]. \qquad (4.6)$$

The expression on the right-hand side of this can easily be remembered as 'number of terms times the average of the first and last terms'.

Example 4.8
Again using the data of Example 4.1 with $n = 5$, the first term is 6 and the last term is 22, so formula (4.6) gives

$$S_5 = 5\frac{[6+22]}{2} = 5 \times 28/2 = 70$$

as before.

It is sometimes convenient to use a zero subscript to label the initial term (as we noted in connection with Figure 4.1) and sum over $(n+1)$

terms, with j running from 0 to n. In this case the rule 'number of terms times the average of the first and last terms' still applies, and it gives:

$$\sum_{j=0}^{n} a_j = (n+1) \frac{[a_0 + a_n]}{2}$$

(4.7)

$$= (n+1)\left[a_0 + \frac{n}{2}d\right].$$

In choosing between formulas (4.5) or (4.6) and formula (4.7), the user must decide whether the first term to be included in the sum corresponds to a_0 or a_1.

Example 4.9
A company has four machines of a certain type. Each machine requires a particular part to be replaced every month. The company can only buy the spare parts in batches of fifty and has just taken delivery of a batch immediately after fitting the last remaining parts to the four machines, so that the current stock level is fifty. If it costs £3 per month to store one of these spare parts, find the total cost of storing these parts over the next 12 months.

Solution
Let a_0 denote the stock at the start of the process. The stock remains at this level throughout the first month, so (working in £1 units) the storage cost in this first month is $3a_0$. At the end of the first month, the stock goes down to $a_0 - 4 = a_1$ and it remains at this level until the end of the second month, so the cost in the second month is $3a_1$ and the total cost for the first 2 months is $3(a_0 + a_1)$. During the third month the stock is $a_1 - 4 = a_2$, the cost for the third month alone is $3a_2$ and the total cost for the first 3 months is $3(a_0 + a_1 + a_2)$.

Extending this reasoning to cover 12 months, we see that the total storage cost will be $3(a_0 + a_1 + a_2 + \ldots + a_{11})$, where the terms in brackets represent the sum of 12 terms of an AP with initial term a_0 (which we know equals 50) and constant common difference $d = -4$ (notice the negative sign, which indicates a decrease). We can call this sum of bracketed terms S and evaluate it by using formula (4.7) with $n = 11$:

$$S = (n+1)\left[a_0 + \frac{n}{2}d\right] = 12\left[50 + \frac{11}{2}(-4)\right]$$

$$= 12[50 - 22] = 12 \times 28 = 336.$$

Multiplying by the unit storage cost (£3 per month) we find the required total cost of storage to be £3S = £3 × 336 = £1008.

It is much more efficient to use the formula rather than to calculate the stock levels for each of the 12 months, add up these 12 values and then multiply by 3 – but the numerical result is exactly the same, because

$$3(50 + 46 + 42 + \ldots + 10 + 6) = 3 \times 336 = 1008.$$

4.4   Geometric progression (GP)

In Section 4.1, we saw that any sequence characterized by having a *common constant difference* between successive terms is an *arithmetic progression* (AP). Another type of sequence, which in business mathematics is even more important than the AP, is called the *geometric progression* (GP); this is characterized by having a *common constant ratio* between successive terms.

Example 4.10
Check whether the following sequence is a GP.

3, 6, 12, 24, 48.

Solution
Ratio (second term)/(first term) = 6/3 = 2
Ratio (third term)/(second term) = 12/6 = 2
Ratio (fourth term)/(third term) = 24/12 = 2
Ratio (fifth term)/(fourth term) = 48/24 = 2.

Clearly there is a common constant ratio of 2 between successive terms, and therefore the sequence is a GP.

To distinguish the GP from the AP, we shall denote the typical term of the GP (or possible GP) by u_j rather than a_j.

In general, for any GP, we denote the common constant ratio by r. The typical term of the GP may then be expressed in terms of r and the first term. To develop the general formula for the typical term, u_j, let us look again at the sequence in Example 4.10 above.

The first term was $u_1 = 3$
the second term was $u_2 = u_1 \times 2 = 3 \times 2$
the third term was $u_3 = u_2 \times 2 = 3 \times 2^2$
the fourth term was $u_4 = u_3 \times 2 = 3 \times 2^3$
the fifth term was $u_5 = u_4 \times 2 = 3 \times 2^4$.

The general term of this GP was therefore of the form

$$u_j = 3 \times 2^{j-1} \quad \text{for} \quad j = 1, 2, \ldots$$

For any GP that has first term $u_1 = a$ and common ratio r, the corresponding formula for the general term is

$$u_j = ar^{(j-1)} \quad \text{for} \quad j = 1, 2, \ldots \tag{4.8}$$

Remember that, by Rule 1.9 of Chapter 1, any quantity raised to the power 0 takes the value unity, so if we put $j = 1$ in formula (4.8) we get

$$u_1 = ar^0 = a,$$

which agrees with our definition of a as being the first term. If we put $j = 2$ in formula (4.8), we find that $u_2 = ar = u_1 \times r$ and so $u_2/u_1 = r$. Similarly, $u_3/u_2 = r$ and in general:

$$u_{j+1}/u_j = r \quad \text{for} \quad j = 1, 2, \ldots \tag{4.9}$$

To check whether a sequence is a GP, we see if it satisfies equation (4.9).

Example 4.11
Check whether the following sequence is a GP.

5, 15, 30, 45.

Solution
$u_2/u_1 = 15/5 = 3$, $u_3/u_2 = 30/15 = 2$, $u_4/u_3 = 45/30 = 1.5$.
  These ratios are not equal, so the sequence is not a GP.

4.5   Sum of terms of a GP

As in the case of the AP, it is convenient to have a formula with which we can evaluate the sum of a given number of terms of a GP without having to list the terms involved and add them one at a time.
  The sum of the first n terms of the typical GP may be written as

$$S_n = u_1 + u_2 + u_3 + \ldots + u_{n-1} + u_n. \tag{4.10}$$

Using formula (4.8) with $j = 1$ to n, we see that equation (4.10) is equivalent to

$$S_n = a + ar + ar^2 + \ldots + ar^{n-2} + ar^{n-1}. \tag{4.11}$$

Hence multiplying each term of (4.11) by r gives

$$rS_n = \quad ar + ar^2 + ar^3 + \ldots \quad + ar^{n-1} + ar^n. \tag{4.12}$$

The right-hand sides of equations (4.12) and (4.11) differ only in their first and last terms, so that if we subtract one from the other the middle terms cancel out and we have:

$$S_n - rS_n = a + ar + ar^2 + \ldots + ar^{n-2} + ar^{n-1}$$
$$- ar - ar^2 - \ldots \qquad - ar^{n-1} - ar^n$$
$$= a - ar^n.$$

Hence

$$S_n(1 - r) = a(1 - r^n). \qquad \textbf{(4.13)}$$

Dividing both sides of equation (4.13) by $(1 - r)$ we get:

$$S_n = \frac{a(1 - r^n)}{(1 - r)}. \qquad \textbf{(4.14)}$$

Note that the numerator (top) and denominator (bottom) on the right-hand side of formula (4.14) will be positive so long as r is less than 1. To avoid negative terms on both the top and the bottom, when r is greater than 1 it is convenient to use formula (4.15), which is exactly equivalent to formula (4.14):

$$S_n = \frac{a(r^n - 1)}{(r - 1)}. \qquad \textbf{(4.15)}$$

Example 4.12
Use the appropriate formula for S_n to evaluate the sum of the following terms: 128, 64, 32, 16, 8, 4.

Solution
Using formula (4.9) we find that the terms form a GP with common ratio $r = 0.5$; since this is less than 1 we shall use formula (4.14) to evaluate the sum. The first term (a) is 128 and the number of terms (n) is 6, so (4.14) gives

$$S_6 = 128(1 - 0.5^6)/(1 - 0.5)$$
$$= 128 \times 0.984\,375/0.5$$
$$= 252$$

which, in this case, can be checked by summing the six original terms. However, as we saw in the case of the AP, when there is a large number of terms it is much more efficient to use the formula rather than explicitly sum the terms.

4.6 Notation for interest calculations

The result for the sum of terms of a GP, which we obtained in the previous section, has important applications in financial problems which involve the payment of interest. In this section we introduce the terminology and notation which are widely used to deal with this sort of problem. However, readers should note that different conventions may be found in literature aimed at particular groups of users.

As our starting point, let us consider someone who borrows a sum of money on the understanding that interest will become payable on the loan at fixed equal periods until the original sum is repaid. This original sum of money, before any interest is added to it, is called the *principal* and will be denoted by P.

The *interest rate* represents the sum to be charged as interest at the end of a period expressed as a proportion of the total sum due to the lender at the start of that period. We shall call this proportion i per period. When the period is 1 year, the interest rate is quoted 'per annum', which is abbreviated to p.a. The interest rate will often be multiplied by 100 and expressed as a percentage; for example, an interest rate of 5% p.a. implies that $i = 5/100 = 0.05$. The *total interest payable over n periods* will be denoted by I_n.

It is convenient to have a name to describe the total amount of money paid by the borrower to the lender if the debt is repaid in full after n periods. This sum will be the principal plus the total interest after n periods. In this chapter we shall call this the *amount* after n periods and denote it by A_n, so that

$$A_n = P + I_n. \tag{4.16}$$

Some authors use A_n to denote an annuity and prefer to use S_n for the amount, as we have done in other chapters. However, since the convention of using S_n to denote a sum of the first n terms of a sequence, as in (4.2) above, is also widely used, this could lead to confusion in this chapter. This is an example of the need for flexibility in notation, which we mentioned in the Preface.

There are two main systems for calculating the relationship between principal and interest, but equation (4.16) applies whichever of the systems is used.

The system which is easier to deal with from a mathematical point of view is called *simple interest*. Under this system the borrower pays the same fixed proportion of the principal as interest at the end of each period. The principal is P, the proportion is i (the interest rate) and so each periodic payment is P times i. Thus, after n periods the total interest will be

$$I_n = nPi \quad \text{(simple interest)}. \tag{4.17}$$

The second system for interest calculations is described below in Section 4.7.

4.7 Compound interest

Let us now suppose that the borrower defers all the interest payments until the principal itself is repaid. The lender will then charge interest on the principal (as would be done under the simple interest system) and also upon the total unpaid (or 'accrued') interest. This system, under which the borrower pays *interest upon accrued interest*, is called *compound interest*. If interest for a year is added to the total sum outstanding and the interest for the following year is then calculated on the principal plus accrued interest, we say that it is *compounded annually* and this is the system that we shall look at first.

In order to calculate the total interest, we need to find the amount at the start of each year ('opening amount') and calculate the interest incurred in that year as a fixed proportion i of that amount. Adding the interest to the opening amount gives the amount at the end of the year ('closing amount'). At the start of the first year, the opening amount is simply P because no interest has yet been incurred. For subsequent years, the opening amount will be the closing amount from the end of the previous year. With this in mind, we can draw up Table 4.2 to show how to calculate interest and update the amount.

Table 4.2 shows us that the amount after n years will equal the principal multiplied by a factor $(1 + i)^n$. This gives us the *basic formula for compound interest*:

$$A_n = P(1 + i)^n. \tag{4.18}$$

Substituting the expression on the right-hand side of equation (4.18) for A_n in equation (4.16), we obtain an expression for the total interest accrued after n years under the compound interest system:

$$I_n = A_n - P = P(1 + i)^n - P$$

$$= P[(1 + i)^n - 1] \quad \text{(compound interest)}. \tag{4.19}$$

Equation (4.19) is the compound interest counterpart of equation (4.17) for simple interest. Since simple interest only involves paying interest

Table 4.2 Calculations for annual compounding of interest.

Year	Opening amount	Interest for the year	Closing amount = opening amount + interest for year
1	P	Pi	$P + Pi = P(1 + i) = A_1$
2	A_1	$A_1 i$	$A_1 + A_1 i = A_1(1 + i) = P(1 + i)^2 = A_2$
3	A_2	$A_2 i$	$A_2 + A_2 i = A_2(1 + i) = P(1 + i)^3 = A_3$
.	.	.	.
.	.	.	.
.	.	.	.
n	A_{n-1}	$A_{n-1} i$	$A_{n-1} + A_{n-1} i = A_{n-1}(1 + i) = P(1 + i)^n = A_n$

on the principal, we find that for any given P, i and n the compound interest system always results in more total interest being paid.

Example 4.13
Find the amount and the total interest paid over 6 years on a loan of £500 when the interest rate is 10% p.a. and interest is compounded annually. Also find the total interest that would have been paid under the simple interest system.

Solution
Working in £1 units, $P = 500$. Interest rate, $i = 10/100 = 0.10$. Number of years, $n = 6$.
By equation (4.18), the amount after 6 years is

$A_6 = 500(1 + 0.10)^6 = 500 \times 1.10^6$

$= 500 \times 1.771\,561 = 885.78$ (to nearest penny).

To find the total interest (I_6), we may simply subtract the principal (500) from this amount or – if we did not specifically want to know the amount – we could obtain the same figure by using equation (4.19):

$I_6 = 500[1.771\,561 - 1]$

$= 500 \times 0.771\,561 = 385.78$ (to nearest penny).

Under the simple interest system, equation (4.17) would have given:
$I_6 = 6 \times 500 \times 0.10 = 300$.
In this case, therefore, paying interest as soon as it became due would reduce the total interest payment by nearly £86. The borrower

would have to weigh this saving against the advantage of not having to repay anything until the end of the 6 year period and meanwhile being able to use the money for some other purpose.

To see how compound interest is related to the theory of the GP, we can think of I_n as the sum of the interest payments in individual years:

$$I_n = Pi + A_1i + A_2i + \ldots + A_{n-1}i$$
$$= Pi + P(1+i)i + P(1+i)^2i + \ldots + P(1+i)^{n-1}i,$$

which is in the form of the sum of n terms of a GP with first term $a = Pi$ and constant common ratio $r = (1+i)$, which will be greater than 1 because i will be positive. Hence the appropriate formula for the sum of n terms of a GP is (4.15), which gives:

$$I_n = S_n = \frac{a(r^n - 1)}{(r-1)}$$

with $a = Pi$ and $r = (1+i)$. Hence

$$I_n = \frac{Pi[(1+i)^n - 1]}{[(1+i) - 1]} = \frac{Pi[(1+i)^n - 1]}{i}$$

$$= P[(1+i)^n - 1],$$

which is the same as (4.19).

When interest is compounded annually, it is only necessary to specify the interest rate which we have denoted by i. However, when interest is reckoned at any interval other than a full year, we need to distinguish between i (which is then called the *nominal rate of interest* or *rate quoted*) and what is called the *effective rate of interest* or *rate paid*, denoted by j. If compounding takes place m times a year, the relationship between i and j is as follows:

$$1 + j = \left(1 + \frac{i}{m}\right)^m . \tag{4.20}$$

Example 4.14
Find the effective rate of interest that corresponds to a nominal rate of 12% p.a. when compounding takes place twice a year (once every 6 months).

Solution
Nominal rate, $i = 12/100 = 0.12$; number of payments per year, $m = 2$.

By (4.22):

$$1 + j = (1 + 0.12/2)^2$$
$$= (1.06)^2.$$

Hence

$$j = (1.06)^2 - 1$$
$$= 1.1236 - 1 = 0.1236,$$

so the effective rate is 12.36% p.a., which is greater than the nominal rate of 12% p.a.

Note that j will always be larger than i if m is greater than 1, that is if compounding takes place more than once a year. In Chapter 5 we shall see what happens when the frequency of compounding is increased to such an extent that we are continually updating the amount of principal plus interest, but for the time being we may note that the general effect of increasing the frequency of compounding (m) is to increase the difference between the nominal and effective rates of interest.

Example 4.15
Suppose that the frequency of compounding is increased to twelve times a year (once a month) and repeat the calculations for Example 4.14.

Solution
We now have $1 + j = (1 + 0.12/12)^{12} = (1.01)^{12}$.
    Hence

$$j = (1.01)^{12} - 1 = 0.1268 \quad \text{to four decimal places,}$$

so the effective rate would have risen to 12.68%, which is 0.68% above the nominal rate. Thus it would clearly be less expensive to pay interest annually rather than monthly if the same nominal rate of interest is to apply.

ADDITIONAL EXAMPLES

A4.1   Check that each of the following sequences is an arithmetic progression and, by identifying the first term and common difference, write down a formula for the sum of the first *n* terms of the sequence. Check the formula for *n* = 3 by adding the first three terms of the sequence.

(i)   100, 135, 170, 205, ...
(ii) 200, 178, 156, 134, ...

A4.2   Check that each of the following sequences is a geometric progression and, by identifying the first term and common ratio, write down a formula for the sum of the first *n* terms of the sequence. Check the formula for *n* = 3 by adding the first three terms of the sequence.

(i)   100.0, 120.0, 144.0, 172.8, ...
(ii) 500, 400, 320, 256, ...

A4.3   At the beginning of January, a maintenance department has in stock 27 units of a particular kind of spare part. At the end of each month, until June, a new unit is fitted to each of four similar machines. At the beginning of June a fifth machine is installed; after that all five machines require a new unit at the end of each month. Each unit costs £20 per month to store.

(i)   Find the total cost over the whole year of storing the spare parts if 24 additional units are delivered at the end of April.
(ii) Find the effect on the total annual storage cost if delivery of the 24 units is delayed until the end of July. Would you recommend this delay?

A4.4   A small company wishes to invest £3000 now in order to finance a project costing £5000 in 4 years' time. What rate of interest would the company require in order to achieve this?

A4.5   As the result of a successful takeover bid, the Knudsen Bolt Company has recently been acquired by a multinational conglomerate that now wishes to sell it off. A large engineering company has made a cash offer of £1.7 million. The present management of Knudsen can raise £1.0 million now and offer to supplement this with four guaranteed payments of £0.25 million each at yearly intervals over the next 4 years. Assuming an interest rate of 15% p.a. over the next 4 years, should this offer be sufficient to secure a management buyout?

5

Logarithms and exponentials

Introduction

In Chapter 4 we used the compound interest formula

A_n or $S_n = P(1 + i)^n$

to obtain the value to which a given sum P will increase at a specified rate of interest i over n periods of time when n is known. In some cases it is necessary to look at the problem from a different point of view. For example, we might wish to know how long it would take for an asset to double in value with a specified rate of interest. This means that we are now given S, P and i but need to find n in the formula above. Finding the unknown value of an exponent, like this n, requires us to carry out the reverse of raising a number to a power. In such cases, we need to use *logarithms* as well as exponents. These are explained in the following sections of this chapter. Use a calculator to confirm the numerical values in the examples.

5.1   Logarithms and exponents

The rules given in Chapter 1 for dealing with powers or indices were listed as follows.

Rule 1.6

To multiply quantities represented by the same base with different exponents, simply add the exponents:

$$a^m \times a^n = a^{m+n}.$$

Rule 1.7

To raise a term involving an exponent to a power, multiply the exponent by the power:

$$(a^m)^n = a^{mn}.$$

Rule 1.8

For different bases with the same exponent, note the following:

$$a^n b^n = (ab)^n; \qquad a^n/b^n = (a/b)^n.$$

Rule 1.9

Any quantity raised to the power 0 takes the value unity:

$$a^0 = 1.$$

It is most important to remember this rule, since it is frequently used.

In Rule 1.6 given above, we could evaluate the functions a^m and a^n and then multiply them to obtain the answer or apply the rule of adding the exponents.

Call the first quantity $y_1 = a^m$ and the second quantity $y_2 = a^n$. Multiply these two to give the answer

$$y_1 \times y_2 = a^m \times a^n = a^{m+n}.$$

Example 5.1
Evaluate $10^{1.5} \times 10^{2.6}$.

Solution
Let $y_1 = 10^{1.5}$ and $y_2 = 10^{2.6}$.

Either: Evaluate y_1 and y_2 on your calculator using the x^y key:

$$y_1 = 31.622\,777$$

$$y_2 = 398.107\,17$$

$$y_1 \times y_2 = 31.622\,777 \times 398.107\,17 = 12\,589.254.$$

Or: Use Rule 1.6 and add the indices:

$$y_1 \times y_2 = 10^{1.5} \times 10^{2.6} = 10^{4.1}.$$

Use the x^y key to evaluate $10^{4.1}$:

$$y_1 \times y_2 = 10^{4.1} = 12\,589.254.$$

Division is carried out in a similar fashion.

Example 5.2
Evaluate

$$\frac{10^{2.6}}{10^{1.5}}.$$

Solution
Let $y_1 = 10^{1.5}$ and $y_2 = 10^{2.6}$.
   We want to evaluate

$$\frac{y_1}{y_2} = \frac{10^{2.6}}{10^{1.5}}.$$

This can be done either by using Rule 1.6 or by finding the numerical value of the numerator and denominator, then dividing.

Alternative A   Use Rule 1.6:

$$\frac{y_2}{y_1} = 10^{2.6} \times 10^{-1.5} = 10^{2.6-1.5} = 10^{1.1}.$$

Use the x^y key on the calculator to evaluate the answer as

$$10^{1.1} = 12.589\,54.$$

Alternative B   Evaluate the numerator and denominator separately, and then divide. Use the x^y key to evaluate

$$y_2 = 10^{2.6} = 398.107\,17$$

$$y_1 = 10^{1.5} = 31.622\,777.$$

Then divide

$$\frac{y_2}{y_1} = \frac{398.107\,17}{31.622\,777} = 12.589\,254.$$

From Example 5.2 above, it can be seen that the rules for dealing with powers can be of use in multiplication and division problems. Before the advent of pocket calculators, most cumbersome arithmetic was dealt with by using these rules. Tables of values of 10^x and its inverse were used instead of calculators but the procedure was exactly the same as in Alternative A above. The tables were called 'logarithmic tables'.

5.2 How logarithms work

Consider what is meant by our value $y_1 = 10^{1.5}$ in Example 5.2. This means that the number 10 is raised to the power 1.5. We know that $10^1 = 10$ and $10^2 = 100$, so $10^{1.5}$ must be between 10 and 100 as we have already shown when y_1 was evaluated in Alternative B. This procedure of raising a number to a power can be written in more general terms as

$$y = a^x \qquad\qquad (5.1)$$

and we could substitute any value for a and x.

The number a is called the *base* and x is called the *logarithm of y to the base a*, written as

$$x = \log_a(y) \qquad\qquad (5.2)$$

and usually read as 'x equals log to the base a of y'.

Taking the logarithm is the *inverse* (reverse procedure) of raising to a power and is used whenever an equation to be solved has the variable whose value is sought in the exponent (power).

Example 5.3
Solve the equation $31.622\,777 = 10^x$.

Solution
Compare $31.622\,777 = 10^x$

with $y = a^x$.

We have $y = 31.622\,777$ and $a = 10$.

The inverse is

$$x = \log_a(y).$$

Substituting for a and y gives

$$x = \log_{10}(31.622\,777).$$

The key marked 'log' on the calculator evaluates the logarithm to the base 10 of the number shown in the display before the key is pressed. Use this to evaluate x in this example.

Enter   31.622 777

Press   log

Answer   1.5 appears in the display.

Thus

$$1.5 = \log_{10}(31.622\,777).$$

To check the answer, reverse the process and use the x^y key to raise 10 to the power 1.5; you will obtain the answer 31.622 777.

The 10^x key
Since there is frequently a need to evaluate numbers of the type 10^x, a key for this is provided on the calculator. This procedure is the inverse of taking a log to the base 10 and so the 10^x key is usually positioned beside the 'log' key.

Logarithms using bases other than 10 can be used but very few other bases are of any practical use. In the following examples the bases 2 and 3 have been used and the logarithms calculated, together with their inverses. The graphs of each curve are given in the following diagram (Figure 5.1).

Example 5.4
Use the base $a = 2$. Use a calculator to find the following values of y.
Putting $a = 2$ into equation (5.1) gives

$$y = 2^x \tag{5.3}$$

and putting $a = 2$ into equation (5.2) gives

$$x = \log_2(y). \tag{5.4}$$

Column 1 By equation (5.3)	Column 2 By equation (5.4)
$y = 2^1 = 2$	$x = 1 = \log_2(2)$
$y = 2^{1.5} = 2.8284$	$x = 1.5 = \log_2(2.8284)$
$y = 2^2 = 4$	$x = 2 = \log_2(4)$
$y = 2^{2.5} = 5.6569$	$x = 2.5 = \log_2(5.6569)$
$y = 2^3 = 8$	$x = 3 = \log_2(8)$

Looking at the two columns and their related equations in the table you can see that in column 1 the object is to find y for a given value of x. The graph is drawn in the usual manner in Figure 5.1 with the given x-values along the horizontal axis and their corresponding y-values along the vertical axis. In column 2 the object is to find x for a given value of y. That is, the usual roles of x and y have been reversed. Here we are trying to determine the inverse, the power to which the base, 2, has been raised. The graph in Figure 5.2 has the given values of y along

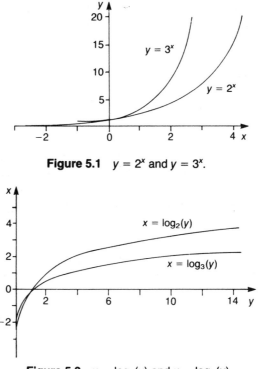

Figure 5.1 $y = 2^x$ and $y = 3^x$.

Figure 5.2 $x = \log_2(y)$ and $x = \log_3(y)$.

the horizontal axis and their corresponding values of x along the vertical axis.

A few values of x and y have been listed above. The complete graph was drawn by a computer which evaluated y for values of x spaced at intervals 0.01 units apart. In practice, when drawing such a graph without a computer you would need more points than those listed above, with more values calculated in regions where the curvature of the graph was greatest.

Example 5.5
Take the base $a = 3$. Use a calculator to confirm the following values of y.

Putting $a = 3$ into equation (5.1) gives

$$y = 3^x \tag{5.5}$$

and putting $a = 3$ into equation (5.2) gives

$$x = \log_3(y). \tag{5.6}$$

The same method as that used in Example 5.4 above has been used to find the sample of points listed in the table below. Many more points were found in order to draw the graphs, which are shown in Figures 5.1 and 5.2.

By equation (5.5)	By equation (5.6)
$y = 3^{0.5} = 1.7321$	$x = 0.5 = \log_3(1.7321)$
$y = 3^1 = 3$	$x = 1.0 = \log_3(3)$
$y = 3^{1.5} = 5.1962$	$x = 1.5 = \log_3(5.1962)$
$y = 3^2 = 9$	$x = 2.0 = \log_3(9)$
$y = 3^{2.5} = 15.5885$	$x = 2.5 = \log_3(15.5885)$

Comment
The graph of $y = 3^x$ is much steeper than that of $y = 2^x$. In general, providing $a > 1$, the greater the value of a the steeper the curve will be.

Example 5.6
Use the base $a = 10$. Use the 10^x key on the calculator to confirm the following values of y.

Putting $a = 10$ into equation (5.1) gives

$$y = 10^x \tag{5.7}$$

and putting $a = 10$ into equation (5.2) gives

$$x = \log_{10}(y) \qquad \qquad \textbf{(5.8)}$$

By equation (5.7)	By equation (5.8)
$y = 10^0 = 1.0$	$x = 0 = \log_{10}(1)$
$y = 10^{0.5} = 3.1623$	$x = 0.5 = \log_{10}(3.1623)$
$y = 10^{0.75} = 5.6234$	$x = 0.75 = \log_{10}(5.6234)$
$y = 10^1 = 10$	$x = 1.0 = \log_{10}(1.0)$
$y = 10^2 = 100$	$x = 2.0 = \log_{10}(100)$
$y = 10^{2.6} = 398.1072$	$x = 2.6 = \log_{10}(398.1072)$

In Examples 5.4, 5.5 and 5.6 above, x is referred to as the *logarithm* of y to the *base a*, and y is called the *anti-logarithm* of x. These terms are usually abbreviated to *log* and *anti-log*.

The shape of the curve of the function $y = a^x$ depends upon the value of a. Since $a^0 = 1.0$ no matter what value is given to a, all such curves will pass through the point ($x = 0$, $y = 1.0$). Sketches of the curves for positive values of a are given in Figure 5.3.

Note
Figures 5.3(a) and (b) show $y = a^x$ for a range of x values near zero, but in theory we could evaluate y for x ranging from infinity (written with the symbol ∞) to minus infinity ($-\infty$).
It is possible to determine values of $y = a^x$ for negative values of x. The graph of $y = 2^x$ in Figure 5.3(a) shows y approaching zero as x approaches $-\infty$. This is true for all graphs of $y = a^x$ where $a > 1$. In Figure 5.3(b) we have $a = 1/2$, that is $a < 1$. Here y approaches zero as x tends to $+\infty$.

In practice it is often important to know the values of y at the extremes when x gets very large or very small. For example, a knowledge of what is expected to happen to demand at the start and end of a product life cycle is necessary for production and investment planning. When in doubt about the value of any function as x tends to an extreme value, simply key a very large negative or positive value of x into your calculator. The display will show 'E' for 'error' if the resulting value of the function is close to either $+\infty$ or $-\infty$. Try calculating the value of the function $y = a^x$ for $a = 2$ and $x = 999\,999\,9$ to demonstrate this statement. Now try calculating the value of the same function with $a = 1/2$ and $x = -999\,999\,9$.
Your calculator can be used in a similar fashion to demonstrate that

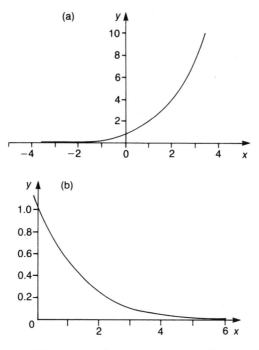

Figure 5.3 (a) $y = a^x$ for $a = 2$. (b) $y = a^x$ for $a = \frac{1}{2}$.

$\log_a(x)$ does not exist for any negative values of x. Logarithms only exist for positive values of the base, a, and for positive, non-zero values of x. If the base, a, is greater than 1 then $\log_a(x)$ approaches or tends to $-\infty$ as x approaches zero. The base, a, can in theory take any positive value, but for most practical applications only two values are used, $a = 10$ and $a = e$ (which will be explained in Section 5.4 below). The base $a = 10$ was used for multiplying and dividing complicated numbers before the advent of calculators. Some quantities such as noise are measured using a base of 10 (an increase of 1 decibel in noise level means a tenfold increase in sound). Logarithms to the base 10 are sometimes called 'common logarithms' in order to distinguish them from those with other bases. The logarithm with the base $a = e$, called the 'natural logarithm', is used most often nowadays. On a calculator, the two types of logarithm are usually distinguished by using 'ln' for the log to the base e and 'log' for the log to the base 10.

Example 5.7
Use the $\log_{10}$ key and the 10^x key on the calculator to multiply 92.5 by 361.7.

Solution

Find $\log_{10}$ for both numbers by using the 'log' key. The results, correct to eight figures, are as follows:

$\log_{10}(92.5) = 1.966\,141\,7$ and $\log_{10}(361.7) = 2.558\,348\,5$.

These equations are in the form of equation (5.2) with $a = 10$, so they could alternatively be written in the form of equation (5.1):

$92.5 = 10^{1.966\,141\,7}$ and $361.7 = 10^{2.558\,348\,5}$.

By Rule 1.6 for indices,

$$92.5 \times 361.7 = 10^{1.966\,141\,7} \times 10^{2.558\,348\,5}$$
$$= 10^{1.966\,141\,7 + 2.558\,348\,5}$$
$$= 10^{4.524\,490\,2}.$$

Now use the 10^x key to evaluate the right-hand side:

$10^{4.524\,490\,2} = 33\,457.247$ to eight figures

$\qquad\qquad = 33\,457.25$ to seven figures (or two decimal places).

Straightforward multiplication shows that

$92.5 \times 361.7 = 33\,457.25$ exactly.

5.3   Rules for combining logarithms

The following rules for manipulating logarithms apply no matter what base value is used.

Rule 5.1

$\log(A . B) = \log(A) + \log(B)$.

Rule 5.2

$$\log\left(\frac{A}{B}\right) = \log(A) - \log(B).$$

Rule 5.3

$\log(A^n) = n . \log(A)$.

Rule 5.4

Logarithms do not exist for negative values of *x*.

These rules have a variety of applications, for example Rule 5.3 will be used in Chapter 7 for finding the derivative of the function $y = \log(A^n)$. Whenever a function involves logarithms it is worth looking at these rules to see if the possibility exists for simplifying that function.

5.4   The exponential function and continuous compounding

In Chapter 4, we explained the basic equation for compound interest, equation (4.19), and the relationship between nominal and effective rates of interest when compounding was carried out *m* times per year, equation (4.20). Combining these two equations, we obtain the following expression for the future value (or amount), A_n, of a principal *P* at the end of *n* full years when interest at a nominal rate of *i* per annum is compounded *m* times per year:

$$A_n = P\left(1 + \frac{i}{m}\right)^{mn}. \tag{5.9}$$

Equation (5.9) has been used to draw the graphs in Figure 5.4, which shows how the value of £1 increases with time for an annual interest rate of *i* = 0.30, or 30%, and various frequencies of compounding. In Figure 5.4(a) the interest is compounded annually, in Figure 5.4(b) it is compounded every 6 months, in Figure 5.4(c) quarterly and in Figure 5.4(d) monthly. It can be seen that, as the frequency of compounding increases (i.e. the interval becomes shorter), the stepped appearance of the graph becomes less marked until eventually, if the interval is very short, the plot of A_n against time becomes a smooth curve. Compare the shape of the curve in Figure 5.4(d) with that of the curve in Figure 5.3(a). It can then be seen that, if we were to draw a curve of A_n against time for daily compounding, the shape of this curve would be very similar to that of

$$y = a^x. \tag{5.10}$$

All curves where the compounding may be considered to be virtually

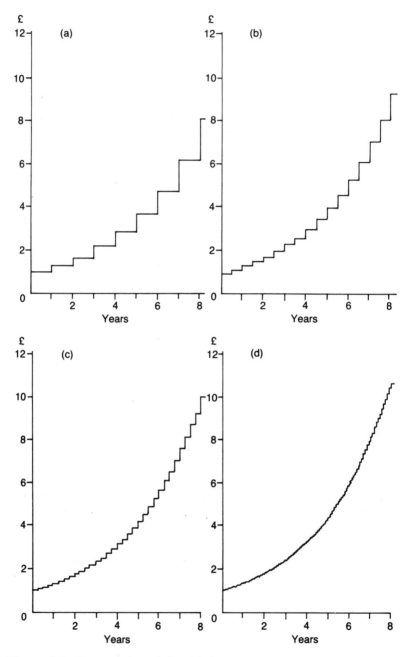

Figure 5.4 Future value of £1. (a) Annual compounding, (b) 6 monthly, (c) quarterly, (d) monthly.

continuous will be of this shape. This type of growth is referred to as *exponential growth* since the value of a^x is always the same as that given by the *exponential function*.

The exponential function

$$y = e^x \tag{5.11}$$

occurs naturally in many instances. It is sometimes referred to as the 'natural exponential function'. A key marked e^x is provided on scientific calculators for evaluating the function. To evaluate, say, e^2 simply proceed as follows:

Enter   2 on the display

Press e^x

Answer   7.389 056 1 appears in the display.

To find the value of $e = e^1$ simply follow the above procedure entering 1 on the display and pressing the e^x key. The value $e = 2.718\,281\,8$ appears in the display. This is the value rounded to seven decimal places. To be exact, the value of e has an infinite number of decimal places but is always rounded to a finite number in practice. Like π, the constant ratio between the circumference and diameter of a circle, the quantity e is a fundamental mathematical quantity.

The graph of $y = e^x$ is shown in Figure 5.5. As you can see, it is much the same shape as the graphs of $y = 2^x$ and $y = 3^x$ in Figure 5.1. The curve passes through the point $(x = 0, y = 1)$ and becomes steeper as the value of x increases.

Consider the function

$$y = Ae^{rx}. \tag{5.12}$$

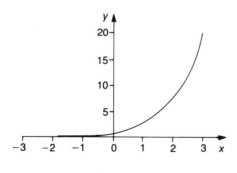

Figure 5.5 $y = e^x$.

This has a shape similar to that of the curve in Figure 5.5 but with a different slope to the line. When $x = 0$, then $y = A$, and thus the curve passes through the point $(x = 0, y = A)$. The parameter A is sometimes referred to as the initial value of y. The parameter r governs the rate at which y changes for any given change in x, that is r governs the slope of the curve. Example 5.8 below illustrates what happens to the shape of the curve if the value of r is increased.

Example 5.8
Draw and compare the two curves $y = 5e^{2x}$ and $y = 5e^{0.5x}$.

Solution
First calculate the values of y for each value of x in the usual fashion.

The curves are shown in Figure 5.6. It can be seen that the values of y increase much more rapidly with changes in x for the curve $y = e^{2x}$ than for the curve $y = e^{0.5x}$. In general the larger the value of r in equation (5.12) the more rapidly y increases.

A situation where prices are subject to high inflation may be assumed to follow the continuous growth curve, since prices will be increasing by significant amounts daily. The price to be paid x units of time hence for an asset which is presently worth £A is given by the formula

$$y = Ae^{rx}.$$

Compare this with the value of an asset presently worth £A compounded over x units of time at an effective rate j per unit of time.

$$y = A(1 + j)^x. \tag{5.13}$$

To make the comparison easier, write equation (5.12) in the form

$$y = A(e^r)^x. \tag{5.14}$$

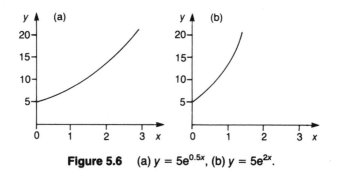

Figure 5.6   (a) $y = 5e^{0.5x}$, (b) $y = 5e^{2x}$.

You can now see that the term e^r in equation (5.14) performs the same function as the term $1 + j$ in equation (5.13), namely it controls the rate at which the value of the asset increases. The difference is that in a compound interest situation the value increases in steps at the end of each time period whilst in the continuous growth situation there is a smooth increase in growth, since there are no distinct divisions between time periods. Figure 5.7(a) shows the future value of an asset presently worth £2 compounded daily at an effective annual rate of 40%, or $j = 0.4$. Figure 5.7(b) shows the value of an asset presently worth £2 which is subject to continuous growth at a rate of 40% annually. It can be seen that there is no distinguishable difference between the two curves in these two figures when they are drawn to this degree of accuracy.

5.5 Nominal interest rates and effective interest rates

Equations (5.13) and (5.14) in the preceding section represent the formula for interest compounded periodically and that for interest compounded continuously. In drawing Figure 5.7(a) we put $1 + j = 1.4$ and in drawing Figure 5.7(b) we put $e^r = 1.4$. If com-

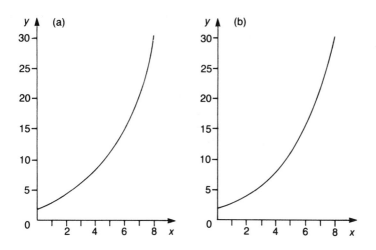

Figure 5.7 (a) $y = 2(1 + j)^x$ with $j = 0.4$, (b) $y = 2e^{rx}$ with $e^r = 1.4$.

pounding is carried out so frequently that we may assume that it is continuous, we can make the general statement that

$$1 + j = e^r.$$

Rearranging this gives

$$j = e^r - 1, \tag{5.15}$$

where j is the effective rate for periodic compounding and r is the nominal rate for continuous compounding.

As we have already seen for the case of compounding a fixed number of times per period, in the case of continuous compounding the effective rate will be greater than the nominal rate.

For example, assume that £1 is compounded continuously at a nominal rate of 40% per annum, so that $r = 0.40$. After 1 year, its value will be

$$e^{0.40} = 1.4918.$$

The effective rate of interest over that year will therefore be

$$j = e^{0.40} - 1$$
$$= 1.4918 - 1$$
$$= 0.4918 \quad \text{or} \quad 49.18\%,$$

which is appreciably higher than the nominal rate of 40%.

Exercise
Try proving for yourself that a nominal rate of 5% with continuous compounding yields an effective rate of 5.13% rounded to two decimal places.

To summarize the contents of this section: simply remember that the nominal rate of interest is the rate quoted and the effective rate of interest is the rate actually paid. For continuous compounding, the nominal rate represents the value of r in the formula for exponential growth; the effective rate will be greater than this.

5.6 Negative growth

In all of the preceding examples that involve the exponential function, the value of the asset has always been increasing. In real life it is possible for the value of an asset to decrease. This is dealt with simply by giving a negative sign to the parameter, r, which controls the rate of growth. A negative increase is, in fact, the opposite and is a decrease.

The graph of the function

$$y = Ae^{-rx} \qquad\qquad (5.16)$$

will always be similar in shape to that shown in Figure 5.8. The initial value when $x = 0$ is $y = Ae^{-0}$. Thus the curve will always pass through the point $(x = 0, y = A)$. Figure 5.8 shows the graph of $y = 8e^{-0.6x}$. From the graph it can be seen that when x is very large, y will be very small. This is true for all negative exponential curves. Try using a calculator to evaluate e^{-20} and you will obtain the answer $2.061\ 153\ 6 \times 10^{-9}$, which is $0.000\ 000\ 002\ 06$, in the usual notation. For most practical purposes the value of e^{-20} may be regarded as zero. As the value x increases, the value of y decreases. In mathematical terminology we say that the value of y tends to zero as the value of x tends to infinity.

The notation exp
Because typing or printing functions like e^{-x} is not easy, the notation exp is used instead of e.

Thus the function e^{-rx} would be written as

$$\exp(-rx),$$

which is much easier to type or print. The exp is an abbreviation of the word exponential.

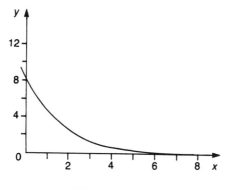

Figure 5.8 $y = 8\exp(-0.6x)$.

Example 5.9

An asset has a present value of £100 000. The value of the asset is continually decreasing and obeys the model

$$y = 100e^{-0.5x}.$$

where y is the value of the asset in thousands of pounds at a time x years from now.

Draw the graph of the value against time for this asset. Use the graph to determine how long it will take for the asset to halve in value. How long will it take for the value of the asset to depreciate to £100?

Solution

The values of y for various values of x must be calculated. This is done by using the e^x key on the calculator and the $+/-$ key to change the sign of the exponent. An example of using the method for finding the value of y when $x = 2.5$ is given.

The function to be evaluated is

$$y = 100e^{-0.5x},$$

working in units of £1000.

Enter	2.5	
Press	$\times$	
Enter	0.5	
Press	$=$	1.25 appears in the display
Press	$+/-$	-1.25 appears in the display
Press	e^x	0.286 504 8 appears in the display.

We now have $\exp(-0.5 \times 2.5) = 0.2865$ which has to be multiplied by 100 to obtain the value $y = 28.650\,48$ when $x = 2.5$. In other words, in $2\frac{1}{2}$ years' time the asset which is presently worth £100 000 will be worth £28 650.48.

Note that rounding to the nearest whole number may be dangerous in cases such as this because we are working in units of thousands of pounds. Since this graph cannot be drawn to a greater accuracy than three decimal places, this accuracy has been chosen in the subsequent calculations.

The other values of y were calculated in a similar fashion. The graph of the function $y = 100\exp(-0.5x)$ is shown in Figure 5.9 together with the table of calculations used to find the values of y.

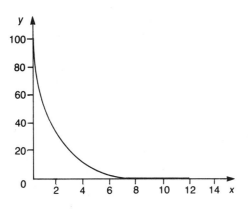

Figure 5.9 $y = 100\exp(-0.5x)$.

x	$0.5x$	$e^{-0.5x}$	$y = 100e^{-0.5x}$
0	0	1	100
1.0	0.5	0.606 531	60.653
2.0	1.0	0.367 879	36.788
3.0	1.5	0.223 130	22.313
4.0	2.0	0.135 335	13.534
6.0	3.0	0.049 787	4.979
8.0	4.0	0.018 316	1.832
10.0	5.0	0.006 738	0.674
12.0	6.0	0.002 479	0.248
15.0	7.5	0.000 553	0.055

From the graph, the value of x when $y = £50\,000$ can be read as $x = 1.4$ years. Clearly the graph needs to be drawn to a larger scale in order to improve the accuracy with which readings from it may be made. Try doing this for yourself.

The value of x when $y = £100$ is the value corresponding to $y = 0.1$ thousands on our graph scale. This cannot be easily read but is approximately $x = 14$ years.

From Example 5.9 above, it can be seen that accurate answers cannot be obtained graphically to some questions. It is clearly necessary in some instances to be able to evaluate the time taken to achieve a given value of the asset. That is, to evaluate x for a given value of y. This is the inverse of raising to a power. As explained earlier in the chapter (equations (5.1) and (5.2)), the inverse of raising to a power is to take the logarithm.

The Essence of Mathematics for Business

If we have raised the exponential, e, to a power we need to take the logarithm to the base e to determine x, that is to find

$$x = \log_e(y). \tag{5.17}$$

This is usually written as

$$x = \ln(y) \tag{5.18}$$

where $\ln(y)$ is understood to mean the logarithm of y to the base e. As we have noted above in Section 5.2, there is an 'ln' key on the calculator which evaluates $\ln(y)$. The e^x key is usually next to the 'ln' (logarithm to the base e) key.

Example 5.10
The value of an asset obeys the model

$$y = 100 \times \exp(-0.5x),$$

where y is measured in units of £1000 and x in years.

(i) Calculate how long it will take for the asset to halve in value.
(ii) Calculate how long it will take for the value of the asset to depreciate to £100 or less.

Solution

(i) How long to halve in value? Half the present value is $y = £50\,000$. Put $y = 50$ into the equation and evaluate x:

$$50 = 100e^{-0.5x}$$
$$\frac{50}{100} = e^{-0.5x}$$
$$0.5 = e^{-0.5x}.$$

Take the logarithm to the base e of both sides, using the 'ln' key to evaluate the left-hand side:

$$\ln(0.5) = -0.5x$$
$$-0.6931 = -0.5x$$

and so

$$x = \frac{-0.6931}{-0.5} = 1.386.$$

It will take 1.4 years or approximately a year and 5 months for the asset to halve in value.

(ii) How long to reach less than £100? Put $y = 0.10$ thousand into the equation:

$$0.1 = 100e^{-0.5x}$$
$$\frac{0.1}{100} = e^{-0.5x}$$
$$0.001 = e^{-0.5x}.$$

Take the log to the base e of both sides, using the 'ln' key for the left-hand side:

$$\ln(0.001) = -0.5x$$
$$-6.9077 = -0.5x$$
$$13.8155 = x.$$

It will take 13.8 years for the asset to depreciate to £100.

Which logarithm to use?
We have used logarithms to the base 10 (log), as well as logarithms to the base e (ln). The question often arises as to which logarithm to use when. The answer is simply to use the base 10 logarithm where the equation to be solved includes terms of the type 10^x and logarithms to the base e where e^x is involved.

If neither 10^x nor e^x is included in the equation to be solved then it does not matter which base is used; the answer will be the same whichever is used.

5.7 Application

Hyperinflation
If the rate of inflation is very high, prices can rise daily. In such cases, prices can be treated as changing continually rather than in steps as they would when inflation is low. With any continual growth, we generally use some model involving the exponential function. If there is no ceiling to the growth, and the underlying growth rate is constant, the exponential model

$$y = Ae^{rt} \tag{5.19}$$

is appropriate.

Example 5.11
A country has a rate of inflation of 80% per annum. Price rises may be regarded as continuous. If an item costs £50 today, how much will it cost in 5 years' time?

How long will it be before the item costs three times its present purchase price?

Solution
The price rises are continuous and so the exponential model is appropriate. The rate is 80% per annum or $r = 0.80$ if we take the year as our time unit. The present price is £50 and so the initial value is $A = 50$. Putting these parameters into the model in equation (5.28) gives

$$y = 50 \times \exp(0.8t)$$

where t is measured in years.

To find the price in 5 years' time, substitute $t = 5$ in the model.

$$y = 50 \times \exp(0.8 \times 5)$$
$$y = 50 \times \exp(4.0) = 50 \times 54.5982 = 2729.9075.$$

In 5 years' time the item will cost £2729.91 to purchase.

How long before the price triples?

Here we know that the price after some time, t, is $y = £3 \times 50$, that is triple the initial price. We have to find the value of t for which $y = £150$. Substitute $y = 150$, $A = 50$ and $r = 0.8$ in the model:

$$150 = 50e^{0.8t}.$$

The unknown, t, is in the exponent and so logarithms must be used. Simplify and then take the ln of both sides. Since the equation involves the exponential function it is necessary to use logarithms to the base e (natural logarithms).

$$\frac{150}{50} = e^{0.8t}$$

$$3 = e^{0.8t}.$$

Take the ln of both sides:

$$\ln(3) = \ln(e^{0.8t})$$
$$1.0986 = 0.8t$$

$$\frac{1.0986}{0.8} = t$$

$$t = 1.3733 \text{ years.}$$

It will take 1.37 years or approximately a year and 4 months for the price of the item to triple.

In Example 5.11 above, an inflation rate of 80% per annum was in force. If goods cost 80% more to buy in 1 year's time, it follows that the purchasing power of the currency will be reduced by 80%. This reduction in purchasing power can also be described using the exponential model with a negative rate of growth. The model is

$$y = A \times \exp(-rt). \tag{5.20}$$

Example 5.12
A currency has a rate of inflation of 80% per annum. How long will it take for the purchasing power of the currency to fall to one-quarter of its value today?

Solution
The rate of decline of the purchasing power is 80% or $r = -0.80$. Take an initial value of $A = 1$ and find out how long it will take for this to fall to a value of 1/4. That is, we need to determine t in the equation

$$1/4 = 1 \times e^{-0.8t}$$

or

$$e^{-0.8t} = 0.25.$$

Take the natural logarithms of both sides since the exponential function appears in the equation.

$$-0.8t = \ln(0.25)$$

$$-0.8t = -1.3863$$

$$t = \frac{-1.3863}{-0.8} = 1.7329.$$

(Remember that dividing a negative quantity by a negative quantity results in a positive quantity.)

It will take 1.73 years, or about a year and 9 months, for the purchasing power of the currency to reduce to one-quarter of its present-day purchasing power.

ADDITIONAL EXAMPLES

Use a calculator to obtain the relevant values of e^x and $\ln(x)$ in the following questions. The term 'log' refers to logarithm to the base 10 and the term 'ln' refers to logarithm to the base e.

A5.1 (i) Plot the graph of $y = e^x$ between $x = 0$ and $x = 4$.
(ii) Plot the graph of $y = e^{-x}$ between $x = 0$ and $x = 4$.
(iii) Plot the graph of $y = e^{2x}$ between $x = 0$ and $x = 2$.

A5.2 (i) Plot the graph of $y = \ln(x)$ between $x = 0.1$ and $x = 4$.
(ii) Plot the graph of $y = \ln(2x)$ between $x = 0.1$ and $x = 4$.
(iii) Plot the graph of $y = \ln(x^2)$ between $x = 0.1$ and $x = 4$.

A5.3 Simplify the expressions:

(i) $f(x) = 2\ln(x-1) + \ln(x+1) - 2\ln(x^2-1)$.
(ii) $f(x,y) = 2\log_a(x-y) + 3\log_a(x+y) - 2\log_a(x^2-y^2)$.

A5.4 Solve the equation $(0.56)^{x-1} = (0.37)^{2x+1}$.

A5.5 Solve the equation $(0.35)^{x+1} = (0.52)^{x-1}$.

A5.6 A growth function is defined as $P = be^{ct}$, where P is the price of a basket of goods, b is the initial value of the goods and c is the continuous rate of inflation; $b = £100$ and $c = 2\%$ per month. Plot the growth function over a period of 2 years. What would you expect to pay for the basket of goods:

(i) after a period of 6 months has elapsed,
(ii) after a period of 18 months has elapsed?

A5.7 An asset, A, has a present value of £10 000 which depreciates exponentially. The value of the asset at the end of t years is given as

$$y = 10\,000e^{-0.1t}.$$

(i) Calculate the value of the asset A after 5 years and after 10 years.
(ii) How long will it take for the asset to halve in value?
(iii) Sketch the graph of y against t for values of t between 0 and 10 years. How much has the value of asset A depreciated over the first 10 year period?

A5.8 On a particular section of road, the daily number of vehicles, N, appears to be following a *logistic* growth curve,

$$N = 10\,000/[1 + 9\exp(-0.03t)],$$

where t is the time in months since the road was reopened after improvements.

It is estimated that when the daily traffic flow reaches 3000 vehicles planning for a new road should be set in motion. How long will it take for the traffic flow to reach 3000 vehicles per day?

A5.9 A firm wishes to reduce the workforce at one of its factories by 'natural wastage' and eventually to close the factory. Using W to denote the size of the workforce, the present value of W is 1200 and it is assumed that t months after announcing the intended closure the value will be given (to a good approximation) by

$$W = 1200\exp(-0.1t).$$

(i) Calculate the size of the workforce after
    (a) 6 months   (b) 12 months.
(ii) How long will it take for the workforce to reduce to half its present size?
(iii) The factory must close when only 100 people are left. How long will it take to reach this situation?

A5.10 In a model for stock control, demand is assumed to be governed by certain probability laws and excess demand may be backlogged until more stock is delivered. A particular model of this kind relates the level of stock at which an order should be placed, r ('the reorder level'), to the order quantity, Q, by

$$\exp(-r/M) = piQ/(xM)$$

where M is mean demand per month, p purchasing cost per unit, i interest rate per month and s cost per unit of shortage which causes a backlog.
    Evaluate r given that $k = 5, p = 12, M = 20, s = 25, i = 0.01$ and $Q = 200$.

6

Matrices

Introduction

Management information is often presented as an array of numbers laid out in rows and columns. A simple example is shown below in Table 6.1.

Table 6.1 Present numbers of grade 1 and grade 2 workers at factories 1, 2 and 3.

	Factory 1	Factory 2	Factory 3
Grade 1	27	45	39
Grade 2	58	75	66

This kind of layout is used in *spreadsheets*, where the rows are usually numbered and the columns denoted by different letters. We shall consider both rows and columns to be numbered, starting from the top left-hand corner of the array, so that in our example row 1 relates to grade 1, row 2 to grade 2 and columns 1, 2 and 3 to factories 1, 2 and 3 respectively.

From a mathematical point of view, the whole array of numbers in the body of the table is called a *matrix* (the plural is *matrices*) and the individual numbers in the array are called *elements* of the matrix (some authors call these *components* rather than elements). The meaning of each element is determined by its position in the matrix, so that in Table 6.1 the entry in row 1 and column 2 tells us that there are 45 grade

1 workers at factory 2, whereas the entry in row 2 and column 1 tells us that there are 58 grade 2 workers at factory 1.

The basic data on present numbers of workers might be used to calculate wages or to study the effects of projected changes in the workforce – all of which would involve certain arithmetic operations (addition, multiplication, etc.) on the elements of the original matrix. When we have a small matrix it is not too much trouble to write out the required operations in full, but for large matrices this is time consuming and it is usually unnecessary if we use the special matrix notation which is described in the next section. However, before we go any further, we must state a general rule that applies to all matrix work.

Rule 6.1

When considering the elements of a matrix, always think of *rows before columns*.

6.1   Matrix notation

It is usual to denote a matrix by some capital letter – for example, we might use the letter **A** to denote the matrix corresponding to the array of numbers in Table 6.1. If the elements of the matrix are displayed in full, then they are enclosed in large (usually square) brackets, so that the workforce matrix would be written:

$$\mathbf{A} = \begin{bmatrix} 27 & 45 & 39 \\ 58 & 75 & 66 \end{bmatrix}.$$

Rule 6.2

The *size* of a matrix is *the number of rows by the number of columns*, written in that order (rows before columns).

Since **A** has two rows and three columns, its size is 2×3 ('two by three'); do not multiply this out and call it 6. Specifying the size of the matrix is like specifying the size of the spreadsheet on which we are going to work. In general, if we say that a matrix is of size $m \times n$, this means that it has m rows and n columns; it tells us nothing about the numerical value of the elements. If the number of rows equals the number of columns, for example the size is $m \times m$, then we have a *square matrix*.

Rather than write the numerical values of each element, we often denote a typical element by the small (lower-case) letter corresponding to the capital letter which denotes the whole matrix – so we would use a for the typical element of matrix **A** – and this small letter is labelled with a double subscript.

Rule 6.3

For the typical matrix element a_{ij}, the *first subscript* (i) shows the *row* and the *second subscript* (j) shows the *column* in which the element is located. (Once again, rows before columns.)

For the typical element of an $m \times n$ matrix, the first subscript could take values from 1 to m and the second subscript could take values from 1 to n. The general form of the 2×3 workforce matrix would therefore be:

$$\mathbf{A} = \begin{bmatrix} a_{11} & a_{12} & a_{13} \\ a_{21} & a_{22} & a_{23} \end{bmatrix}. \tag{6.1}$$

Later in this chapter, we shall want to refer to all the elements in a particular row of a matrix or to all the elements in a particular column. Rather than introduce special letters for this purpose, we shall use a *dot notation* in which one of the subscripts is replaced by a dot.

To illustrate this, consider the first row of **A** in (6.1), which contains the elements a_{11}, a_{12} and a_{13}. They all belong to row 1, so they all have 1 as their first subscript. If we want to refer to row 1 as a whole, we simply write $a_{1.}$, with the dot indicating that the second subscript ranges over all possible values – which would be 1 to 3 for this particular matrix.

Rule 6.4

Whenever a subscript that denotes a row or column is replaced by a dot, this means that all possible values of that subscript are to be considered.

Thus a_2. means 'all of row 2', $a_{.1}$ means 'all of column 1' and so on.

$$a_1. = [a_{11} \quad a_{12} \quad a_{13}]$$
$$a_2. = [a_{21} \quad a_{22} \quad a_{23}]$$
$$a_{.1} = \begin{bmatrix} a_{11} \\ a_{21} \end{bmatrix}. \qquad (6.2)$$

Rule 6.5

Whenever a matrix consists of a single row or column, it is called a *vector*. If it consists of a single row, it is called a *row vector*; if it consists of a single column, it is called a *column vector*.

Thus in (6.2), a_1. and a_2. are row vectors and $a_{.1}$ is a column vector. Notice that, as an exception from the general convention about using capital letters to denote matrices, row and column vectors may be denoted by small letters.

The elements in a matrix contain more information than just their numerical values. This extra information is provided by their *position within the matrix*. For example, if we are told that $a_{12} = 45$ in the workforce matrix, the full meaning of this is that 45 is the number of workers in grade 1 at factory 2. The numerical value (45 in this case) cannot be separated from the row and column information. Because of this, the elements of a matrix cannot be interchanged at random – they must retain appropriate row and column identification. In matrix work, any numerical value which does not have an associated row and column position is called a *scalar*. From the matrix point of view, a scalar may be thought of as a 1×1 matrix, that is a matrix with just one element; since the 1×1 matrix contains just one numerical value, no ambiguity will arise if we do not quote the row and column position of this value within the 1×1 matrix.

It is most important to understand that, although matrices are made up of elements which have numerical values, they are not numbers themselves. Nevertheless we can define various arithmetic operations on matrices which correspond to similar operations on ordinary numbers (scalars). In the matrix context, these operations involve carrying out ordinary arithmetic on the individual elements but using special rules which are particularly concerned with the *position* of the elements. For this reason, the rules of algebra for ordinary quantities (scalars) cannot be automatically transferred to matrices.

As we shall see later in this chapter, the benefit of using matrix notation is that it provides us with a very compact way of describing patterns of arithmetic operations which involve many matrix elements at the same time. It does not reduce the amount of arithmetic required to get numerical answers to problems, but by reducing the amount of detail that is displayed it enables us to get a better understanding of the underlying pattern of operations.

6.2 Equality, addition and subtraction of matrices

Rule 6.6

If we have two matrices, **A** and **B**, we say that '**A** equals **B**', which is written **A** = **B**, if the two matrices are the *same size* and each element of **A** is *equal to the element in the corresponding position* in **B**.

Suppose that we have two matrices, **A** and **B**, as shown in (6.3) below.

$$\mathbf{A} = \begin{bmatrix} 19 & 25 \\ 20 & 16 \end{bmatrix}, \qquad \mathbf{B} = \begin{bmatrix} 10 & 12 \\ 15 & 11 \end{bmatrix}. \tag{6.3}$$

Although the matrices in (6.3) are the same size (both are 2×2), all their elements are different, so these two matrices are not equal.

To take a less obvious example, consider the matrices **F** and **G** below.

$$\mathbf{F} = \begin{bmatrix} 1 & 2 \\ 3 & 4 \end{bmatrix}, \qquad \mathbf{G} = \begin{bmatrix} 5 & 2 \\ 3 & 4 \end{bmatrix}. \tag{6.4}$$

Only the top left-hand elements of these two matrices are different, but this is sufficient for us to say that $\mathbf{F} \neq \mathbf{G}$ because we cannot say that *each* element of **F** is equal to the element in the corresponding position in **G**.

Now suppose that we define another matrix, **C**, which is to be equal to *the sum of* **A** *and* **B** – this is written **C** = **A** + **B**. Again, **A** and **B** must be the same size. We evaluate the elements of **C** by adding the corresponding elements of **A** and **B** according to Rule 6.7 below.

Rule 6.7

If **C** = **A** + **B**, then each element of **C** is the sum of the elements in the corresponding positions in **A** and **B**:

$$c_{ij} = a_{ij} + b_{ij}.$$

Matrices

Referring back to the numerical values in (6.3), this rule gives:

$$C = \begin{bmatrix} 19+10 & 25+12 \\ 20+15 & 16+11 \end{bmatrix} = \begin{bmatrix} 29 & 37 \\ 35 & 27 \end{bmatrix}.$$

If we define **D** to be the *difference between* **A** *and* **B**, we would write this as **D** = **A** − **B** and evaluate the elements of **D** by applying Rule 6.8, which is an obvious modification of Rule 6.7.

Rule 6.8

If **D** = **A** − **B**, then each element of **D** is the difference between the elements in the corresponding positions in **A** and **B**:

$d_{ij} = a_{ij} - b_{ij}.$

Using the numerical values from (6.3), this gives:

$$D = \begin{bmatrix} 19-10 & 25-12 \\ 20-15 & 16-11 \end{bmatrix} = \begin{bmatrix} 9 & 13 \\ 5 & 5 \end{bmatrix}.$$

Rules 6.7 and 6.8 still apply if there are negative signs associated with some of the elements in the two matrices which are to be added or subtracted.

Example 6.1
Suppose that the matrix **A** shown below is the actual workforce matrix based on the present state of affairs shown in Table 6.1 and **C** is the matrix showing corresponding projected changes in workforce over the next 6 months.

$$A = \begin{bmatrix} 27 & 45 & 39 \\ 58 & 75 & 66 \end{bmatrix}, \quad C = \begin{bmatrix} 3 & -5 & 11 \\ -8 & 0 & -6 \end{bmatrix}.$$

The forecast for the workforce in 6 months' time is then the present workforce plus the projected change in workforce. This forecast can then be written as a matrix, call it **F**, such that

F = **A** + **C**.

139

Think of this as shorthand for 'Forecast = Actual + Changes'. Applying Rule 6.7, we find that:

$$\mathbf{F} = \begin{bmatrix} 27+3 & 45-5 & 39+11 \\ 58-8 & 75+0 & 66-6 \end{bmatrix} = \begin{bmatrix} 30 & 40 & 50 \\ 50 & 75 & 60 \end{bmatrix}.$$

The rules for adding and subtracting matrices are so close to the rules for adding and subtracting scalars that they usually cause no problems for newcomers to matrix theory. The only new point to bear in mind is that the matrices to be added or subtracted must be the same size, so that we cannot, for example, subtract a 4 × 2 matrix from a 2 × 3 matrix.

6.3 Multiplication of matrices

For multiplying matrices, we have different rules according to whether the multiplier is a scalar or another matrix. To develop the rule for multiplying by a scalar, we consider the following extension of Example 6.1.

Example 6.2
The entire workforce **F**, defined in Example 6.1, is to be tripled over the next 2 years. Find the eventual size of the workforce in each grade at each factory when this expansion is complete.

Solution
When we say that the entire workforce is to be tripled, this means that each element of the workforce will be three times as large when the expansion is complete. In matrix terms, this is written as follows:

$$3\mathbf{F} = 3 \times \begin{bmatrix} 30 & 40 & 50 \\ 50 & 75 & 60 \end{bmatrix}$$

$$= \begin{bmatrix} 3\times 30 & 3\times 40 & 3\times 50 \\ 3\times 50 & 3\times 75 & 3\times 60 \end{bmatrix} = \begin{bmatrix} 90 & 120 & 150 \\ 150 & 225 & 180 \end{bmatrix}.$$

Reading off the elements of the last matrix, we see that we shall eventually have 90 grade 1 workers at factory 1, 120 grade 1 workers at factory 2, and so on. The meaning of the positions within the matrix remains the same but each of the 'number of workers' entries has been multiplied by the scalar 3.

Rule 6.9

Multiplication of a matrix by a scalar implies that the value of each element of the matrix is multiplied by the scalar. The position of individual elements is not affected and the size of the matrix is not altered.

It is conventional to write the scalar before the matrix (and to omit the multiplication sign) but it could be written after the matrix without affecting the result because, whichever way we write it, each element is to be multiplied by the same scalar but retains its position within the matrix.

When we multiply a matrix by another matrix, again we usually omit the multiplication sign, so that **AB** denotes '**A** multiplied by **B**'. As we shall see when we have stated the detailed rule for evaluating the product of two matrices, the order in which we write them is most important, so that **AB** ('**A** multiplied by **B**') is not the same thing as **BA** ('**B** multiplied by **A**') if **A** and **B** are matrices.

Matrix multiplication is sometimes perceived as being a complicated process but it is quite straightforward if we follow Rule 6.1 and think of rows first and columns second. This is because the basic pattern that we follow in finding the product of two matrices is to multiply *rows of the first matrix* by *columns of the second matrix*. To be more precise, we go from left to right, *along rows of the first matrix* and *down columns of the second matrix*, calculating products of successive pairs of terms and adding these together. The simplest case is where the first matrix is a row vector and the second a column vector, but each of them must have the same number of elements, as in Example 6.3 below.

Example 6.3
Given that **A** and **B** are as shown below, find the product **AB**.

$$A = [2 \quad 4 \quad 6], \qquad B = \begin{bmatrix} 5 \\ 7 \\ 9 \end{bmatrix}.$$

Solution
To find the product, we multiply the first element of **A** by the first element of **B**, the second element of **A** by the second element of **B**, the third element of **A** by the third element of **B** – and then add:

$$AB = [2 \times 5 + 4 \times 7 + 6 \times 9] = [10 + 28 + 54] = [92].$$

Now **AB** is a matrix, which we have emphasized by enclosing its single element in a square bracket, but because of what we said in Section 6.1 about matrices with just one element we treat it as a scalar and simply write the result as

AB = 92.

This example illustrates two points which we shall see result from the general rules for matrix multiplication. The first point is that both **A** and **B** have the same number of elements; the second point is that the product of the row vector and the column vector is a 1×1 matrix which we treat as an ordinary (scalar) number.

Rule 6.10

If two matrices are to be multiplied together, their sizes must be such that

number of columns in first matrix = number of rows in second matrix.

If this rule is obeyed, the matrices are said to be *conformable* for multiplication and the product is defined. If it is not obeyed, the product is not defined.

The method of multiplication that we used in Example 6.3 is extended to enable us to multiply any pair of matrices which are conformable. Suppose that **C** is the matrix which is the product of any two conformable matrices **A** and **B**, so that **C** = **AB**. The elements of **C** are found by multiplying rows of **A** by columns of **B**, until we have covered all possible pairs of rows and columns. The row of **A** and column of **B** which combine to give a particular element of **C** will have the same row number and column number as that element.

Thus,

row 1 of **A** and column 1 of **B** give the element in row 1 and column 1 of **C**,

row 1 of **A** and column 2 of **B** give the element in row 1 and column 2 of **C**,

row 2 of **A** and column 1 of **B** give the element in row 2 and column 1 of **C**,

row 2 of **A** and column 2 of **B** give the element in row 2 and column 2 of **C**,

and so on.

Example 6.4
Find the elements of the product matrix $\mathbf{C} = \mathbf{AB}$, given that

$$\mathbf{A} = \begin{bmatrix} 2 & 4 & 6 \\ 1 & 2 & 3 \end{bmatrix} \quad \text{and} \quad \mathbf{B} = \begin{bmatrix} 5 & 3 & 2 \\ 7 & 1 & 4 \\ 9 & 3 & 1 \end{bmatrix}.$$

Solution
Let c_{ij} denote the element in row i and column j of $\mathbf{C}$, and use the dot notation for rows of $\mathbf{A}$ and columns of $\mathbf{B}$.
First consider row 1 of $\mathbf{C}$:

$$c_{11} = a_1.b_{.1} = 2 \times 5 + 4 \times 7 + 6 \times 9 = 92;$$

$$c_{12} = a_1.b_{.2} = 2 \times 3 + 4 \times 1 + 6 \times 3 = 28;$$

$$c_{13} = a_1.b_{.3} = 2 \times 2 + 4 \times 4 + 6 \times 1 = 26.$$

There are no more columns in $\mathbf{B}$, so we have found all the elements in row 1 of $\mathbf{C}$.
Now consider row 2 of $\mathbf{C}$:

$$c_{21} = a_2.b_{.1} = 1 \times 5 + 2 \times 7 + 3 \times 9 = 46;$$

$$c_{22} = a_1.b_{.2} = 1 \times 3 + 2 \times 1 + 3 \times 3 = 14;$$

$$c_{23} = a_1.b_{.3} = 1 \times 2 + 2 \times 4 + 3 \times 1 = 13.$$

We have now used all the rows of $\mathbf{A}$ with all the columns of $\mathbf{B}$, so there are no further elements to be evaluated. The complete product matrix is therefore

$$\mathbf{C} = \begin{bmatrix} 92 & 28 & 26 \\ 46 & 14 & 13 \end{bmatrix}.$$

We multiplied the 2×3 matrix $\mathbf{A}$ by the 3×3 matrix $\mathbf{B}$ and so obtained the 2×3 product matrix $\mathbf{C}$. In general, the size of any product matrix can be found by applying Rule 6.11 below.

Rule 6.11

If $\mathbf{A}$ is an $m \times n$ matrix and $\mathbf{B}$ is an $n \times r$ matrix, so the product $\mathbf{AB}$ is defined by Rule 6.10 (columns of $\mathbf{A}$ = rows of $\mathbf{B}$ = n), then the product $\mathbf{AB}$ is a matrix of size $m \times r$. In other words:

number of rows in product matrix = number of rows in first matrix;

number of columns in product matrix = number of columns in second matrix.

These must match

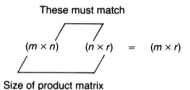

$$(m \times n) \quad (n \times r) \quad = \quad (m \times r)$$

Size of product matrix

Figure 6.1 Rules for multiplying an $(m \times n)$ and an $(n \times r)$ matrix.

We can combine Rules 6.10 and 6.11 into the diagram shown in Figure 6.1.

Applying Rule 6.10 to the matrices in Example 6.3, we see that **A** is of size 1×3 and **B** is of size 3×1. Hence **A** has three columns and **B** has three rows, so the product **AB** is defined. In practice, this means that each element of the row vector **A** finds a partner in the column vector **B** when we come to multiply and add. Applying Rule 6.11, **A** has one row and **B** has one column, so the product **AB** has one row and one column – in other words it is simply a scalar. The result would still have been a scalar if **A** had been a row vector with any other number of columns, provided that **B** was a column vector with an equal number of rows.

Example 6.5
Given that **P** is a 3×2 matrix, **Q** is a 2×3 matrix and **R** is a 2×4 matrix, check whether the matrices are conformable for multiplication to get the following products:

   (i) **PQ**;   (ii) **QR**;   (iii) **PR**;   (iv) **QP**.

In the cases where they are conformable, find the size of the product matrix.

Solution
(i)   **P** is 3×2 and **Q** is 2×3, so there are two columns in **P** to match the two rows in **Q** and they are therefore conformable. The product **PQ** will have three rows (like **P**) and three columns (like **Q**). In terms of Figure 6.1, we can summarize this as:

the product **PQ** is of size $(3 \times 2)(2 \times 3) = (3 \times 3)$.

(ii)   **Q** is 2×3 and **R** is 2×4, so the number of columns in **Q** does not match the number of rows in **R**; therefore they are not conformable. Summarizing:

$(2 \times 3)(2 \times 4)$ does not match, so **QR** is not defined.

(iii)   **P** is 3×2 and **R** is 2×4, so the two columns in **P** do match the two rows in **R** and they are conformable. The product **PR** will have three rows (like **P**) and four columns (like **R**). Summarizing:

the product **PR** is of size $(3 \times 2)(2 \times 4) = (3 \times 4)$.

(iv)   **Q** is 2×3 and **P** is 3×2, so the three columns of **Q** do match the three rows of **P** and they are conformable. The product **QP** will have two rows (like **Q**) and two columns (like **P**). Summarizing:

the product **QP** is of size $(2 \times 3)(3 \times 2) = (2 \times 2)$.

Notice that **QP** is a different size from **PQ**, which we found in (i) to be 3×3. This emphasizes that the order in which we consider the matrices is important.

We can now summarize the method that we used in Example 6.4 into a general rule for finding the product of any two conformable matrices: **A** which is of size $m \times n$ and **B** which is of size $n \times r$.

Rule 6.12

If **C** = **AB**, the typical element in row i and column j of **C** is the product of row i of **A** with column j of **B**; in other words, it is the sum of products of all a elements that have first suffix i with all b elements that have second suffix j:

$c_{ij} = a_{i.}b_{.j}$

$\quad = a_{i1}b_{1j} + a_{i2}b_{2j} + \ldots + a_{in}b_{nj}.$

Rule 6.12 just tells us how to find a single typical element of **C**. To find the entire $m \times r$ product matrix, we must apply this rule for each possible value of i and j, which will eventually involve multiplying each row of **A** by each column of **B**.

Example 6.6
Evaluate the elements of the product matrix **C** = **AB**, when **A** and **B** are as shown below.

$$\mathbf{A} = \begin{bmatrix} 1 & 2 & 3 \\ 4 & 5 & 6 \\ 7 & 8 & 9 \end{bmatrix}, \qquad \mathbf{B} = \begin{bmatrix} 10 & 40 & 70 \\ 20 & 50 & 80 \\ 30 & 60 & 90 \end{bmatrix}.$$

Solution
Both **A** and **B** are 3×3 matrices, so the number of columns in **A** does equal the number of rows in **B**; Rule 6.10 is satisfied and we can therefore calculate the product. Rule 6.12 says that we require products of *rows of* **A** *with columns of* **B**. For clarity, the sums representing the separate row and column products are shown in brackets, but this is not a standard convention.

$$
\mathbf{C} = \mathbf{AB} = \begin{bmatrix} 1 & 2 & 3 \\ 4 & 5 & 6 \\ 7 & 8 & 9 \end{bmatrix} \begin{bmatrix} 10 & 40 & 70 \\ 20 & 50 & 80 \\ 30 & 60 & 90 \end{bmatrix}
$$

$$
= \begin{bmatrix} (1 \times 10 + 2 \times 20 + 3 \times 30) & (1 \times 40 + 2 \times 50 + 3 \times 60) & (1 \times 70 + 2 \times 80 + 3 \times 90) \\ (4 \times 10 + 5 \times 20 + 6 \times 30) & (4 \times 40 + 5 \times 50 + 6 \times 60) & (4 \times 70 + 5 \times 80 + 6 \times 90) \\ (7 \times 10 + 8 \times 20 + 9 \times 30) & (7 \times 40 + 8 \times 50 + 9 \times 60) & (7 \times 70 + 8 \times 80 + 9 \times 90) \end{bmatrix}
$$

$$
= \begin{bmatrix} 140 & 320 & 500 \\ 320 & 770 & 1220 \\ 500 & 1220 & 1940 \end{bmatrix}.
$$

Notice that, because in this case we are dealing with two square matrices of the same size, the number of columns in **B** equals the number of rows in **A**, so Rule 6.10 would again have been satisfied if we had wished to work out a product taking **B** as the first matrix and **A** as the second. However, as the next example shows, the result would be quite different from what we have just found.

Example 6.7
With **A** and **B** as defined in Example 6.6, calculate the product **D** = **BA**.

Solution
We now require products of *rows of* **B** *with columns of* **A**.

$$
\mathbf{D} = \mathbf{BA} = \begin{bmatrix} 10 & 40 & 70 \\ 20 & 50 & 80 \\ 30 & 60 & 90 \end{bmatrix} \begin{bmatrix} 1 & 2 & 3 \\ 4 & 5 & 6 \\ 7 & 8 & 9 \end{bmatrix}
$$

$$= \begin{bmatrix} (10 \times 1 + 40 \times 4 + 70 \times 7) & (10 \times 2 + 40 \times 5 + 70 \times 8) & (10 \times 3 + 40 \times 6 + 70 \times 9) \\ (20 \times 1 + 50 \times 4 + 80 \times 7) & (20 \times 2 + 50 \times 5 + 80 \times 8) & (20 \times 3 + 50 \times 6 + 80 \times 9) \\ (30 \times 1 + 60 \times 4 + 90 \times 7) & (30 \times 2 + 60 \times 5 + 90 \times 8) & (30 \times 3 + 60 \times 6 + 90 \times 9) \end{bmatrix}$$

$$= \begin{bmatrix} 660 & 780 & 900 \\ 780 & 930 & 1080 \\ 900 & 1080 & 1260 \end{bmatrix}.$$

These last two examples show that matrix algebra is unlike ordinary algebra in that we get a different result if we multiply in a different order. To get $C = AB$ we took **A** as the first matrix, whereas to get $D = BA$ we took **A** as the second matrix. To distinguish these two cases, we say that to get $C = AB$ (the product in which **A** comes first) we use **A** as the *premultiplier* of **B** but to get $D = BA$ (the product in which **A** comes last) we use **A** as the *postmultiplier*. Alternatively, we could say that to find **AB** we *postmultiply* **A** by **B** but to get **BA** we *premultiply* **A** by **B**.

Rule 6.13

If **A** and **B** are two matrices for which the product **AB** is defined by Rule 6.10, it does not follow automatically that the product **BA** is defined. Even if **BA** is defined, in general **AB** does not equal **BA**.

One of the main reasons for using matrix notation is to avoid writing long strings of terms like those in the solutions to Examples 6.6 and 6.7, so we must make a clear distinction between, on the one hand, the detailed 'number crunching' which is involved in evaluating the elements of a product matrix and, on the other hand, the understanding of which elements of the original matrices are being combined.

Although we have shown the detailed arithmetic in the last two examples, readers should realize that in practice a computer program (a 'matrix package') would be used to carry out the large number of multiplication and addition operations. The matrix package might be part of a spreadsheet package or part of a general-purpose package for statistical or scientific computing. However, as with any computer software, the potential user should understand what the package is going to do before entrusting it with any data. People using a matrix package for the first time are often puzzled about its requirements for entering rows and columns of data so that they are read in the correct order. If you are in this situation, we suggest that you get the package to solve the problems in Examples 6.5 and 6.6, and check that it gives the answers that we obtained above.

6.4   Transposing matrices

When we initially define a matrix, the definition of rows and columns is usually somewhat arbitrary. For example, in Table 6.1 we might well have chosen to list the factories in rows and the workers in columns, rather than the other way about. If we later want to multiply the matrices and check them for conformability, we may find that they are the wrong size – or rather that they are the wrong shape; if only we could turn rows into columns – and columns into rows – then they might become conformable.

Because we frequently need to turn matrices round like this, a standard notation has been developed. Suppose that we start with the matrix $\mathbf{A}$, which has m rows and n columns, and its typical element in row i and column j is a_{ij} as usual.

The *transpose* of $\mathbf{A}$ is a new matrix formed from $\mathbf{A}$ by interchanging rows and columns, so that row i of $\mathbf{A}$ becomes column i of the new matrix and column j of $\mathbf{A}$ becomes row j of the new matrix.

We shall denote the transpose by putting a superscript dash against the name of the original matrix, so that $\mathbf{A}'$ denotes the transpose of $\mathbf{A}$. This convention is widely used but in some scientific work a superscript T is used instead of the dash, so in that convention $\mathbf{A}^{T}$ would represent the transpose of $\mathbf{A}$.

Because we have transposed rows and columns, $\mathbf{A}'$ will have n rows and m columns and the typical element in its row i and column j, say a'_{ij}, will be the element that was in row j and column i of the original matrix $\mathbf{A}$:

$$a'_{ij} = a_{ji}.$$

A little thought shows that if we take the transpose of the transpose we shall find ourselves with the original matrix. We can state this as a formal rule.

Rule 6.14

$(\mathbf{A}')' = \mathbf{A}$.

Translation: The transpose of the transpose is the original matrix.

Example 6.8
Given the matrices $\mathbf{A}$ and $\mathbf{B}$ shown below, find their transposes, $\mathbf{A}'$ and $\mathbf{B}'$. Also find the product matrices $\mathbf{AB}$ and $\mathbf{B}'\mathbf{A}'$.

$$\mathbf{A} = \begin{bmatrix} 4 & 9 & 7 \\ 1 & 5 & 3 \end{bmatrix}, \qquad \mathbf{B} = \begin{bmatrix} 6 & 5 \\ 0 & 8 \\ 2 & 1 \end{bmatrix}.$$

Solution

$$\mathbf{A}' = \begin{bmatrix} 4 & 1 \\ 9 & 5 \\ 7 & 3 \end{bmatrix} \qquad \mathbf{B}' = \begin{bmatrix} 6 & 0 & 2 \\ 5 & 8 & 1 \end{bmatrix}$$

$$\mathbf{AB} = \begin{bmatrix} (4 \times 6 + 9 \times 0 + 7 \times 2) & (4 \times 5 + 9 \times 8 + 7 \times 1) \\ (1 \times 6 + 5 \times 0 + 3 \times 2) & (1 \times 5 + 5 \times 8 + 3 \times 1) \end{bmatrix} = \begin{bmatrix} 38 & 99 \\ 12 & 48 \end{bmatrix}$$

$$\mathbf{B}'\mathbf{A}' = \begin{bmatrix} (6 \times 4 + 0 \times 9 + 2 \times 7) & (6 \times 1 + 0 \times 5 + 2 \times 3) \\ (5 \times 4 + 8 \times 9 + 1 \times 7) & (5 \times 1 + 8 \times 5 + 1 \times 3) \end{bmatrix} = \begin{bmatrix} 38 & 12 \\ 99 & 48 \end{bmatrix}.$$

We see from this that $\mathbf{B}'\mathbf{A}'$ is the transpose of $\mathbf{AB}$, which we would write as $(\mathbf{AB})'$. It might perhaps have been expected that $(\mathbf{AB})'$ would equal $\mathbf{A}'\mathbf{B}'$, but even without doing the detailed arithmetic we see that this cannot be so because the size of $\mathbf{A}'\mathbf{B}'$ would be 3×3 whereas $(\mathbf{AB})'$ is 2×2. This is another example of matrix algebra giving results that we might not expect from ordinary algebra. In fact our result in Example 6.7 comes from the following general rule.

Rule 6.15

If $\mathbf{A}$ and $\mathbf{B}$ are any matrices which are conformable for multiplication, so that the product $\mathbf{AB}$ is defined, then:

$(\mathbf{AB})' = \mathbf{B}'\mathbf{A}'$.

Translation: To find the transpose of a product of two matrices, reverse the order of the product and then transpose each of the matrices.

Example 6.9

Suppose that Table 6.1 included additional information regarding the weekly wages of workers (£250 for grade 1 and £200 for grade 2 at any of the factories) as shown below in Table 6.2.

Show how the calculation of the weekly wage bill at each factory can be expressed compactly in matrix form.

Solution

The data in the body of Table 6.2 consist of two parts – three columns representing numbers of workers, which we have already defined to be matrix **A**, and the final column of wage rates, which we can call 'the wage vector' and denote by **w**.

$$\mathbf{A} = \begin{bmatrix} 27 & 45 & 39 \\ 58 & 75 & 66 \end{bmatrix}, \qquad \mathbf{w} = \begin{bmatrix} 250 \\ 200 \end{bmatrix}.$$

Without using matrices, it is clear that we would find the total weekly wage bill at each factory by multiplying the number of workers of each grade by their wage rate and adding the results for both grades, so that we would finish up with three separate totals – one for each factory. This must involve some kind of multiplication of **A**, which is of size 2×3, and **w**, which is a column vector of size 2×1.

Because we know that the number of columns in **A** does not equal the number of rows in **w**, we cannot form the product **Aw**. However, if we transpose **w**, we can form **w'A**, the product of a 1×2 vector and a 2×3 matrix, which will therefore have one row (like **w'**) and three columns (like **A**).

$$\mathbf{w'A} = \begin{bmatrix} 250 & 200 \end{bmatrix} \begin{bmatrix} 27 & 45 & 39 \\ 58 & 75 & 66 \end{bmatrix} = \begin{bmatrix} 18\,350 & 26\,250 & 22\,950 \end{bmatrix}.$$

The three columns of the row vector **w'A** represent the three factories, like the corresponding columns of **A**. The elements of **w'A** are the total wage bills: £18 350 at factory 1, £26 250 at factory 2 and £22 950 at factory 3.

Table 6.2 Present numbers of workers and wage rates.

Grade	Factory 1	Factory 2	Factory 3	Weekly wage
1	27	45	39	250
2	58	75	66	200

If we are not concerned about keeping columns to represent factories, we could transpose the result into a column vector $(\mathbf{w}'\mathbf{A})'$. Using Rules 6.15 and 6.14, we see that

$$(\mathbf{w}'\mathbf{A})' = \mathbf{A}'(\mathbf{w}')' \quad \text{by Rule 6.15}$$
$$= \mathbf{A}'\mathbf{w} \quad \text{by Rule 6.14.}$$

This tells us that we would get the same numerical totals if we premultiplied the unchanged $\mathbf{w}$ by the transposed $\mathbf{A}$, but the totals would be arranged in a column rather than a row.

The whole idea of using matrices in this example may seem like the proverbial use of a sledgehammer to crack a nut. However, the example itself is very oversimplified in comparison with real-life wage calculations. Suppose that an actual company had twenty factories, each employing eight grades of workers. Even if we assume that all the workers are on a fixed weekly wage, writing out all the arithmetic for the total wage bills would involve $20 \times 8 = 160$ multiplications and the corresponding sums. All that we need to do to indicate this algebraically is to define a 20×8 workforce matrix $\mathbf{A}$ and an 8×1 wage vector $\mathbf{w}$, and then the required totals will be the elements of $\mathbf{w}'\mathbf{A}$, just as they were in our oversimplified example.

We emphasize again that matrices provide a compact way of describing complicated patterns of operations on arrays of numbers. The pattern may remain the same even if the sizes of the arrays increase, in which case we can still use the same underlying matrix models.

6.5 Matrix formulation of simultaneous equations

There are several possible ways that we might have defined the result of multiplying two matrices together. The advantage of the convention which we described in Section 6.3 is that it leads to a particularly convenient way of dealing with simultaneous equations and other common problems in algebra. To understand its advantages, we look again at some problems from Chapter 3.

Example 6.10
In Example 3.7, we had to solve a set of simultaneous equations that was originally stated in the form:

$$3x + 4y + 3z = 10$$

$$5x + 7y - 4z = 12$$

$$2x + 3y - 2z = 5.$$

Rewrite these equations in matrix form.

Solution
The left-hand side of each equation is in the form of known numerical coefficients multiplied by the unknown variables x, y and z respectively. We can think of the coefficients as forming a matrix A and the variables as forming a column vector w:

$$A = \begin{bmatrix} 3 & 4 & 3 \\ 5 & 7 & -4 \\ 2 & 3 & -2 \end{bmatrix}, \qquad w = \begin{bmatrix} x \\ y \\ z \end{bmatrix}.$$

Notice that negative elements in A correspond to negative coefficients in the original equations. Having defined A and w like this, we can express all the left-hand side terms as a matrix product Aw, because the standard convention for matrix multiplication gives

$$Aw = \begin{bmatrix} 3x & 4y & 3z \\ 5x & 7y & -4z \\ 2x & 3y & -2z \end{bmatrix}.$$

If we then define b as a column vector of the known values on the right-hand sides of the original equations,

$$b = \begin{bmatrix} 10 \\ 12 \\ 5 \end{bmatrix},$$

we can write the complete set of equations as a single matrix equation:

$$Aw = b.$$

In order to generalize from Example 6.10, we need to recognize that the original equations contained three types of terms: (1) the known coefficients that went into the matrix A, (2) the unknown variables that went into the column vector w, and (3) the known values that went into the column vector **b**. The coefficients in **A** can be denoted by using small a with the appropriate row and column subscripts as usual. Since the unknown variables are all of the same type, it is preferable to denote them by the same letter – with subscripts to indicate whether we are referring to the first, second or third variable – so we write x_1, x_2 and x_3 instead of the original x, y and z. Similarly, the elements of **b** may be written as b_1, b_2 and b_3 instead of the particular values 10, 12 and 5 in Example 6.10, so that we now have:

$$A = \begin{bmatrix} a_{11} & a_{12} & a_{13} \\ a_{21} & a_{22} & a_{23} \\ a_{31} & a_{32} & a_{33} \end{bmatrix}, \quad x = \begin{bmatrix} x_1 \\ x_2 \\ x_3 \end{bmatrix}, \quad b = \begin{bmatrix} b_1 \\ b_2 \\ b_3 \end{bmatrix}. \quad \text{(6.5)}$$

The corresponding equations, in the non-matrix form, will be:

$$a_{11}x_1 + a_{12}x_2 + a_{13}x_3 = b_1$$
$$a_{21}x_1 + a_{22}x_2 + a_{23}x_3 = b_2 \quad \text{(6.6)}$$
$$a_{31}x_1 + a_{32}x_2 + a_{33}x_3 = b_3.$$

Comparing (6.5) and (6.6), we see that the first equation in (6.6) is equivalent to saying that the first element of **b** is equal to the first row of **A** times **x**. Using the dot notation, we can write this as:

row 1 of **A** times $x = a_1 . x = b_1$.

Similarly, for the second and third equations:

row 2 of **A** times $x = a_2 . x = b_2$

row 3 of **A** times $x = a_3 . x = b_3$

and the whole set of equations in (6.6) can be summarized by saying that we premultiply the vector **x** by the square coefficient matrix, **A**, and put the result equal to **b**. Thus we get a single matrix equation:

$$Ax = b, \quad \text{(6.7)}$$

which immediately conveys the idea of the **b** being made up in some way of a product of the **a** and the **x**. To be more precise, equation (6.7) consists of the known coefficient matrix **A** which is postmultiplied by the unknown vector **x** to give the known vector **b**.

What we now require is a method of solving the matrix equation so that we can find the numerical values of the elements of the unknown vector **x**. We shall see that the solution can also be written in matrix form and the methodology behind it can be applied to solve almost any number of ordinary simultaneous equations such as those in (6.6) above, provided that the number of equations equals the number of unknown x. The only practical limitation is the capacity of the computer that will be required to carry out the necessary arithmetic and store the results.

To understand how the solution might be obtained, we go back and look again at the methods that we developed in Chapter 2 for solving ordinary algebraic equations involving a scalar variable, x. As an example, let us consider

$$2x = 6.$$

The most obvious way to solve this is to divide both sides by the coefficient 2:

$$\frac{2}{2}x = \frac{6}{2}, \quad \text{so} \quad x = 3.$$

Alternatively, we could multiply both sides by the reciprocal of the coefficient 2:

$$2^{-1} \times 2x = 2^{-1} \times 6.$$

Using the results of Section 1.7, we find that $2^{-1} \times 2 = 1$ and $2^{-1} \times 6 = 3$, so we get that $x = 3$ as before.

These two methods of solving $2x = 6$ are essentially the same: both involve operating upon the coefficient of the unknown variable so as to make it unity, remembering that any operation upon the left-hand side of the equation must also be applied to the right-hand side in order to preserve the balance of the equation.

In matrix algebra, division of one matrix by another is not defined. However, we know that, provided the matrices are conformable, multiplication is defined and we can solve an equation of the type $Ax = b$ by premultiplying both sides of the equation by a special matrix whose effect is analogous to that of the reciprocal of the coefficient in the simple algebraic equation – it effectively cancels out the coefficient matrix A on the left-hand side. This special matrix is called the *inverse* of A.

6.6 The identity matrix and the inverse

Before we can define the inverse, we need to introduce a particularly simple kind of square matrix. Any square matrix in which all the elements on the diagonal from top left to bottom right are one and all the other elements are zero is called an *identity matrix* (or sometimes a *unit matrix*) and is denoted by **I**. For example, the 3 × 3 identity matrix is

$$\mathbf{I} = \begin{bmatrix} 1 & 0 & 0 \\ 0 & 1 & 0 \\ 0 & 0 & 1 \end{bmatrix}. \tag{6.8}$$

The effect of multiplying any conformable matrix by **I** is to leave that matrix unchanged. For example, if we premultiply the vector **x** from (6.5) by **I** as defined in (6.8), we get the following:

$$\mathbf{Ix} = \begin{bmatrix} 1 & 0 & 0 \\ 0 & 1 & 0 \\ 0 & 0 & 1 \end{bmatrix} \begin{bmatrix} x_1 \\ x_2 \\ x_3 \end{bmatrix}$$

$$= \begin{bmatrix} x_1 + 0 + 0 \\ 0 + x_2 + 0 \\ 0 + 0 + x_3 \end{bmatrix} = \begin{bmatrix} x_1 \\ x_2 \\ x_3 \end{bmatrix} = \mathbf{x}. \tag{6.9}$$

If **A** is an $n \times n$ matrix and **I** is an $n \times n$ identity matrix, then the inverse of **A** is defined to be another $n \times n$ matrix, denoted by $\mathbf{A}^{-1}$, such that premultiplying or postmultiplying **A** by $\mathbf{A}^{-1}$ gives **I**. Note that **A** must be a *square matrix* for its inverse to exist.

Rule 6.16

$\mathbf{A}^{-1}\mathbf{A} = \mathbf{I}$ and $\mathbf{AA}^{-1} = \mathbf{I}$.

Translation: If a square matrix is premultiplied or postmultiplied by its inverse, the result is an identity matrix.

We can now return to the problem of solving the matrix equation $\mathbf{Ax} = \mathbf{b}$. From Rule 6.16, we know that $\mathbf{A}^{-1}\mathbf{A} = \mathbf{I}$ and from equation (6.9) we know that $\mathbf{Ix} = \mathbf{x}$, so if both sides of $\mathbf{Ax} = \mathbf{b}$ are premultiplied by $\mathbf{A}^{-1}$ we get:

$$\mathbf{A}^{-1}\mathbf{Ax} = \mathbf{A}^{-1}\mathbf{b},$$

which simplifies to $\mathbf{Ix} = \mathbf{A}^{-1}\mathbf{b}$ or

$$\mathbf{x} = \mathbf{A}^{-1}\mathbf{b}. \tag{6.10}$$

Thus equation (6.10) tells us that we can solve equation (6.7) provided that we know the inverse of the coefficient matrix **A**.

General methods for finding the inverse are too complicated to be considered in this book but we shall look briefly at a simple rule for inverting 2×2 matrices which is given in Section 6.8 below. Larger matrices would normally be inverted by using a special package on a computer.

For the time being, we may adapt Rule 6.14 to provide a rule for testing whether some matrix, say **M**, is the inverse of a given matrix **A**.

Rule 6.17

If **A** is a square matrix and **M** is another square matrix of the same size, then **M** is the inverse of **A** if

$$\mathbf{MA} = \mathbf{I} \quad \text{or} \quad \mathbf{AM} = \mathbf{I}.$$

Example 6.11
Given matrices **A** and **M** as below, use Rule 6.17 to test whether **M** is the inverse of **A**.

$$\mathbf{A} = \begin{bmatrix} 2 & 6 \\ 1 & 4 \end{bmatrix}, \quad \mathbf{M} = \begin{bmatrix} 2 & -3 \\ -\frac{1}{2} & 1 \end{bmatrix}.$$

Solution
Premultiply **A** by **M**:

$$\mathbf{MA} = \begin{bmatrix} 2 & -3 \\ -\frac{1}{2} & 1 \end{bmatrix} \begin{bmatrix} 2 & 6 \\ 1 & 4 \end{bmatrix}$$

$$= \begin{bmatrix} (2 \times 2 - 3 \times 1) & (2 \times 6 - 3 \times 4) \\ (-\frac{1}{2} \times 2 + 1 \times 1) & (-\frac{1}{2} \times 6 + 1 \times 4) \end{bmatrix} = \begin{bmatrix} 1 & 0 \\ 0 & 1 \end{bmatrix},$$

which is an identity matrix, so **M** is the inverse of **A**.

Before we look at examples of using an inverse matrix to write down the solution of simultaneous equations in matrix form, we need to remember the cautionary note in Section 3.5 about independence between the equations. We can check whether the equations are independent by calculating what is called the *determinant* of the coefficient matrix **A**. If this determinant is zero, the equations are not independent and, furthermore, the inverse of **A** is not defined.

6.7 Determinants

A determinant is a number which is calculated according to certain rules from the elements of a square matrix. We enclose the elements between a pair of plain vertical lines to distinguish the determinant, which is a scalar (ordinary number), from the original matrix, which is a collection of numbers arranged in a particular way rather than a number itself. If the original matrix is **A**, which is 2×2, we shall call the determinant det **A** and define it as follows:

$$\det \mathbf{A} = \begin{vmatrix} a_{11} & a_{12} \\ a_{21} & a_{22} \end{vmatrix} = a_{11}a_{22} - a_{12}a_{21}. \tag{6.11}$$

Instead of det **A**, the notation $|\mathbf{A}|$ is widely used for the determinant of matrix **A**. The rule for evaluating a determinant which has two rows and two columns, like this one, may be written in terms of its elements as follows.

Rule 6.18

The determinant of the 2×2 matrix

$$\mathbf{A} = \begin{bmatrix} \text{top left} & \text{top right} \\ \text{bottom left} & \text{bottom right} \end{bmatrix}$$

is a scalar whose value is given by

det **A** = (top left times bottom right) minus (bottom left times top right).

There are more complicated rules for evaluating the determinants of larger square matrices. They can be built up from Rule 6.18, but they are seldom needed in practical management problems because any large determinants that arise would be evaluated by a computer package.

Example 6.12
Use Rule 6.18 to evaluate the determinant of

$$\mathbf{A} = \begin{bmatrix} 5 & 9 \\ 4 & 6 \end{bmatrix}.$$

Solution

$|\mathbf{A}|$ or $\det \mathbf{A} = 5 \times 6 - 4 \times 9 = 30 - 36 = -6.$

Note that, in this particular case, the result is negative even though all the elements of $\mathbf{A}$ are positive. In general, the determinant may be positive or negative or zero.

If $\det \mathbf{A}$ is zero, the inverse of matrix $\mathbf{A}$ does not exist and we say that the matrix $\mathbf{A}$ is *singular*. Any set of simultaneous equations whose coefficient matrix is singular will not yield a solution because the zero determinant indicates that the equations are not independent – hence there are too many unknown variables.

Example 6.13
By evaluating the determinant of the coefficient matrix, check whether the following pair of simultaneous equations can be solved:

$$3x_1 + 7x_2 = 20$$
$$6x_1 + 14x_2 = 40.$$

Solution
The coefficient matrix is

$$\mathbf{A} = \begin{bmatrix} 3 & 7 \\ 6 & 14 \end{bmatrix},$$

so by Rule 6.18:

$$\det \mathbf{A} = 3(14) - 6(7) = 42 - 42 = 0.$$

Hence $\mathbf{A}$ is singular and the equations cannot be solved.

Looking again at the two equations, it is clear that each term in the second equation is simply twice the corresponding term in the first equation, so the two equations are clearly not independent. Thus we are left with just one equation in two unknowns, and this cannot be solved.

As we saw in Chapter 3, the relationship between the coefficients may be less obvious than it is in this case, but evaluating the determinant will reveal any lack of independence. Even if the determinant is not exactly zero, if it is very small it can cause problems in solving a set of simultaneous equations; in this case the coefficient matrix is said to be 'ill-conditioned', a term which we first introduced at the end of Section 3.5. One way in which the coefficient matrix may become ill-conditioned is by containing a mixture of very large and very small coefficients; it is sometimes possible to remove this ill-conditioning by rescaling some of the unknown variables so that all the coefficients become more or less the same size. Computer packages which handle matrices will normally output error messages if a matrix is ill-conditioned or singular; the user should be very cautious in interpreting any results obtained under these conditions.

6.8   The inverse of a 2 × 2 matrix

In general, provided that det A is not zero, the elements of the inverse of a 2 × 2 matrix are related to those of the original matrix by

$$\mathbf{A}^{-1} = \frac{1}{\det \mathbf{A}} \begin{bmatrix} a_{22} & -a_{12} \\ -a_{21} & a_{11} \end{bmatrix}. \tag{6.12}$$

This result, equation (6.12), can be used directly to solve pairs of simultaneous equations. It may be useful in cases where we have several sets of equations that have the same coefficient matrix but different vectors **b** on the right-hand side. This situation is illustrated in Example 6.14.

Example 6.14
Suppose that two kinds of machine require servicing. Each service involves work by a fitter and by an electrician, although it does not matter whether a fitter or an electrician works first on a particular machine. We shall also assume that fitters and electricians can work simultaneously without interfering with each other.

   The total amount of time that fitters and electricians are available for this work is fixed by their other commitments, and the manager wants to find the number of each type of machine that can receive both types of service if all the available time is used.

   Each machine of type 1 requires 2 hours' work by a fitter and 1 hour by an electrician. Each machine of type 2 requires 6 hours' work by a fitter and 4 hours by an electrician. In week 1, fitters are available for 40 hours and electricians for 20 hours. In week 2, fitters are available for 30 hours and electricians for 20 hours. We want to find the number of machines of type 1 (say x_1) and of type 2 (say x_2) that can be serviced in each week.

Solution
Using the methods which we developed in Chapter 3, we write down equations which balance the fitters' time and the electricians' time in each week.

Week 1:   Fitters: $2x_1 + 6x_2 = 40$
           Electricians: $x_1 + 4x_2 = 20$

Week 2:   Fitters: $2x_1 + 6x_2 = 30$
           Electricians: $x_1 + 4x_2 = 20.$

In each week we have the same coefficient matrix, which is the matrix we considered in Example 6.11:

$$\mathbf{A} = \begin{bmatrix} 2 & 6 \\ 1 & 4 \end{bmatrix}.$$

From Rule 6.16

$$\det \mathbf{A} = 2 \times 4 - 1 \times 6 = 2$$

and from equation (6.12) we then find that

$$\mathbf{A}^{-1} = \frac{1}{2}\begin{bmatrix} 4 & -6 \\ -1 & 2 \end{bmatrix}.$$

Hence

$$\mathbf{A}^{-1} = \begin{bmatrix} 2 & -3 \\ -\frac{1}{2} & 1 \end{bmatrix},$$

as we proved in Example 6.11. Then,

$$\text{in week 1: } \mathbf{b} = \begin{bmatrix} 40 \\ 20 \end{bmatrix}; \quad \text{in week 2: } \mathbf{b} = \begin{bmatrix} 30 \\ 20 \end{bmatrix}.$$

We now use equation (6.10), which told us that $\mathbf{x} = \mathbf{A}^{-1}\mathbf{b}$, so the solution for $\mathbf{x}$ in each week will be obtained by premultiplying the appropriate $\mathbf{b}$ by $\mathbf{A}^{-1}$.

$$\text{Week 1: } \begin{bmatrix} x_1 \\ x_2 \end{bmatrix} = \begin{bmatrix} 2 & -3 \\ -\frac{1}{2} & 1 \end{bmatrix}\begin{bmatrix} 40 \\ 20 \end{bmatrix} = \begin{bmatrix} 2\times40-3\times20 \\ -40/2+20 \end{bmatrix} = \begin{bmatrix} 20 \\ 0 \end{bmatrix}.$$

$$\text{Week 2: } \begin{bmatrix} x_1 \\ x_2 \end{bmatrix} = \begin{bmatrix} 2 & -3 \\ -\frac{1}{2} & 1 \end{bmatrix}\begin{bmatrix} 30 \\ 20 \end{bmatrix} = \begin{bmatrix} 2\times30-3\times20 \\ -30/2+20 \end{bmatrix} = \begin{bmatrix} 0 \\ 5 \end{bmatrix}.$$

Hence the manager could plan to service twenty type 1 but no type 2 machines in week 1 and five type 2 but no type 1 machines in week 2. For other weeks, when the availability of fitters and electricians is different, the calculation could be repeated – premultiplying an appropriate vector **b** by the same $\mathbf{A}^{-1}$ as long as the times required by each type of machine remained the same.

The *pattern* of calculation would remain exactly the same if we were to consider a problem with n types of machine requiring n types of servicing, for any value of n. Obviously, for large values of n there would be much more detailed arithmetic to do, but in each case we could describe what had to be done by writing the simple matrix equation

$$\mathbf{x} = \mathbf{A}^{-1}\mathbf{b}$$

and getting a computer package to do the 'number crunching' that is required to evaluate the elements of the vector **x**.

6.9 Summary

If we have any set of simultaneous equations in any number of unknown variables, provided that we have as many equations as there are unknown variables, the problem of solving for **x** remains essentially the same. Although the sizes of **A**, **x** and **b** may change, the equations

$$\mathbf{Ax} = \mathbf{b} \quad \text{and} \quad \mathbf{x} = \mathbf{A}^{-1}\mathbf{b}$$

still express the relationship between them.

Matrix algebra provides the way for extending the algebraic models that we have considered in earlier chapters to provide more realistic management models that take account of many variables. Input–output analysis, manpower planning and market research are just a few of the areas in which large amounts of data are used in model building. Matrices usually provide the most efficient way to describe and manipulate this sort of data and computer packages are used to do the detailed arithmetic. The mathematics behind these packages is very specialized and there is no need for the average user to know the details, but it is essential to understand such basic ideas as the size of a matrix, premultiplication and postmultiplication, the transpose, the determinant, the inverse, singularity and ill-conditioning.

If no matrix package is readily available, sets of two, three or four simultaneous equations can be solved reasonably quickly and accur-

The Essence of Mathematics for Business

ately by using the methods which we described in Chapter 3. It should be understood therefore that the matrix methods complement rather than replace those other methods, which remain as basic tools for solving a variety of practical problems.

ADDITIONAL EXAMPLES

A6.1 Evaluate the following determinants.

(i) $\begin{vmatrix} 2 & -4 \\ 7 & -3 \end{vmatrix}$ (ii) $\begin{vmatrix} 2 & 9 \\ 0 & 8 \end{vmatrix}$

(iii) $\begin{vmatrix} 0.2 & 9.0 \\ -1.2 & 2.3 \end{vmatrix}$.

A6.2 Find the product **AB**, given that

$$A = \begin{bmatrix} 2 & 1 \\ 3 & 4 \end{bmatrix}, \qquad B = \begin{bmatrix} 0 & 3 & 7 \\ 1 & 8 & 9 \end{bmatrix}.$$

A6.3 An industrial cleaning contractor negotiates contracts which may run for up to 3 years or be cancelled at 1 month's notice. At the end of any given year, t, there are $a(t)$ contracts less than 1 year old, $b(t)$ between 1 and 2 years old, and $c(t)$ between 2 and 3 years old.

Existing contracts give rise to new ones in such a way that the numbers of type a, b and c contracts at the end of year t are linked to those expected at the end of the next year, $t + 1$, by the matrix equation

$$[a(t) \ b(t) \ c(t)] \ P = [a(t + 1) \ b(t + 1) \ c(t + 1)],$$

where **P**, which is called the 'projection matrix', is defined to be:

$$P = \begin{bmatrix} 0.2 & 0.9 & 0 \\ 0.6 & 0 & 0.8 \\ 0.4 & 0 & 0 \end{bmatrix}.$$

(i) Taking last year as $t = 0$, and given that $a(0) = 112, b(0) = 80$ and $c(0) = 56$, find the total number of contracts, $a(1) + b(1) + c(1)$, expected at the end of this year, when $t = 1$.
(ii) Apply the projection matrix to the values expected for $t = 1$ in order to find the total number of contracts expected at the end of next year, when $t = 2$.

A6.4 A team of economists working on an input–output model for three industries has produced the following equation which relates the output of industry i (denoted by x_i) to the final demand for the product of that industry (denoted by d_i) for $i = 1$ to 3:

$$Tx = d,$$

where

$$x = \begin{bmatrix} x_1 \\ x_2 \\ x_3 \end{bmatrix}, \qquad d = \begin{bmatrix} d_1 \\ d_2 \\ d_3 \end{bmatrix},$$

and T is called the 'technology matrix'.
Given that

$$T^{-1} = \begin{bmatrix} 1.292 & 0.549 & 0.531 \\ 0.389 & 1.398 & 0.708 \\ 0.230 & 0.372 & 1.327 \end{bmatrix},$$

find values of the outputs from each industry which would satisfy the original equation when the final demands are:

(i) $d_1 = 8, d_2 = 6, d_3 = 5$;
(ii) $d_1 = 10, d_2 = 9, d_3 = 7$.

A6.5 A study on the impact of TV commercials for Tusko toothpaste has shown that, at t weeks after a commercial has been shown, expected daily sales S (measured in £1000 units) can be represented by an equation of the form

$$S = b_0 + b_1 t + b_2 t^2. \tag{1}$$

Statistical investigation has shown that the b coefficients in equation (1) satisfy the matrix equation

$$Ab = g, \tag{2}$$

where

$$A = \begin{bmatrix} 3 & 9 & 35 \\ 9 & 35 & 153 \\ 35 & 153 & 707 \end{bmatrix}, \qquad b = \begin{bmatrix} b_0 \\ b_1 \\ b_2 \end{bmatrix}, \qquad g = \begin{bmatrix} 86 \\ 282 \\ 1126 \end{bmatrix}.$$

Show that C is the inverse of A, where

$$C = \frac{1}{32} \begin{bmatrix} 167 & -126 & 19 \\ -126 & 112 & -18 \\ 19 & -18 & 3 \end{bmatrix}.$$

Then premultiply each side of equation (2) by C in order to solve it for b and hence evaluate b_0, b_1 and b_2.

7

Differentiation

Introduction

This chapter and the next are concerned with *differentiation*; Chapter 9 is concerned with the related topic of *integration*. These two topics are generally considered together under the heading *calculus*, which is short for 'differential and integral calculus'. Differentiation is the process of finding the *rate at which changes take place*. The result of the differentiation process is called a *derivative*. Familiar examples of derivatives are speed and acceleration. The speed of a vehicle measures the rate at which distance is covered in a given period of time and it represents the derivative of distance with respect to time. The acceleration of a vehicle is a measure of the rate at which the speed of the vehicle is changing and so it is the derivative of speed with respect to time.

In a business environment, it might be appropriate to consider derivatives when a firm introduces a new product. If the level of sales can be described mathematically as a function of time then differentiating this function will give the rate at which sales change with time. If the total cost of production varies with the level of production, rising for some levels and falling for others, the rate at which the total costs change in response to changes in the production level would be determined by differentiation. The change in total cost brought about by a unit change in production level is known as the *marginal cost*; as we obtain the marginal cost by differentiation, it is a derivative.

Other derivatives are widely used in economics. For example, the *price elasticity of demand* measures the amount by which demand changes with change in price, so it is the derivative of demand with respect to price.

Now let us go back and look again at some of the functions considered in Chapter 2.

First let us take the function $y = 2x - 2$, which was first shown in Figure 2.2(b) and is reproduced in Figure 7.1.

The rate at which y changes for a unit change in x is 2. This is the slope of the line. This rate of change, or slope, of a straight line is the same no matter what value of x is considered. If two lines have the same slope but different intercepts (cross the y-axis at different points) they are parallel to one another.

Now consider the cubic function $y = x^3 + x^2 - 0.25x - 0.25$ which was plotted in Figure 2.5 on page 42.

Looking at Figure 2.5, we can see that the slope of the line varies as the value of x varies. Thus, when $x = 1$ the slope is positive, so an increase in x would cause an increase in y. When $x = -0.5$ the slope is negative, so an increase in x would cause a decrease in y. In many cases we are interested in locating what are called *turning points* on a curve; as we said in Chapter 2, these are simply points at which the curve changes direction to go down instead of up or vice versa.

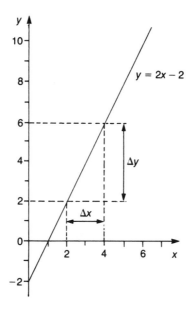

Figure 7.1

7.1 The slope of a straight line

The slope or gradient of a straight line can be determined by finding the change in y for a given change in x.

Consider the straight line $y = 2x - 2$, which is shown in Figure 7.1. Let us choose any two points on the line, for example the points ($x = 2$, $y = 2$) and ($x = 4$, $y = 6$). These two points can be used to find the slope of the line. This is done by comparing the change in y brought about by a given change in x.

Here the value of x has increased from 2 to 4; Δx denotes this change in x (where Δ is the Greek letter 'delta'). The value of y has increased from 2 to 6; this change in y is denoted by Δy.

So in this case the change in x is

$$\Delta x = 4 - 2 = 2$$

and the corresponding change in y is

$$\Delta y = 6 - 2 = 4.$$

Thus a change of two units in x has caused a change of four units in y. The slope of the line is given by the ratio

$$\text{slope} = \frac{\Delta y}{\Delta x} = \frac{6 - 2}{4 - 2} = \frac{4}{2} = 2.$$

The above result can be generalized for any straight line as Rule 7.1.

Rule 7.1

The slope of a straight line is given by the ratio

$$\frac{\Delta y}{\Delta x}$$

where Δx is the difference between any two values of x and Δy is the corresponding difference between the two corresponding values of y that lie on the straight line.

Example 7.1
Find the slope of the line $y = -2x + 8$.

Solution

If the function is not too complicated it is a good idea to draw the curve, and we have done this in Figure 7.2.

Consider the straight line in Figure 7.2 and apply Rule 7.1, that is find the change in y brought about by a change in x. It is usually easier to use integer values of x so that the arithmetic involved in finding the corresponding values of y is as simple as possible. We have chosen $x = 1$ and $x = 2$.

When $x = 1$ then $y = -2 \times 1 + 8 = 6$.
When $x = 2$ then $y = -2 \times 2 + 8 = 4$.

Then changes in x and y are $\Delta x = 2 - 1 = 1$ and $\Delta y = 4 - 6 = -2$. The slope is the rate at which y changes with changes in x,

$$\text{slope} = \frac{\Delta y}{\Delta x} = \frac{4-6}{2-1} = \frac{-2}{1} = -2.$$

The slope of this line is -2. This means that each time x increases by one unit y decreases by two units. The slope is the same at every point on a straight line. This means that any two values of x could have been chosen and the same result obtained. Try repeating Example 7.1 taking the values $x = 3$ and $x = 5$ to prove that Rule 7.1 will again give the slope -2.

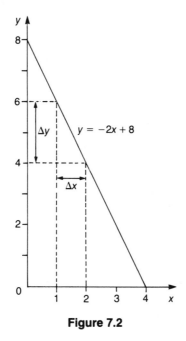

Figure 7.2

7.2   Finding the equation of a straight line

Since the slope of a straight line can be found using two points on that line, the equation of a straight line can be found using the same information.

As we saw in Chapter 2, the equation of a straight line is always of the form

$$y = ax + b, \tag{7.1}$$

where a is the slope and b is the intercept. If necessary refer back to Section 2.2 to refresh your memory.

The slope, a, is found using the method of Example 7.1 above. Once we know the slope and the coordinates of one point through which the line passes, the value of the intercept, b, can be determined using simple algebra.

Example 7.2
A straight line is known to pass through the points (3, 4) and (5, 8). (Remember that the convention is that the first figure in the bracket relates to the horizontal axis and the second figure to the vertical axis.) Determine the equation of the line.

Solution
First find the slope of the line using the method of Example 7.1 above.

To find the value of a   As x changes from 3 to 5 so y changes from 4 to 8.

$$\text{slope} = a = \frac{\Delta y}{\Delta x} = \frac{8-4}{5-3} = \frac{4}{2} = 2.$$

To find the value of b   Having found the slope the next step is to find the intercept, b. We were told that the line passes through the point ($x = 3$, $y = 4$) and have found that the slope is $a = 2$. Put these values into equation (7.1) above.

$$y = ax + b$$

$$4 = 2 \times 3 + b.$$

The only unknown quantity is b. This can be found by collecting up the terms.

$$b = 4 - 6 = -2.$$

The equation of this straight line is therefore

$y = 2x - 2.$

7.3 A numerical method for finding the slope of a curve

For finding the slope of a straight line, the method based on Rule 7.1 is easy to use since the slope is the same for any value of x. However, this no longer applies if we consider the curve $y = x^2 - 6x + 8$, shown in Figure 2.4 (p. 40). Here the slope changes from being negative to being positive. The minimum value of y is $y = -1$; this occurs when $x = 3$. As x moves further away from 3, the curve becomes progressively steeper, so clearly the slope of the line depends upon the value of x.

Tangents and chords
A *chord* is a straight line joining any two points on a curve; it will usually cross (or 'cut') the curve at each of these points (Figure 7.3).

A *tangent* to a curve at point P is a straight line which just touches but does not cross the curve at that point.

The slope or gradient of a curve
If a tangent is drawn at a point P on a curve, then the slope of this tangent is said to be the slope or gradient of the curve at the point P.

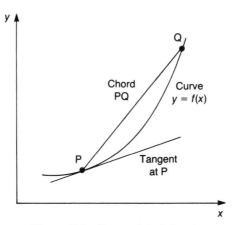

Figure 7.3 Tangent and chord.

In Example 7.3 below the slope of the curve is determined numerically at the specified point ($x = 1$, $y = 4$). This provides a numerical illustration of the algebraic method of finding the slope of a curve. Example 7.4 gives the algebraic equivalent of the numerical method which enables us to find the slope at any point on the curve.

Example 7.3
Find the slope of the curve

$$y = f(x) = 4x^2$$

at the point (1,4).

Solution
Consider the chord PQ_1 in Figure 7.4(a) (not drawn to scale). We can find the slope of this chord by using the method employed in Example 7.1. The slope of PQ_1 is an approximation to the slope of the tangent to the curve at the point P, which is what we are seeking.

When $x = 1.0$ then $y = 4x^2 = 4 \times 1^2 = 4$.
When $x = 1.5$ then $y = 4x^2 = 4 \times 1.5^2 = 9.0$
The change in x is $PR_1 = \Delta x = 1.5 - 1.0 = 0.5$.
The change in y is $R_1 Q_1 = \Delta y = 9.0 - 4.0 = 5.0$.
The slope of the chord PQ_1 is thus

$$\frac{\Delta y}{\Delta x} = \frac{R_1 Q_1}{PR_1} = \frac{9-4}{1.5-1} = \frac{5}{0.5} = 10.$$

We have found the slope of the chord PQ_1 as an approximation to the slope of the curve at the point P but this is not a very good approximation. If the point Q had been closer to P the approximation would have been better.

Consider the slope of the chord PQ_2 in Figure 7.4(b). The point Q_2 is the point $x = 1.2$, $y = 4x^2 = 4 \times 1.2^2 = 5.76$. The slope of PQ_2 is found as before.

When $x = 1.0$ then $y = 4.0$.
When $x = 1.2$ then $y = 5.76$.
The length $PR_2 = \Delta x = 1.2 - 1.0 = 0.2$.
The length $R_2 Q_2 = \Delta y = 5.76 - 4.0 = 1.76$.
The slope of PQ_2 is thus

$$\frac{R_2 Q_2}{PR_2} = \frac{\Delta y}{\Delta x} = \frac{1.76}{0.2} = 8.8.$$

From Figure 7.4(b) it can be seen that the slope of the chord PQ_2 is a

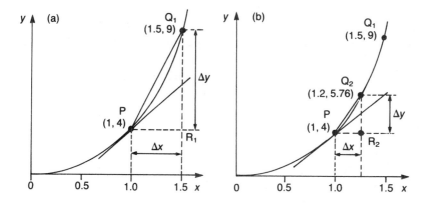

Figure 7.4 Chord as approximation to slope of curve at P. (a) Chord PQ$_1$, (b) chord PQ$_2$.

better approximation to the slope of the curve than the slope of the chord PQ$_1$. If a point even closer to P, say Q$_3$, had been considered the approximation would be even better. In Table 7.1 we have considered a sequence of points Q$_3$, Q$_4$, Q$_5$, Q$_6$ which move progressively closer to the point P. In each case, Δx and Δy have been evaluated and used to find the slope or gradient of the curve.

Looking across the bottom row of Table 7.1, we can see that the gradient of the chord approaches the gradient of the tangent as the point Q$_i$ gets closer to P. In other words, as the value of Δx gets smaller the value of $\Delta y / \Delta x$ becomes closer to the true slope of the curve. In this case the value of $\Delta y / \Delta x$ is getting closer to 8.0 as Δx gets closer to zero. That is, at the point P where $x = 1$ and $y = 4$, the slope of the curve is 8.0. In mathematical jargon the procedure used here for finding the slope of the curve is described as 'finding the limit of $\Delta y / \Delta x$ as Δx tends towards zero'.

Table 7.1

Point Q$_i$	Q$_1$	Q$_2$	Q$_3$	Q$_4$	Q$_5$	Q$_6$
x-value at Q$_i$	1.5	1.2	1.1	1.01	1.001	1.000 1
y-value at Q$_i$	9.0	5.76	4.84	4.0804	4.008 004	4.000 800 04
Diff. Q$_i$R$_i$ = Δy	5.0	1.76	0.84	0.0804	0.008 004	0.000 800 04
Diff. PR$_i$ = Δx	0.5	0.20	0.10	0.01	0.001	0.000 1
Gradient $\Delta y / \Delta x$	10	8.8	8.4	8.04	8.004	8.000 4

Clearly the slope of the curve varies as the value of x varies. It is not practical to use the method above to calculate the slope of a non-linear curve each time a new value of x is considered. A formula giving the slope of the curve for any value of x is needed so that the x-value of interest may be substituted into that formula to find the required slope. The method of Example 7.3 has been expressed in algebraic terms in Example 7.4 below in order to find the formula for the slope of the curve at any value, x.

Example 7.4
Use the algebraic equivalent of the method illustrated in Example 7.3 to find the equation for the slope of the curve

$$y = f(x) = 4x^2$$

at any point P.
   Use this equation to confirm that the slope at the point $(1,4)$ is exactly 8.

Solution
The method used in Example 7.3 was to find the slope of the chord PQ and then see what happened to the slope as the point Q moved nearer to P. In other words, we saw what happened as Δx moved towards zero (Figure 7.5).

Find the slope of the chord PQ   The height of the curve is defined as

$$y = f(x) \quad \text{at the value } x \text{ on the horizontal axis,}$$
$$\text{and} \quad y = f(x+h) \quad \text{at the value } x+h \text{ on the horizontal axis.}$$

At the point P with coordinates x and $f(x)$, we have

$$f(x) = 4x^2.$$

At the point Q with coordinates $x+h$ and $f(x+h)$, substituting $(x+h)$ instead of x we find that

$$f(x+h) = 4(x+h)^2 = 4(x^2 + 2xh + h^2) = 4x^2 + 8xh + 4h^2.$$

Hence

$$\Delta y = f(x+h) - f(x) = 4x^2 + 8xh + 4h^2 - 4x^2 = 8xh + 4h^2,$$
$$\Delta x = (x+h) - x = h.$$

The slope of the chord PQ is therefore

$$\frac{\Delta y}{\Delta x} = \frac{RQ}{PR} = \frac{f(x+h) - f(x)}{h} = \frac{8xh + 4h^2}{h} = 8x + 4h.$$

Differentiation

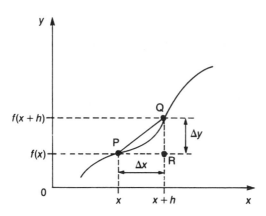

Figure 7.5 Finding the slope of the chord PQ on the general curve y = f(x).

Find the slope of the curve The slope is found by making $\Delta x = h$ progressively smaller, that is by taking the limit as h tends to zero, abbreviated to $\lim_{h\to 0}$. We write the expression for the slope as

$$\text{slope} = \lim_{h\to 0} [8x + 4h].$$

The limit of the contents of the square bracket as h tends to zero is found by putting all h-values in the bracket equal to zero, so that putting $h = 0$ in this case we have

$$\text{slope} = \lim_{h\to 0} [8x + 4h] = 8x.$$

The formula for the slope of the curve $y = 4x^2$ at any point P is then

$$\text{slope} = 8x.$$

When $x = 1$, the slope of the curve is $8x = 8 \times 1 = 8$, the same result as in Example 7.3. Since we have a general formula, we can find the slope at any other points on the curve: the slope at $x = 2$ is $8x = 8 \times 2 = 16$, the slope at $x = -2$ is -16, and so on.

Example 7.4 above showed how the slope of a curve could be found by taking the limit of the slope of a chord through a point P on that curve. The general algebraic equivalent of this method is given below in Rule 7.2.

7.4   The general method of differentiation

This process of taking the limit of $\Delta y/\Delta x$ as Δx tends towards zero is called differentiation. The result of the process of differentiation is called the derivative of y with respect to x (or simply the derivative of y if there is only one other variable involved). This is written as

$$\frac{dy}{dx}$$

which is spoken as 'dee y by dee x'.

Once the equation of the derivative has been found it is easy to evaluate the slope of the curve for any value of x.

We need to find the algebraic equivalent of Δy and Δx. Suppose that y is some function of x, say

$$y = f(x).$$

The value of y for any specified x is found by substituting the x-value into the formula. If the size of x is increased by a small amount, h, then x becomes $x + h$ and y becomes $f(x + h)$.

Using the same procedure as in Example 7.4 where the point P was given as $[x, y = f(x)]$ and the point Q was given as $[(x + h), f(x + h)]$:

The difference in x was $\Delta x = (x + h) - x = h$.
The difference in y was $\Delta y = f(x + h) - f(x)$.
The gradient of the chord PQ was

$$\frac{\Delta y}{\Delta x} = \frac{f(x + h) - f(x)}{h}$$

and the derivative with respect to x is the limit of the gradient of this chord as h tends to zero.

Rule 7.2

The derivative of y with respect to x is defined as the limit of the gradient of the chord PQ as h tends to zero. This is written as

$$\frac{dy}{dx} = \lim_{h \to 0} \left[\frac{f(x + h) - f(x)}{h} \right] \tag{7.2}$$

where $\lim_{h \to 0}$ means the limit as h tends to zero of the contents of the square bracket.

7.5   Rules for derivatives

Clearly it is better to have a formula for the gradient of a curve of the type obtained in Example 7.4 above than to be obliged to recalculate the slope from first principles for each value of x in which we might be interested. Fortunately there are rules which enable us to avoid going back to first principles as in equation (7.2) when we want to find the derivative of a mathematical function. These rules are usually set out in tabular form. Generally speaking, it is easier to apply the rules if you think of the meaning of the process in words rather than in algebraic symbols. Many of the most useful functions involve products of several terms. In order to stress this in the following sections we shall use the dot notation introduced in Chapter 1 to indicate the multiplication of algebraic quantities. Where there might be a possibility of confusing the dot for multiplication with the decimal point, the ordinary multiplication sign, ×, will be used. The notation $\ln(x)$ will be used to denote logarithm to the base e (the natural logarithm) of x.

Rule 7.3

If $y = a.x^n$, then

$$\frac{dy}{dx} = a.n.x^{n-1}.$$

Translation: Leave the constant, a, alone. Multiply by the power of x and reduce this power by 1.

Rule 7.4

If $y = \log_e(x)$ or $y = \ln(x)$, then

$$\frac{dy}{dx} = \frac{1}{x}.$$

Translation: The derivative of $\ln(x)$ is $1/x$.

Rule 7.5

If $y = \ln(ax)$, then

$$\frac{dy}{dx} = \frac{1}{x}.$$

Translation: The derivative of $\ln(ax)$ is also $1/x$. The explanation for this apparent contradiction with Rule 7.4 is given in Section 8.5 under the heading 'Function of a function'.

Rule 7.6

If $y = \ln(x^b)$, then

$$\frac{dy}{dx} = \frac{b}{x}.$$

Translation: The derivative of the natural logarithm of x raised to a power is that power divided by x. This is a direct application of Rule 5.3 which tells us that $\ln(x^b) = b\ln(x)$.

Rule 7.7

If $y = e^{ax}$, then

$$\frac{dy}{dx} = ae^{ax}.$$

Translation: The derivative of the exponential of a constant times x is that constant multiplied by the *unchanged* exponential term. (Note that, as a general rule, the power of the exponential term *never* changes during the process of differentiation or integration.)

Rule 7.8

If $y = a$, then

$$\frac{dy}{dx} = 0.$$

Translation: The derivative of a constant term (containing no x) is zero. By definition, a constant has no rate of change.

Differentiation

There are many more functions than those listed above. We have given those which are used most often in basic mathematics. The next section deals with different applications of the above derivatives and so this list of derivatives will be needed for reference purposes as we go through the examples.

An example of each rule is given below and in the next section. In each example the translation in word form is given in order to emphasize the thinking involved in the application of the relevant rule.

Example 7.5
Differentiate the function $y = 4x^2$ and hence find the slope of the curve when $x = 1.5$.

Solution
Since this function, $y = 4x^2$, involves a term with x raised to a power, we see that Rule 7.3 is the rule to use and we have $a = 4$ and $n = 2$:

$$y = 4x^2 = ax^n.$$

Leave the constant ($a = 4$) alone, multiply by the power ($n = 2$), then reduce the power by 1:

$$\frac{dy}{dx} = 4 \times 2x^{2-1} = 8x^1 = 8x.$$

When $x = 1.5$ the slope is $8 \times 1.5 = 12.0$.

Example 7.6
Find the derivative of the function

$$y = 5x^{1/2}.$$

Solution
This function contains x raised to a power and so Rule 7.3 applies, with $a = 5$ and $n = 1/2$:

$$y = 5x^{1/2}.$$

Leave the constant ($a = 5$) alone, multiply by the power ($n = 1/2$), then reduce the power by 1:

$$\frac{dy}{dx} = 5 \times \tfrac{1}{2}x^{1/2-1}.$$

Hence

$$\frac{dy}{dx} = 2.5 \times x^{-1/2}.$$

This answer could also be written as

$$\frac{dy}{dx} = 2.5 \times \frac{1}{x^{1/2}} \quad \text{or} \quad \frac{2.5}{\sqrt{x}}.$$

7.6 The derivative of the reciprocal of a function

When the function to be differentiated contains the reciprocal of a function (i.e. 'one over' that function), the first step in the differentiation process should be to rewrite the function so that all of the terms in x are above the 'fraction line'. Remember that when a term is moved from below the fraction line to above the line or vice versa, the sign of the power is reversed.

Example 7.7
Find the slope of the curve

$$y = \frac{5}{x^3}$$

when $x = 2.0$.

Solution
First rewrite the function.

$$y = \frac{5}{x^3} = 5x^{-3}.$$

Since the function contains x raised to a power, use Rule 7.3 with $a = 5$ and $n = -3$.

Leave $a = 5$ alone, multiply by the power $n = -3$ and then reduce the power by 1.

$$\frac{dy}{dx} = 5 \times (-3)x^{-3-1} = -15x^{-4} = \frac{-15}{x^4}.$$

Mathematically speaking, either means of expressing the solution is correct. The advantage of expressing the solution as a fraction is that it is easier to visualize what happens at the extremes when very small or very large values of x occur. Most people find it easier to evaluate a term mentally in the form of a fraction than to deal with an identical term expressed as a negative power of x. In the above example, when x

is very large dy/dx is virtually zero and as x moves closer to zero the slope dy/dx approaches $-\infty$.

Example 7.8
Find the derivative of the function

$\quad y = \ln(3x).$

Solution
Since the function to be differentiated involves a natural logarithm, one of Rules 7.4 to 7.6 applies. Our function corresponds to Rule 7.5 with $a = 3$. The derivative is therefore

$$\frac{dy}{dx} = \frac{1}{x}.$$

Example 7.9
Find the derivative of the function

$\quad y = \ln(x^4).$

Solution
Here Rule 7.6 with $b = 4$ is used. The derivative is b/x, so

$$\frac{dy}{dx} = \frac{4}{x}.$$

This is the same as applying Rule 5.3 to the function and then differentiating.
The function is $\quad y = \ln(x^4) = 4\ln(x).$
Then we leave the multiplying constant alone and differentiate $\ln(x)$ according to Rule 7.4:

$$\frac{dy}{dx} = \frac{4}{x}.$$

It does not matter which method you use. Choose the one that you find easiest to deal with.

Example 7.10
Find the gradient of the function

$\quad y = e^{6x}.$

Solution
Use Rule 7.7 with $a = 6$:

$$\frac{dy}{dx} = 6.e^{6x}.$$

Note that the exponential term does not change on differentiation.

Example 7.11
Differentiate the function

$$y = 7e^{3x}$$

with respect to x.

Solution
Use Rule 7.7 with $a = 3$ to differentiate the exponential term, leaving the multiplying coefficient, 7, untouched.
   Multiply by the coefficient of x and leave the exponential untouched.

$$\frac{dy}{dx} = 7 \times 3e^{3x} = 21e^{3x}.$$

If the function consists of the sum (or difference) of a number of terms, the derivative of the sum is simply the sum (or difference) of the derivatives of the individual terms.

Example 7.12
Find the slope of the curve

$$y = \frac{2}{e^{3x}} + \frac{7}{4x^5} + 3.$$

Solution
First rewrite the expression without the fractions in x.

$$y = 2e^{-3x} + \frac{7}{4}x^{-5} + 3.$$

Use Rule 7.7 with $a = -3$ for the first term, Rule 7.3 with $a = 7/4$ and $n = -5$ for the second term, and Rule 7.8 for the third term.

$$\frac{dy}{dx} = 2(-3)e^{-3x} + \frac{7}{4}(-5)x^{-6} + 0.$$

Differentiation

Hence

$$\frac{dy}{dx} = -6e^{-3x} - \frac{35}{4}x^{-6}.$$

Writing the terms with negative exponents as fractions, the solution may be given as

$$\frac{dy}{dx} = -\frac{6}{e^{3x}} - \frac{8.75}{x^6}.$$

ADDITIONAL EXAMPLES

A7.1 Find the gradients of the following curves at the points specified:
  (i) $y = 2x^2$ at the point (2,8);
  (ii) $y = x^2 - 1$ at the point (3,8);
  (iii) $y = 2x + x^2$ at the point (1,3);
  (iv) $y = 5x^2$ at the point (1,5).

A7.2 Differentiate the functions:
  (i) $y = 5x^8$;

  (ii) $y = \frac{6}{x^2}$;

  (iii) $y = 2x^{3/4}$;
  (iv) $y = 10x^{1/2} - 9x^{1/3}$;
  (v) $f(x) = 6x^4 + 3x^3 - 2x^2 + 5x - 6$;

  (vi) $f(x) = \dfrac{7x^3 - 5x^2 - 6x + 4}{x^2}$.

A7.3 Differentiate the following functions:
  (i) $y = 6e^{2x}$;
  (ii) $y = 3\ln(x)$;
  (iii) $y = 3e^{-4x}$;
  (iv) $y = 2e^{x/2}$;
  (v) $y = 6e^{2x} + 3\ln(x)$;
  (vi) $y = 4\ln(x^3)$;
  (vii) $y = 4\ln(3x)$.

A7.4 Cumulative demand, D, for a type of novelty item produced by the Watt Fun Company is thought to vary with time, t, according to the model

$$D = 50t - 0.08t^2,$$

where t is measured in days from the time that the product was launched on to the market.

(i) Differentiate D to find an expression for the rate at which cumulative demand is increasing with time.

(ii) In a sensible model, cumulative demand should never decrease as time increases. Use this fact to find the largest number of days for which the model is valid.

(iii) When the company launched the product, it had 7500 items in stock. Find how many days it will take for the stock to drop to 100 items, assuming orders are satisfied immediately. Explain whether there is more than one feasible solution to this problem.

8

More about differentiation

Introduction

Chapter 7 explained the basic method of differentiating simple functions but it is often necessary to deal with more complicated functions. The way that we approach this is to build on and extend the methods developed in Chapter 7. Once these basic 'building blocks' of differentiation have been mastered, it should be possible to use them systematically to find the derivative of almost any function you encounter. We have dealt in this book only with functions of a single variable; if a function contains more than one variable then the same basic 'building blocks' are used with further extensions of the techniques presented in Chapter 7 and in this chapter.

8.1   The second and higher derivatives

Consider the function $y = f(x)$ which represents the curve of y against x on a graph.

The process of differentiating once determines the slope at any point on the curve. This slope gives the rate at which y changes as x changes. Sometimes the rate at which the slope changes is of as much interest as the value of the slope at a particular point. For example, the rate of inflation measures the rate at which prices change over a given period of time; this is found by taking the derivative of price with respect to time. Quite often the economic point of interest is whether or not the rate of inflation is slowing down or speeding up. In this case we look for the change in the rate of inflation over a given period; this entails differentiating the rate of inflation function with respect to time. Since this latter derivative is the result of a second differentiation process it is known as the *second derivative* of price with respect to time.

In general the quantity obtained by differentiating once is called the first derivative. If the differentiation is repeated, we get the second derivative. If it is repeated again, we get the third derivative, a further repetition gives the fourth derivative and so on. The procedures for finding the second and subsequent derivatives are essentially the same as those used for finding the first derivative but the starting point is always the previous derivative rather than the original function. In some cases, the higher derivatives will be zero and non-existent.

The first derivative is denoted by $\dfrac{dy}{dx}$.

The second derivative is denoted by $\dfrac{d^2y}{dx^2}$.

The third derivative is denoted by $\dfrac{d^3y}{dx^3}$,

and so on. The notation for the second derivative is spoken as 'dee 2 *y* by dee *x* squared', the third derivative is spoken as 'dee 3 *y* by dee *x* cubed', etc.

The first derivative gives the rate of change of *y* with *x*, the second derivative gives the rate of change of the first derivative which is itself the rate of change of *y* with *x*; in other words, the second derivative gives the 'acceleration' or 'deceleration' of *y* whereas the first derivative gives the 'speed'. Another way of looking at it is to consider the second derivative as the rate at which the slope of the line changes as *x* changes. It is often essential to know both the first and second derivatives in order to make sense of a business situation. For example, if the rate of inflation is slowing down, this can mean that prices are still rising but not rising as fast as they once were or that prices are actually falling, depending upon whether point A or point B on the curve in Figure 8.1 is being considered. At point A, prices are still increasing with time but the curve is becoming flatter, that is the rate of change of the rate of inflation (the second derivative of price with respect to time) is decreasing. At point B, prices are falling as time increases and the rate of change of the rate of inflation (the second derivative) is still

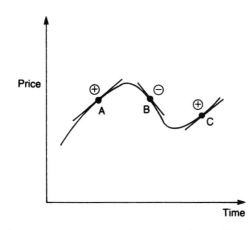

Figure 8.1 Sketch graph of price versus time: ⊕, positive slope; ⊖, negative slope.

decreasing (getting more negative). At point C, where prices are starting to rise once more, the rate of change of the rate of inflation is increasing, that is the second derivative is increasing.

Example 8.1
Find the second derivative of the function

$$y = x^5.$$

Solution
Split the calculation into two stages.
   Using Rule 7.3 with $a = 1$ and $n = 5$ gives the first derivative as

$$\frac{dy}{dx} = 5x^4.$$

Now take dy/dx as the starting point for the second stage. The application of Rule 7.3 with $a = 5$ and $n = 4$ this time gives the second derivative as

$$\frac{d^2y}{dx^2} = 5 \times 4x^3 = 20x^3.$$

This second derivative of $20x^3$ allows us to calculate the rate at which the slope of the curve is changing at any given point on that curve simply by substituting the given value of x into the expression $20x^3$.

Example 8.2

Find the second derivative of the function

$$y = 3e^{2x}$$

Solution

The first derivative is found using Rule 7.7 with $a = 2$. Ignore the multiplying coefficient, multiply by a and leave the exponential term unchanged.

$$\frac{dy}{dx} = 3 \times 2e^{2x} = 6e^{2x}.$$

The second derivative also uses Rule 7.7 with $a = 2$ but with a multiplying coefficient of 6.

$$\frac{d^2y}{dx^2} = 6 \times 2e^{2x} = 12e^{2x}.$$

It can be seen that the exponential expression for y has a slope that also increases exponentially and that the rate of change of that slope is also exponential. This explains some effects of the exponential model used for hyperinflation, which we considered in Chapter 5. If the under-lying model remains exponential and prices rise exponentially, the rate at which prices rise will also rise exponentially – a sort of snowballing effect. This vicious circle can only be broken if the economic factors which formed the basis of the underlying model can be altered in order to remove the exponential effect.

8.2   Alternative notation for the derivative

The use of the notation

$$\frac{df(x)}{dx}$$

and its variations for the first derivative of the function $f(x)$ can be rather cumbersome to write out. For this reason the notation $f'(x)$ is also used to denote the first derivative with respect to x. The advantage of this notation is that it is easier to extend to the higher derivatives and to cases where we require the value of the derivative at a specified value of x:

$$f'(x) \quad \text{means} \quad \frac{df(x)}{dx},$$

$$f''(x) \quad \text{means} \quad \frac{d^2f(x)}{dx^2},$$

and so on.

If the derivative at a specified value of x is required, then that value of x is written inside the bracket of $f(x)$.

For example, if in Example 8.2 above we had wanted the first derivative

$$f'(x) = 6e^{2x}$$

at the point $x = 0.5$ we would write

$$f'(0.5) = 6e^{2 \times 0.5} = 16.3097 \quad \text{to four decimal places.}$$

Similarly the value of the second derivative at $x = 0.5$ is written as

$$f''(0.5) = 12e^{2 \times 0.5} = 32.6194 \quad \text{to four decimal places.}$$

8.3 Maxima and minima

In Section 2.4 we drew graphs which had peaks and troughs called turning points. It is sometimes necessary to determine accurately the location of these turning points. This is done by using the methods of calculus introduced in the last chapter.

Consider dy/dx in the curve shown in Figure 8.2. From the point A to the point B, the slope is positive. From the point B to the point C, the slope is negative. At the point B the slope is zero. From the point C to the point D, the slope is positive. The slope moves from positive values at point A through zero at point B to negative values as x increases. The point B is called a *maximum*. The slope changes from negative values through zero at point C to positive values at point D. The point C is called a *minimum*.

The points such as B and C on a curve where the slope is zero are generally called *stationary points*. These points can be located by finding the first derivative and then finding the values of x which satisfy the equation

$$\frac{dy}{dx} = 0.$$

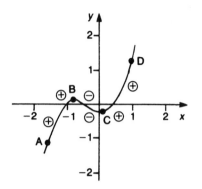

Figure 8.2 Graph of $y = x^3 + x^2 - 0.25x - 0.25$ (cf. Figure 2.5): $\oplus$, positive slope; $\ominus$, negative slope.

The nature of the stationary points can be determined:

1. by arithmetical examination of the slope of the line on either side of the stationary point;
2. by looking at the sign of the second derivative;
3. by examining the graph of the curve.

Consider the function

$$y = x^3 + x^2 - 0.25x - 0.25$$

shown in Figure 8.2.

The approximate location of the stationary points can be found from the graph. A more exact location must be found by using the first derivative as shown in Example 8.3.

The second derivative gives the rate of change of the slope; that is, it tells us if the slope is increasing or decreasing. If the slope is increasing, then the second derivative will be positive. If the slope is increasing at a stationary point then that point is a minimum – like point C in Figure 8.2. If the slope is decreasing at a stationary point then that point is a maximum – like point B. The sketches in Figure 8.3 illustrate the effect which changes in the slope have on the sign of the second derivative.

Example 8.3
Find the stationary points of the function

$$y = x^3 + x^2 - 0.25x - 0.25$$

correct to four decimal places.

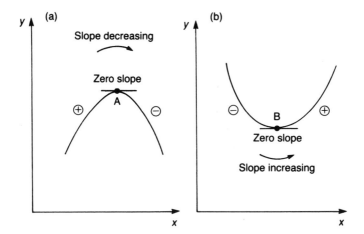

Figure 8.3   (a) Point A is a maximum. (b) Point B is a minimum.

Solution
The first step is to find the first derivative to obtain the equation for the slope of the curve:

$$\text{slope} = \frac{dy}{dx} = 3x^2 + 2x - 0.25.$$

At a stationary point the slope is zero, so the next step is to determine the values of x for which the slope is zero. This means we have to solve the quadratic equation

$$\text{slope} = 3x^2 + 2x - 0.25 = 0.$$

This equation is solved in the usual way by using Standard Form 2.5 for solving quadratic equations given in Chapter 2.

The standard form is $ax^2 + bx + c \quad\ = 0.$
We have to solve $3x^2 + 2x - 0.25 = 0.$
The roots are

$$x = \frac{-b \pm \sqrt{b^2 - 4ac}}{2a}.$$

A comparison of coefficients gives $a = 3$, $b = 2$, $c = -0.25$, and so

$$x = \frac{-2 \pm \sqrt{4 - 4 \times 3 \times (-0.25)}}{2 \times 3}.$$

The roots are $x = -0.7743$ and $x = 0.1076$, but this is only half the answer.

In order to find the stationary points we need the y-values as well as the x-values, so the next step is to evaluate y at the turning points.

When $x = -0.7743$, $y = (-0.7743)^3 + (-0.7743)^2$
$$-0.25(-0.7743) - 0.25.$$
Hence $y = 0.0789.$
When $x = 0.1076$, $y = (0.1076)^3 + (0.1076)^2$
$$-0.25 \times 0.1076 - 0.25.$$
Hence $y = -0.2641.$

The stationary points are $(-0.7743, 0.0789)$ and $(0.1076, -0.2641)$.

The graph of the curve is shown in Figure 8.2. It can be seen which of the stationary points is a maximum and which is a minimum. If we had not drawn the graph it would have been necessary to determine the nature of the stationary points by using one of the methods described below.

Either use Method 1 Find the second derivative. This measures the rate of change of the slope. If the slope is decreasing then the point is a maximum; if the slope is increasing, the point is a minimum. See Figure 8.3.

$$\frac{d^2y}{dx^2} = 6x + 2.$$

For the stationary point $x = -0.7743$, $y = 0.0789$:

$$\frac{d^2y}{dx^2} = -2.6458.$$

The negative value of the second derivative tells us that the slope is decreasing here, and hence the point $(-0.7743, 0.0789)$ is a maximum. For the stationary point $x = 0.1076$, $y = -0.2641$:

$$\frac{d^2y}{dx^2} = 2.6456.$$

The positive value tells us that the slope is increasing here, and hence the point $(0.1076, -0.2641)$ is a minimum.

Or use Method 2 Find the sign of dy/dx each side of the stationary point.

Use the logic of Figure 8.3 to determine the nature of the stationary point.

The slope is given by the expression

$$\frac{dy}{dx} = 3x^2 + 2x - 0.25.$$

Consider the stationary point $x = -0.7743$, $y = 0.0789$. Examine the slope to the left of this point, at $x = -1$, say.
When $x = -1$,

$$\frac{dy}{dx} = 3(-1)^2 + 2(-1) - 0.25 = 0.75.$$

Now consider the slope to the right of the stationary point, at $x = 0$, say.
When $x = 0$, the slope is

$$\frac{dy}{dx} = -0.25.$$

The slope changes from positive through zero to negative as x increases. From the diagram in Figure 8.3(a) it can be seen that the point $x = -0.7743$, $y = 0.0789$ is a maximum.
Consider the point $x = 0.1076$, $y = -0.2641$ and examine the slope either side of this point. Consider a point to the right of the stationary point, $x = 1$, say.
When $x = +1$, the slope is

$$\frac{dy}{dx} = 4.75.$$

Consider a point to the left of the stationary point, $x = 0$, say.
When $x = 0$, the slope is

$$\frac{dy}{dx} = -0.25.$$

The slope changes from being negative through zero to positive as the value of x increases. From Figure 8.3(b) it can be seen that the point $x = 0.1076$, $y = -0.2641$ is a minimum.
Note that either of these methods for finding the nature of the stationary point may be used. Use the method which you find the easiest.

8.4 Points of inflexion

As we have seen from the graphs in Chapter 2 a point of inflexion occurs when a curve moves in one direction, tends to flatten out and then moves at an increasing rate in the same direction. When the curve flattens out the rate of change of the slope is momentarily zero (so the second derivative will be zero) at a point of inflexion, but the slope itself (the first derivative) need not be zero. If the slope is zero the point is a stationary point or, more fully, a *stationary point of inflexion*. As previously explained the nature of a stationary point must be determined. This can be done by inspection of the graph or by one of the methods already illustrated in Example 8.3.

The curve of the function

$$y = \frac{x^3}{2} - 3x^2 + 6x + 5$$

is shown in Figure 8.4. For points to the left of A, y increases as x increases, that is the slope of the curve is positive. For points to the right of A the slope is also positive. At the point A the slope is a minimum, in this case zero. It is not necessary for the slope to be zero at a point of inflexion, merely that the slope should be numerically a minimum irrespective of the sign of the slope. This means that the curve flattens out at the point of inflexion and then continues in the same direction (Figure 8.5).

Example 8.4
Find the stationary points of the curve

$$y = \frac{x^3}{2} - 3x^2 + 6x + 5.$$

Solution
The graph of the function is shown in Figure 8.4.

To find the stationary point, first find out if there is a value of x for which the slope is zero. The slope is

$$\frac{dy}{dx} = \frac{3}{2}x^2 - 6x + 6.$$

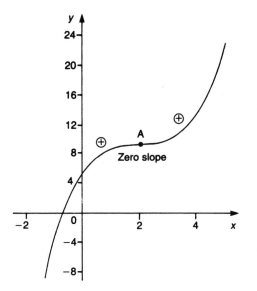

Figure 8.4 Graph of $y = x^3/2 - 3x^2 + 6x + 5$ (cf. Figure 2.6). A is a stationary point of inflexion.

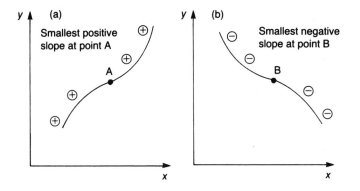

Figure 8.5 Points of inflextion. (a) Smallest positive slope at point A. (b) Smallest negative slope at point B.

To find the point where the slope is zero, solve the equation

$$\frac{3}{2}x^2 - 6x + 6 = 0.$$

To simplify the equation multiply throughout by 2 to remove the fraction and divide throughout by 3 to remove the common factor of 3 in every term. The equation then becomes

$$x^2 - 4x + 4 = 0.$$

This factorizes to

$$(x-2)^2 = 0$$

or

$$(x-2)(x-2) = 0,$$

so there is a repeated root at $x = 2$. Next find the value of y which corresponds to $x = 2$ by substituting $x = 2$ into the equation for y. Thus there is a stationary point at $x = 2, y = 9$.

The second derivative at the point $x = 2, y = 9$ is

$$\frac{d^2y}{dx^2} = 3x - 6 = 0$$

when $x = 2$. This indicates that the slope is a minimum at the stationary point and that the stationary point is a point of inflexion. Inspection of the graph in Figure 8.4 confirms this result.

If the slope to either side of the point $x = 2, y = 9$ is examined using the same method as in Example 8.3 it will be seen to be positive on both sides of this point. As previously stated, this is the major characteristic of a point of inflexion: the slope of the curve has the same sign to either side of the point where the curve flattens out.

8.5   The function of a function rule

When a function is to be differentiated, the first step should be to see if the function can be simplified algebraically. If this can be done, we may find that the expression simplifies to a set of basic terms and the list of derivatives from Chapter 7 can be applied. In some other cases, the function contains bracketed terms and it may be possible to expand the brackets using the techniques explained in Chapter 1. If the brackets cannot be expanded and removed, the function must be differentiated in its original form.

It is easier to explain this technique by means of an example. We have considered the function

$$f(x) = (3x + 1)^2$$

in Examples 8.5 and 8.6 below. In the first case the expression is simplified and then differentiated; in the second example the function is differentiated with the brackets left in place.

Example 8.5
Differentiate the function

$$f(x) = (3x + 1)^2.$$

Solution
First simplify the expression by expanding the brackets.

$$f(x) = (3x + 1)^2 = 9x^2 + 6x + 1.$$

Now differentiate the function term by term, using Rules 7.3 and 7.8.

$$\frac{df(x)}{dx} = 9 \times 2x + 6 \times 1x^0 + 0$$

$$= 18x + 6.$$

Example 8.6
Differentiate the function

$$f(x) = (3x + 1)^2.$$

Solution
The function to be differentiated is of the type

$$f(x) = \text{bracket}^2.$$

We know how to differentiate a squared term using Rule 7.3. Call the bracket contents b, say, and then rewrite the expression in its new form.

Let the bracket contents be $b = 3x + 1$. Then $f(x)$ can be written as

$$F(b) = b^2.$$

The derivative of $F(b)$ with respect to b is

$$\frac{dF(b)}{db} = 2b^1 = 2b.$$

However, we are really seeking $df(x)/dx$.

We have the relationship between b and x and it is easy to differentiate b with respect to x:

$$b = 3x + 1,$$

so

$$\frac{db}{dx} = 3.$$

At this stage we have now found

$$\frac{dF(b)}{db} \quad \text{and} \quad \frac{db}{dx}$$

and need to combine them to find the derivative of $f(x)$ with respect to x. The relationship between the three derivatives is:

$$\frac{df(x)}{dx} = \frac{dF(b)}{db} \times \frac{db}{dx}.$$

Substituting our values into the relationship gives

$$\frac{df(x)}{dx} = 2b \times 3 = 6b.$$

Since the original expression was defined in terms of the original variable x the result must be given in terms of the same variable. To do this substitute $b = 3x + 1$ into the derivative.

$$\frac{df(x)}{dx} = 6(3x + 1) = 18x + 6.$$

This is the same as the result we obtained in Example 8.5, as was expected.

Why 'function of a function'?
In Example 8.6 $F(b)$ was a function of b and b was itself a function of x, so we say that $F(b)$ was a 'function of a function', that is a function of b which was a function of x.

In the above examples it was quicker and easier to expand the bracket and differentiate rather than to replace the bracket and then differentiate. In some cases it is difficult or impossible to expand the bracket. In such cases, for example $y = \sqrt{(3x + 1)}$, the technique of Example 8.6 must be used.
This is generalized in Rule 8.1 below.

Rule 8.1

To differentiate a function of a function, let $y = F(b)$ where b is a function of x.
Then

$$\frac{dy}{dx} = \frac{dF(b)}{db} \times \frac{db}{dx}.$$

Translation: When the function is in the form of a bracket as in Example 8.6 above it is easier to remember the rule in word form. 'Differentiate with respect to the bracket, then multiply by the derivative of the function inside the bracket.'

Example 8.7
Differentiate the function

$$y = \sqrt{(3x + 1)}.$$

Solution
This expression cannot be simplified by expanding the bracket. Hence the function of a function rule must be used.

Let $b = 3x + 1,$ then $y = \sqrt{b} = b^{1/2}.$

Now use Rule 7.3 to differentiate these functions.

$$\frac{db}{dx} = 3x^0 + 0 \qquad\qquad \frac{dy}{db} = \frac{1}{2} b^{1/2-1}$$

$$= 3 \qquad\qquad\qquad\qquad = \frac{1}{2} b^{-1/2}.$$

Next combine these results as

$$\frac{dy}{dx} = \frac{dy}{db} \times \frac{db}{dx} = \frac{1}{2}b^{-1/2} \times 3$$

and substitute for b in terms of the original variable, x:

$$\frac{dy}{dx} = \frac{3}{2}(3x+1)^{-1/2} = \frac{3}{2(3x+1)^{1/2}}.$$

Remember that when moving a term from above the fraction line to below the fraction line or vice versa the sign of the power of the term is reversed.

Example 8.8
Differentiate the function

$$f(x) = 2(6x^2 + 2x + 3)^{1/2}.$$

Solution
The function $f(x)$ contains a bracket which cannot be expanded. Hence the function of a function rule must be used.

Let $u = 6x^2 + 2x + 3$, then $\dfrac{du}{dx} = 6 \times 2x + 2 = 12x + 2 = 2(6x + 1)$.

The original $f(x)$ is equivalent to

$$F(u) = 2u^{1/2}.$$

$$\frac{dF(u)}{du} = \frac{1}{2} \cdot 2u^{1/2-1} = u^{-1/2}.$$

Hence

$$\frac{df(x)}{dx} = \frac{dF(u)}{du} \cdot \frac{du}{dx} = u^{-1/2} \times 2(6x+1) = \frac{2(6x+1)}{u^{1/2}}.$$

Substitute for u:

$$\frac{df(x)}{dx} = \frac{2(6x+1)}{(6x^2+2x+3)^{1/2}}.$$

Now that the function of a function rule has been explained the explanation for the apparent contradiction between Rule 7.4 and Rule 7.5 can be given.

Example 8.9
Differentiate the function

$$y = \ln(ax)$$

where a is a constant.

Solution
This function involves a bracket. Use the function of a function rule.

Let $b = ax$ so that $y = \ln(b)$.

Now $\dfrac{db}{dx} = a$, using Rule 7.3,   and $\dfrac{dy}{db} = \dfrac{1}{b}$, using Rule 7.4.

The required derivative is

$$\frac{dy}{dx} = \frac{dy}{db} \times \frac{db}{dx} = \frac{1}{b} \times a.$$

Substitute $b = ax$ to give

$$\frac{dy}{dx} = \frac{1}{ax} \times a = \frac{1}{x}.$$

It can be seen that this function of a function rule gives us a very powerful tool to use in the differentiation process. More illustrations of its use are given in the additional examples at the end of the chapter.

8.6 The product rule

Thus far we have dealt only with functions which have just one term or bracket involving the independent variable. It is quite common to have functions which are products of two or more factors. Hence we need the *product rule* to deal with such functions. The rule is stated in terms of the product of two functions but can be easily extended by the repeated application of the rule to cover the product of more than two terms.

Rule 8.2

If a function $f(x)$ is the product of two functions of x, called u and v respectively, so that $f(x) = u \cdot v$, then

$$\frac{df(x)}{dx} = \frac{d(u \cdot v)}{dx} = \frac{du}{dx} \cdot v + u \cdot \frac{dv}{dx}.$$

Translation: Once again it is easier to remember this rule in terms of words. In word form the rule is 'differentiate the first term, leaving the second alone, and then add the derivative of the second term, leaving the first alone'.

As with the function of a function rule, this product rule will be illustrated using a function which can be differentiated by expanding the brackets and finding the derivative of each term as well as by applying Rule 8.2.

The function $\qquad f(x) = 3x^2(1 - x^2)$

can be expanded as $\qquad f(x) = 3x^2 - 3x^4.$

Rule 7.3 will be used to differentiate the expanded form and Rule 8.2 will be used to differentiate the function with the bracket in place in its original form.

Example 8.10
Find the derivative with respect to x of the function

$$f(x) = 3x^2(1 - x^2)$$

by simplifying the function and then applying Rule 7.3 to each term.

Solution
The function is expanded as

$$f(x) = 3x^2 - 3x^4.$$

Now use Rule 7.3 to differentiate each term. 'Leave the constant alone, multiply by the power and reduce the power by 1'.

$$\frac{df(x)}{dx} = 3 \times 2x^1 - 3 \times 4x^3$$

$$= 6x - 12x^3.$$

The result can also be written as

$$\frac{df(x)}{dx} = 6x(1 - 2x^2).$$

Example 8.11
Differentiate the function

$$y = f(x) = 3x^2(1 - x^2)$$

using the function of a function rule.

Solution
First split the function into the product of two terms u and v.

$$y = 3x^2.(1 - x^2).$$
Let $u = 3x^2$ and $v = 1 - x^2$.

In order to apply Rule 8.2 we must find du/dx and dy/dx and substitute into the equation for $df(x)/dx$.

$$\frac{du}{dx} = 6x, \qquad \frac{dv}{dx} = -2x.$$

$$\frac{dy}{dx} = \frac{du}{dx}.v + u.\frac{dv}{dx}.$$

$$\frac{dy}{dx} = 6x(1 - x^2) + 3x^2(-2x)$$

$$= 6x - 6x^3 - 6x^3.$$

Hence

$$\frac{dy}{dx} = 6x - 12x^3 = 6x(1 - 2x^2).$$

Clearly in this case it would have been easier to expand the bracket on the right-hand side of $f(x)$ and differentiate the function directly as demonstrated in Example 8.10. If the expression can be easily simplified it is probably better to do this. As a general rule it is best to use the simplest techniques possible. However, in many cases the function cannot be simplified and can only be differentiated by applying Rule 8.2.

Example 8.12
Differentiate the function

$$y = 2x^5 e^{6x}.$$

Solution
First write the function in the standard form as a product of two factors

$$y = u.v,$$

$$\text{so} \quad y = 2x^5.e^{6x}.$$

Let $\quad u = 2x^5 \qquad\qquad \text{and} \quad v = e^{6x}$

$$\frac{du}{dx} = 2 \times 5x^4 \qquad\qquad \frac{dv}{dx} = 6e^{6x}$$

$$= 10x^4$$

$$\frac{dy}{dx} = \frac{du}{dx}.v \quad + u.\frac{dv}{dx}$$

$$= 10x^4.e^{6x} + 2x^5.6e^{6x}.$$

Hence

$$\frac{dy}{dx} = 10x^4 e^{6x} + 12x^5 e^{6x}.$$

The result can be left in this form or it can be simplified using the factorization methods of Chapter 1.

There is a common factor of $2x^4$ and also a common factor of e^{6x} in both terms. These factors can be taken outside of the bracket to give the solution

$$\frac{dy}{dx} = 2x^4(5e^{6x} + 6xe^{6x}),$$

and hence

$$\frac{dy}{dx} = 2x^4 e^{6x}(5 + 6x).$$

8.7 Mixing the function of a function and product rules

Some functions involve both products and brackets. In such cases Rule 8.1 and Rule 8.2 can be used together to differentiate the function. Example 8.13 illustrates this point.

Example 8.13
Differentiate the function

$$y = 3x^2(3x + 1)^{1/2}.$$

Solution
This function cannot be simplified and is the product of two factors. First identify the factors:

$$y = u \cdot v,$$

so $\quad y = 3x^2 \cdot (3x + 1)^{1/2}.$

Let $\quad u = 3x^2 \quad$ and $\quad v = (3x + 1)^{1/2}.$

Use Rule 7.3 to differentiate u with respect to x. Since v contains a bracket which cannot be expanded use the function of a function rule (Rule 8.1) to differentiate this factor with respect to x. This has in fact already been done in Example 8.7 and so the answer is quoted below. If anything complicated arises in a procedure it is common to work it out in detail elsewhere and then substitute the answer into the appropriate place. This avoids the possibility of making errors in copying long algebraic expressions from one line to the next.

$$\frac{du}{dx} = 3 \times 2x^{2-1} = 6x, \qquad \frac{dv}{dx} = \frac{3}{2(3x + 1)^{1/2}}.$$

Substitute the above results into the relationship

$$\frac{dy}{dx} = \frac{du}{dx} \cdot v \qquad + \quad u \cdot \frac{dv}{dx}.$$

$$\frac{dy}{dx} = 6x \cdot (3x + 1)^{1/2} \quad + 3x^2 \cdot \frac{3}{2(3x + 1)^{1/2}}$$

$$= 6x(3x + 1)^{1/2} \quad + \quad \frac{9x^2}{2(3x + 1)^{1/2}}.$$

The algebraic methods demonstrated in Chapter 1 for simplifying fractions can be applied to the solution given above.

$$\frac{6x(3x+1)^{1/2}}{1} + \frac{9x^2}{2(3x+1)^{1/2}} = \frac{6x(3x+1)^{1/2} \times 2(3x+1)^{1/2} + 9x^2 \times 1}{2(3x+1)^{1/2}}$$

$$= \frac{12x(3x+1) + 9x^2}{2(3x+1)^{1/2}} = \frac{36x^2 + 12x + 9x^2}{2(3x+1)^{1/2}}$$

$$= \frac{3x(15x+4)}{2(3x+1)^{1/2}}.$$

As we mentioned before, each presentation of the derivative is correct. The simplified version makes it easier to visualize the shape of the curve of the derivative and hence gives an idea of where the slope is increasing and decreasing and also where it goes to infinity. (Dividing any quantity by zero gives the answer of infinity.) Here, when $x = 0$ and when $x = -4/15$ the slope is zero. When $x = -1/3$ the slope is infinity. The way in which this is calculated is shown below.

$$\frac{dy}{dx} = \frac{3(-1/3)[15(-1/3)+4]}{2[3(-1/3)+1]^{1/2}} = \frac{-1[-5+4]}{2[-1+1]^{1/2}} = \frac{+1}{2 \times 0} = \infty.$$

In a practical application of this model this could never happen, because when the slope becomes very large the value of y is increasing so rapidly that the underlying system, whatever this is, moves out of control. As a system approaches the 'out of control state' all of the standard models and hypotheses begin to break down. For this reason it is important to know what happens to models for extreme values of the independent variable (when x is zero or near infinity).

8.8 Differentiating expressions containing fractions

A quotient is one function divided by another, that is the ratio of two functions. There is a special rule for differentiating quotients but this rule is difficult to remember. Most people prefer to deal with quotients by rewriting them as a product and then using Rule 8.1. The answer obtained is exactly the same as that obtained using the quotient rule but the methodology is a lot simpler.

More about differentiation

Example 8.14
Find the derivative with respect to x of the function

$$y = \frac{1}{(6x^2 + 2x + 3)}.$$

Solution
The first step is to remove the fraction. The expression can be rewritten as

$$y = (6x^2 + 2x + 3)^{-1}.$$

Since this expression contains a bracket which cannot be removed the function of a function rule (Rule 8.1) must be used.

Let $b = 6x^2 + 2x + 3$ and $y = b^{-1}$.

$$\frac{db}{dx} = 6 \times 2x + 2 \times 1 + 0 \qquad\qquad \frac{dy}{db} = (-1)b^{-1-1}$$

$$= 12x + 2 = 2(6x + 1) \qquad\qquad = -b^{-2}.$$

Now use Rule 8.1.

$$\frac{dy}{dx} = \frac{dy}{db}\cdot\frac{db}{dx}$$

$$= -b^{-2}.2(6x + 1).$$

Hence we have slope $= \dfrac{-2(6x+1)}{b^2} = \dfrac{-2(6x+1)}{(6x^2+2x+3)^2}.$

Example 8.15
Find the derivative of the function

$$y = \frac{3x^2}{(1-x^2)^{1/2}}.$$

Solution

$$y = \frac{3x^2}{(1-x^2)^{1/2}} = 3x^2(1-x^2)^{-1/2}.$$

205

Let $\quad u = 3x^2 \quad$ and $\quad v = (1 - x^2)^{-1/2}$.

$$\frac{du}{dx} = 6x \qquad \frac{dv}{dx} = \frac{-1}{2}(1 - x^2)^{-3/2}(-2x)$$

$$= x(1 - x^2)^{-3/2}$$

$$\frac{dy}{dx} = 6x \cdot (1 - x^2)^{-1/2} + 3x^2 \cdot x(1 - x^2)^{-3/2}.$$

This can be rearranged in various ways.
There is a common factor of $3x$.

$$\frac{dy}{dx} = 3x[2(1 - x^2)^{-1/2} + x^2(1 - x^2)^{-3/2}].$$

Take out a factor of $(1 - x^2)^{-3/2}$

$$\frac{dy}{dx} = 3x(1 - x^2)^{-3/2}[2(1 - x^2)^1 + x^2]$$

$$\frac{dy}{dx} = 3x(1 - x^2)^{-3/2}[2 - 2x^2 + x^2].$$

Hence

$$\frac{dy}{dx} = \frac{3x(2 - x^2)}{(1 - x^2)^{3/2}}.$$

It is not essential to rearrange and factorize the answer but, as previously shown, it makes examination of the slope easier. It can be seen that the slope is zero when $x = 0$, when $x = -\sqrt{2}$ and when $x = +\sqrt{2}$. Try putting these values into the equation for the slope, dy/dx, if you are not convinced.

8.9   Continuous functions

If you look back at the graphs shown in the preceding chapters you will see that they all show smooth curves with no sudden changes in direction within the range of values of x drawn. These well-behaved functions of x are said to be *continuous* within those values of x shown on the graph. Not all functions are like this. It is possible to have functions which have sudden changes in direction or are not defined for certain values of x; such functions are said to be *discontinuous*. In order to see what we mean, examine the graph of the function

$y = 2/x$

shown in Figure 8.6. Remember that the result of dividing by zero is infinity.

Look first at the negative values for x. As the x-values move further left along the x-axis the value of y gets progressively smaller. That is

$$\lim_{x \to -\infty} \left[\frac{2}{x} \right] = 0.$$

As the x-values approach the origin at $x = 0$ from the left-hand side the values of y move progressively closer to $-\infty$.

Similarly for the positive x-values: as x approaches the origin from the right-hand side, the value of y approaches $+\infty$. As the x-values increase, the values of y approach the limit of zero when $x = +\infty$. As you can see there is a discontinuity in the curve at the value $x = 0$. The

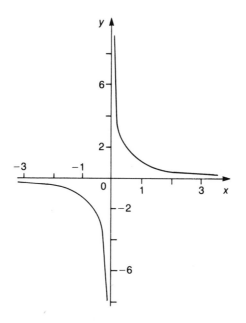

Figure 8.6 Graph of $y = 2/x$.

function $y = 2/x$ is not continuous in the range $x = -3$ to $x = +3$ which we have sketched. There would have been no problems if we had only been interested in values of x between 1 and 3, say, since the function is continuous for this range of x-values.

Functions can exhibit discontinuity in other ways. In Figure 8.7 a sketch is shown of a function which has two values of y when $x = a$. Since the y-value drops suddenly from y_1 to y_2 for the value $x = a$ we say that there is discontinuity at this value of x. Whatever the type of discontinuity, the function cannot be differentiated at that point.

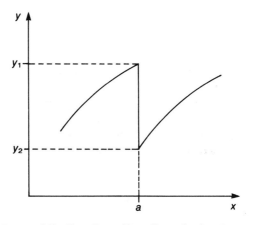

Figure 8.7   Function with a discontinuity at $x = a$.

Note
It is always advisable to draw the graph of the model being examined before attempting to carry out any mathematical analysis. This will have the benefit of providing an easily assimilated picture of what is happening in the model. It will also show up any discontinuities in the model. If discontinuities are shown to exist it usually means that a mistake has been made in constructing the model. The model should mirror the practical situation as closely as possible; if it does not, then it should be discarded in favour of a model which does.

8.10   Partial derivatives

In many practical applications of differentiation, the quantity whose rate of change is being studied will be a function of more than one variable. For example, the total cost of a manufacturing or assembly project may change as a result of changes in the costs of materials and the change in labour costs. Call the amount of material used x, call the amount of labour used z and the total production cost y. If either x or z changes then y will change. Since the value of y depends upon the two variables, x and z, any change in y must necessarily depend upon changes in both of these variables. A special notation is used to denote the changes in these two variables so that it will be immediately apparent that changes in more than one variable contribute to the change in y.

$\dfrac{\partial y}{\partial x}$ denotes the derivative of y with respect to x when z is held constant.

$\dfrac{\partial y}{\partial z}$ denotes the derivative of y with respect to z when x is held constant.

The 'curly dee' (∂) indicates that we are considering derivatives with respect to just one of several possible variables; these are called *partial derivatives*. No special rules are required to evaluate partial derivatives but the 'curly dee' reminds us to treat any variables that are not prefaced by the ∂ as if they were constants. The symbol ∂ should only be used where partial differentiation is involved.

ADDITIONAL EXAMPLES

A8.1 Differentiate the following functions with respect to x.

(i) $y = 5(2x^3 + 1)^8$;

(ii) $y = \dfrac{3}{(x^2 + 1)^{3/2}}$.

A8.2 Find d^2y/dx^2 for the following functions.

(i) $y = (1 + x^2)^{1/2}$;
(ii) $y = 2x^2(1 + x)^4$;
(iii) $y = 3xe^{4x}$.

A8.3 Differentiate the function

$$y = \frac{3x^{1/2}}{(1 + x^2)^2}.$$

A8.4 Locate the stationary points for the following functions. Determine the nature of each stationary point, whether each is a maximum, minimum or point of inflexion.

(i) $y = x^2 - 6x + 3$;
(ii) $y = x^3 - 12x + 5$;
(iii) $y = x^3 - 3x^2 + 3x - 1$.

A8.5 The total cost of producing Purrkyns catfood is related to the quantity produced (q, in units of 100 cans per hour) by the formula

$$TC = q^3 - 12q^2 + 21q + 105.$$

(i) Find the stationary points of the function TC, stating clearly the nature of the stationary point in each case.
(ii) The marginal cost is defined as $MC = dTC/dq$. Find the value of q which will minimize MC.
(iii) If the catfood company is interested in a low average cost per can, would it do better to select the level of production so as to minimize the marginal cost or minimize the total cost?

A8.6 In a simplified model for controlling the stock of a certain chemical used in a manufacturing process, the order quantity, Q, is related to the total cost per month, C, by the following equation:

$$C = \frac{kM}{Q} + pM + \frac{1}{2}piQ,$$

where k is the fixed order cost, p the purchasing cost per unit, M the mean demand per month, and i the interest rate per month.

Use this to obtain an expression for the order quantity which will minimize C. Hence evaluate this optimal order quantity and the total cost per month when $k = £5$, $p = £12$, $M = 20$ and $i = 0.01$.

A8.7 Sales of a certain CD recording are expected to vary with time so that the cumulative total sold at t weeks after the recording is launched, $S(t)$, follows the logistic curve given by the following equation:

$$S(t) = \frac{300\,000}{1 + 500\exp(-0.3t)}.$$

(i) Find the cumulative total sold at 10 weeks after the launch and at 52 weeks after the launch.
(ii) Find an expression for the weekly rate of change in cumulative sales. Evaluate this expression at 52 weeks. What is the practical implication of this result?

A8.8 A study on the benefits of training has shown that, if personnel employed on a particular task are trained for t hours per year, the cost of training (C, in £ per person), is

$C = 200 + 45t$.

The benefit to the company (B, in units of £1000 increased annual revenue per person trained) has been shown to be related to the time spent training by

$B = 110 + 70t - 1.5t^2$.

Find the optimal value of t so as to maximize the net benefit to the company, making allowance for the cost of training.

A8.9 A company is opening a new factory and has advertised for staff. At t days after the advertisement first appeared, the cumulative total of job applications which have been received is given, to a good approximation, by

$$A = \frac{3000}{1 + 25e^{-0.2t}}.$$

(i) Find the daily rate of increase in the cumulative total of applications when $t = 10$, $t = 21$ and $t = 35$ days.

(ii) Suppose that 35 days after the advertisement first appeared it has been found that approximately 25% of the applicants are suitable and 100 posts remain unfilled. Does the model for A suggest that the original advertisement will attract a sufficient number of applicants for all of the posts to be filled?

9

Integration

Introduction

In Chapters 7 and 8 the topic of differentiation was introduced. We saw that the derivative, which is the result of the process of differentiation, gives an algebraic function and that this function can be used to determine the slope at any point on the curve. The slope is important because it tells us the rate of change of the function in question. For example, if price levels are given as a function of time, the rate of inflation at any point in time can be found by differentiating the price function with respect to time. Now consider what happens if we are given an expression for the rate of inflation as a function of time and wish to determine the relationship between price levels and time. In such a case we have the derivative and wish to know the function from which it was derived; to do this we reverse the process of differentiation and we call this new process *integration*.

Integration is a powerful procedure since it allows us not only to reverse the differentiation procedure but also to obtain cumulative values of a continuous function. For example, if daily sales of a product are represented by some continuous function of time, we can determine the cumulative sales over a given period by integrating the sales function over that time period.

9.1   Integration as the reverse of differentiation

Let us first consider a simple example of differentiation.

Example 9.1
Differentiate the function

$$F(x) = 4x^2 + 2$$

with respect to x.

Solution

$$\frac{dF(x)}{dx} = 4 \times 2x^1 + 0 = 8x.$$

Using Rule 7.3, 'multiply by the power and reduce the power by one'.
The function

$$\text{slope} = f(x) = 8x$$

can now be used to evaluate the slope for any value of x.

In Example 9.1 above, the slope was obtained from the given equation
for the curve. If we had been given the slope and asked to find the
equation of the curve, this would necessitate reversing the differentiation procedure; that is, we would start with $f(x)$ and use this to find
$F(x)$. This reversal of the differentiation procedure is called *integration*;
it would lead us back to the quadratic curve with which we started.
   To generalize this, consider any continuous function $F(x)$. Let $f(x)$ be
the derivative of $F(x)$ with respect to x, so that

$$f(x) = \frac{dF(x)}{dx}. \tag{9.1}$$

If $f(x)$ is known then $F(x)$ is said to be the 'integral of $f(x)$ with respect to
x'. This is written as

$$F(x) = \int f(x)\,dx. \tag{9.2}$$

The symbol $\int$ is called the *integral sign* and denotes the process of
integration. The dx signifies that the function $f(x)$ is to be *integrated with
respect to the variable x*. Hence the expression $\int f(x)\,dx$ is read as 'the
integral of $f(x)$ with respect to x'. The function $f(x)$ following the

integral sign is called the *integrand*, which means 'the term to be integrated'.

In Example 9.1, the function $F(x)$ contained the constant $+2$, the derivative of which is zero and hence which disappeared when $F(x)$ was differentiated. As we saw in Chapter 7 *all* constant terms have the same derivative of zero. It follows that knowing the derivative, $f(x)$, of a function gives us no knowledge of any constant term included in that function beyond the fact that it exists. The existence of this constant must be indicated and so a more correct version of equation (9.2) is

$$\int f(x)\,dx = F(x) + C \qquad\qquad (9.3)$$

The term C is called an arbitrary constant or *constant of integration* and can take any value between $-\infty$ and $+\infty$ (including zero). In order to find the value of C we need some additional information. This procedure is illustrated in Example 9.2.

Example 9.2
Integrate the function

$$f(x) = 8x$$

with respect to x, given that the curve for which $f(x)$ is the slope passes through the point ($x = 2$, $y = 18$).

Solution
The slope $f(x) = 8x$ was obtained by applying Rule 7.3, that is '*multiply* by the power then *reduce* the power by 1'.

Reverse this procedure to find the curve, that is '*increase* the power by 1 and *divide* by the new power'.

$$y = F(x) + C = \int 8x\,dx = 8 \times \frac{x^2}{2} + C = 4x^2 + C. \qquad\qquad (9.4)$$

We now know that the curve is a quadratic and have been given the fact that $F(x) + C = 18$ when $x = 2$. Substitute these values of $F(x) + C = 18$ and $x = 2$ into equation (9.4) above:

$$18 = 4 \times 2^2 + C.$$

Rearranging the terms gives

$$C = 18 - 16 = 2$$

and the equation for the curve as

$$y = 4x^2 + 2.$$

Integration

The integrals of other simple functions can also be found by reversing the process of differentiation. A list of the integrals of commonly used simple functions is given below.

9.2 Rules for integration

The following rules are precise reversals of the differentiation rules. Once again it is easier to use the rules in word form.

Rule 9.1

$$\int bx^n \, dx = \frac{bx^{n+1}}{n+1} + C.$$

Translation: Leave the constant, b, alone. Increase the power of x by 1, then divide by the new power.

This rule can be applied to integrating a constant by considering b as representing bx^0, so that $n = 0$ in Rule 9.1.

Rule 9.2

$$\int be^{ax} \, dx = b \times \frac{e^{ax}}{a} + C.$$

Translation: Leave the constant, b, alone. Divide by the coefficient of x in the exponent. *The exponential term remains unchanged.*

Rule 9.3

$$\int \frac{1}{x} \, dx = \log_e(x) + C.$$

Translation: When the integrand is $1/x$, the integral is always the logarithm to the base e of x, that is $\ln(x)$.

Rule 9.4

$$\int \frac{1}{x^n}\,dx = \int x^{-n}\,dx = \frac{x^{-n+1}}{(-n+1)} + C \quad \text{for } n \neq 1.$$

Translation: If the power, n, is not equal to 1 then move the x term above the fraction line, remembering to change the sign of the power, and then apply Rule 9.1 to the result. Increase the power by 1, then divide by the new power. If $n = 1$ then apply Rule 9.3.

Rule 9.5

$$\int \Big(f(x) + g(x) \Big)\,dx = \int f(x)\,dx + \int g(x)\,dx.$$

Translation: If the function to be integrated is the sum of a number of individual terms the procedure is simply to integrate term by term, applying the rules as appropriate, and sum the results.

Example 9.3
Find

$$\int \frac{4}{x^3}\,dx.$$

Solution
Here the function to be integrated is of the form given in Rule 9.4 with $n \neq 1$. First bring the x terms above the fraction line and then integrate.

$$\int \frac{4}{x^3}\,dx = \int 4x^{-3}\,dx = 4 \times \frac{x^{-2}}{(-2)} + C$$

$$= C - \frac{2}{x^2}.$$

Example 9.4
Determine

$$\int e^{2x}\,dx.$$

Solution
Use Rule 9.2 for this integration.

$$\int e^{2x}\,dx = \frac{e^{2x}}{2} + C.$$

Example 9.5
Determine

$$\int \frac{2}{x}\,dx.$$

Solution
Since the function to be integrated involves $1/x$ use Rule 9.3.

$$\int \frac{2}{x}\,dx = 2\ln(x) + C.$$

Example 9.6
Determine

$$\int \left(e^{2x} + \frac{2}{x}\right)dx.$$

Solution
Here we have the sum of two terms and must integrate each term separately as specified in Rule 9.5. The first term involves the exponential and hence Rule 9.2 applies to that term. The second term involves $1/x$ and hence Rule 9.3 applies to that term.

$$\int \left(e^{2x} + \frac{2}{x}\right)dx = \frac{e^{2x}}{2} + 2\ln(x) + C.$$

9.3 The definite integral

Consider the form of the integral given in equation (9.3):

$$\int f(x)\,dx = F(x) + C.$$

This is called an *indefinite integral* since the value of the constant, C, is unknown and the integral cannot be uniquely defined if an unknown is included in the expression.

The value of this integral when $x = a$ is found by substituting $x = a$ in $F(x)$.

$$\int_{x=a} f(x)\,\mathrm{d}x = F(a) + C.$$

The value of this integral when $x = b$ is found by substituting $x = b$ in $F(x)$.

$$\int_{x=b} f(x)\,\mathrm{d}x = F(b) + C.$$

If $b > a$ then the constant, C, can be eliminated by subtracting the first integral from the second. That is

$$\int_{x=b} f(x)\,\mathrm{d}x - \int_{x=a} f(x)\,\mathrm{d}x = F(b) + C - F(a) - C = F(b) - F(a).$$

This is generally written in shortened form as

$$\int_{x}^{b} f(x)\,\mathrm{d}x = \Big[F(x)\Big]_{a}^{b} = F(b) - F(a) \qquad \textbf{(9.5)}$$

and is called the *definite integral* of $f(x)$ with respect to x, between $x = a$ and $x = b$, usually shortened to the definite integral. The definite integral contains no unknown constants in contrast with the indefinite integral which contained the unknown constant, C. The value b is the *upper limit of integration* and the value a is the *lower limit of integration*. The convention is to use square brackets to enclose the algebraic result of the integration with the limits of integration written as shown above. Writing these limits after the square brackets indicates that we should evaluate $F(x)$ at each limit and subtract the result at the lower limit from the result at the upper limit.

Example 9.7
Evaluate

$$\int_{1}^{3} 8x\,\mathrm{d}x.$$

Integration

Solution
First carry out the integration and then evaluate the result at both limits of integration.

$$\int_1^3 8x\,dx = \left[8\cdot\frac{x^2}{2} + C\right]_1^3 = \left[4x^2 + C\right]_1^3$$

$$= \underbrace{[4\times 3^2 + C]}_{\text{value at }x=3} - \underbrace{[4\times 1^2 + C]}_{\text{value at }x=1} = 36 - 4 = 32.$$

Because the constant of integration, C, will always cancel out when we subtract the value of the integral at the lower limit from the value at the upper limit, it is usual to omit this constant when evaluating any definite integral.

9.4 The integral as the area between the curve and the x-axis

Determining the indefinite integral gave us the equation of a curve. Evaluating the definite integral gave us a number. The question of the practical meaning of this number then arises. The definite integral of a function $f(x)$ between the values $x = a$ and $x = b$ gives the size of the area between the curve and the x-axis between these two limits. This area is the cumulative value of the function $f(x)$ between the limits $x = a$ and $x = b$. In statistics where $f(x)$ represents a probability density, the area gives the cumulative probability of obtaining an x-value between a and b. If $f(x)$ represented sales of a product, then the area would represent the cumulative sales between two points in time. If the area between the curve and the x-axis is above the axis, the area is positive; if it is below the axis the area is negative – see Examples A9.2 and A9.3 for a practical illustration of the effects of this statement. In most management contexts the function $f(x)$ will be positive and so the corresponding definite integral will be positive.

Example 9.8
Evaluate the area under the curve $f(x) = 8x$ between $x = 1$ and $x = 3$ using basic geometry to confirm the result in Example 9.7.

Solution
For Example 9.7 the curve which was integrated was $f(x) = 8x$ which is shown in Figure 9.1. In this example the area under the curve could have been evaluated by using elementary geometry.

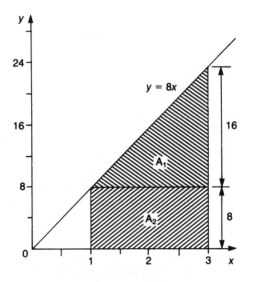

Figure 9.1 Graph of $y = 8x$. Total shaded area is $\int_1^3 8x\,dx$.

The area of the triangle	$A_1 = \frac{1}{2}$ base $\times$ height
	$= \frac{1}{2} \times 2 \times 16 = 16.$
The area of the rectangle	$A_2 =$ base $\times$ height
	$= 2 \times 8 = 16.$
The total area under the curve	$= A_1 + A_2 = 32.$

In this case the fact that the integrand was a linear function, $f(x) = 8x$, meant that the area was easy to evaluate by non-calculus means. In most cases the area under the curve can only be evaluated by using the method of integration.

Example 9.9
Evaluate

$$\int_1^2 x^{1/2}\,dx.$$

Solution
The integrand, the function to be integrated, is x raised to a power, and hence Rule 9.1 must be applied.

$$\int_1^2 x^{1/2}\,dx = \left[\frac{x^{1/2+1}}{3/2}\right]_1^2 = \left[\frac{2}{3}x^{3/2}\right]_1^2.$$

Increase the power by 1 from 1/2 to 3/2 and divide by this new power. Next, evaluate the integral at the upper limit $x = 2$ and the lower limit $x = 1$ and subtract the lower limit value from the upper limit value.

$$\int_1^2 x^{1/2}\,dx = \left[\frac{2}{3}\,(2)^{3/2}\right] - \left[\frac{2}{3}(1)^{3/2}\right]$$

$$= 1.8856 - 0.6667 = 1.2189.$$

Example 9.10
The expected demand, D, for product X varies with time, t, and is represented by the function

$$D = 200e^{-0.2t} \quad \text{for} \quad t > 0.$$

Draw the graph of the expected demand curve against time.
   The expected cumulative demand, C, for product X between times t_1 and t_2 is given by the integral

$$C = \int_{t_1}^{t_2} D\,dt.$$

Determine the cumulative demand between $t_1 = 0$ years and $t_2 = 10$ years. Shade the area corresponding to this cumulative demand on your graph.
   Find the cumulative demand for the time period commencing 10 years from now to the end of the product's life cycle.
   If the present machinery used to manufacture product X will need replacing in 10 years' time at considerable cost, would you recommend the capital investment required for this replacement?

Solution
To sketch the curve first determine the initial value, the value of the demand at time $t = 0$. The curve of demand, D, against time is a negative exponential and thus the demand decreases to virtually zero for large values of t. The sketch is shown below in Figure 9.2.
   The cumulative demand is obtained by integrating D with respect to t between the specified limits. In the first instance, integration between $t_1 = 0$ and $t_2 = 10$ is needed. In the second instance, integrate between $t_1 = 10$ and $t_2 = \infty$. Since integration over two different sets of limits is required, it is better to perform the integration first in terms of t_1 and t_2 and then substitute for these values of t as necessary.

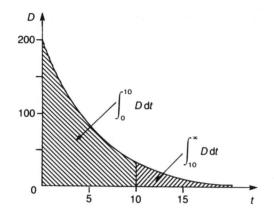

Figure 9.2 Areas under the curve $D = 200 \exp(-0.2t)$.

The integral required is

$$C = \int_{t_1}^{t_2} D \, dt$$

$$= \left[\frac{200e^{-0.2}}{-0.2} \right]_{t_1}^{t_2} = \left[-1000e^{-0.2t} \right]_{t_1}^{t_2}$$

$$= -1000e^{-0.2t_2} - (-1000e^{-0.2t_1})$$

$$C = -1000e^{-0.2t_2} + 1000e^{-0.2t_1}. \tag{9.6}$$

The value of any integral can now be found by substituting the specified values of t into the equation for C above.

The cumulative demand between $t_1 = 0$ and $t_2 = 10$ years is given as

$$C = -1000e^{-0.2 \times 10} + 1000e^{-0.2 \times 0}$$

$$= -1000e^{-2.0} + 1000e^{-0}$$

$$= -1000 \times 0.1353 + 1000 \times 1$$

$$C = -135.3353 + 1000 = 864.6647.$$

The cumulative demand for product X over the first 10 years of the life cycle is expected to be 865 units to the nearest whole number. The shaded area on the graph to the left of $t = 10$ shows the cumulative demand between 0 and 10 years.

To find the cumulative demand from time $t_1 = 10$ years to the end of the life cycle take the value of t_2 as ∞ since in theory this is the upper time limit of the product life cycle, although in fact the demand will be effectively zero long before then (see the graph in Figure 9.2). Take $t_1 = 10$, $t_2 = \infty$ and just substitute these values into equation (9.6).

$$C = -1000e^{-0.2 \times \infty} + 1000e^{-0.2 \times 10}$$

$$= -1000e^{-\infty} + 1000e^{-2.0}$$

$$C = -0 + 135.3353 = 135.3353.$$

Note that $e^{-\infty} = 0$, as can be seen from the graph.

The cumulative demand for product X from time 10 years to the end of the product life cycle is expected to be 135 units to the nearest whole number. This cumulative demand is then shown on the graph as the area under the curve to the right of time $t = 10$ years.

If the present manufacturing machinery will need replacing in 10 years' time it will only be economic to do this if the demand for the product is such that any loans can be serviced or the machinery can be used for other products. With a total expected cumulative demand of 135 units after the investment and demand decreasing exponentially (see the graph of D against t in Figure 9.2) it would not be worth investing heavily in product X in 10 years' time unless the manufacturer could cover the cost of the investment by either setting the selling price at a sufficiently high level or being able to turn spare production capacity over to other products or both.

9.5 A general remark on integration and differentiation

We have dealt with simple mathematical models. In many cases, realistic models may need to be more complicated. However, the same general procedures will still be applicable. There will be a need to differentiate to find rates of change and to integrate to find the cumulative value of a variable. Where the methods of calculus cannot be used, numerical approximations to them will be employed. Generally speaking, it is only possible to integrate a function if it can be obtained by differentiation. If you cannot remember how to integrate a function $f(x)$ then select some functions which look as if they might yield $f(x)$ when differentiated. Differentiate each of them in turn to check, and when you find the right one simply reverse the differentiation in order to find the integral of $f(x)$. In some complicated cases it is impossible to use the methods of calculus to perform the integration or differentiation and numerical methods are used. In statistical applications where the area under the curve is needed and where numerical integration is necessary, tables of the values of such integrals have been calculated using computers and are published as standard books of statistical tables. Clearly it is more accurate to use the exact methods of calculus where possible. Extensive sets of tables setting out the derivatives and integrals for standard mathematical functions are available but, generally speaking, when a function gets very complicated it is time to call in the expert. You will, however, be required to make sense of the expert's results; hence the need to understand the basics of algebra and calculus.

ADDITIONAL EXAMPLES

A9.1 Draw the graph of $y = 2x$ for values of x between $x = -1$ and $x = +1$.
Evaluate

$$\int_{-1}^{1} 2x \, dx.$$

Indicate on the graph the area represented by the integral given.

A9.2 Draw the graph of $y = 2x^2$ between the values $x = -1.2$ and $x = +1.2$.
Evaluate

$$\int_{-1}^{1} 2x^2 \, dx.$$

Shade on the graph the area represented by this integral.

A9.3 Draw the graph of the function $y = 2x^3$ between the values $x = -1.2$ and $x = +1.2$. Evaluate the integral

$$\int_{-1}^{1} 2x^3 \, dx.$$

Shade on the graph the area represented by this integral.

Integration

A9.4 Sketch the curve of the function $y = 1/x^2$ between the values $x = 0.1$ and $x = 1.2$. Evaluate the integral

$$\int_{0.1}^{1} \frac{1}{x^2}\, dx.$$

Explain why the integral of the function $y = 1/x^2$ between the values $x = 0$ and $x = 1.0$ could not arise in practice in the management environment.

A9.5 Find

$$y = \int (3x^2 + 2x + 3)\, dx,$$

given that the curve passes through the point $x = 1, y = 6$.

A9.6 Find

(i) $\displaystyle\int_0^1 e^{2x}\, dx$, (ii) $\displaystyle\int_0^1 e^{-2x}\, dx$, (iii) $\displaystyle\int_1^\infty e^{-2x}\, dx$.

A9.7 Evaluate the following integrals:

(i) $$\int_{0.1}^{1} \frac{1}{x}\, dx,$$

(ii) $$\int_{1}^{20} \left(\frac{1}{x}\right) dx,$$

(iii) $$\int_{-2}^{2} (x^2 + e^{3x} + 2)\, dx,$$

(iv) $$\int \left(\frac{1}{x} + \frac{1}{2}\, e^{x/2}\right) dx.$$

A9.8 Studies on a certain type of machine have shown that the proportion of machines which survive and are in working order t years after purchase is given by

$$p(t) = 1 - 0.025t - 0.001\,25t^2,$$

for t between 0 and 20. Actuarial theory then shows that the average number of future years' service to be expected from a machine now aged *x* years is

$$\frac{1}{p(x)} \cdot \int_x^{20} p(t)\,dt.$$

Find the average number of future years' service to be expected from a machine which is now 8 years old.

A9.9 The cost to a property company of holding a parcel of land for *t* years is given as

$$H = \int_0^t 8\exp(-0.2x)\,dx.$$

Evaluate the cost of holding the land for 3 years, 5 years and 10 years.

A9.10 The Koverup Paint Company produces a type of emulsion paint for which the marginal cost (*MC*) is related to the quantity produced in one batch (*x*, measured in 1000 litre units) by the formula

$$MC = 2x^2 - 16x + 11.$$

The marginal cost is defined as the rate of change in the total cost (*TC*) brought about by a change in the batch size, *x*, so that

$$MC = \frac{d(TC)}{dx}.$$

Integrate *MC* with respect to *x* and hence determine the formula which relates *TC* to batch size, given that *TC* = 50 when *x* = 0, that is there is a fixed cost of 50 which is independent of the batch size.

A9.11 It has been predicted that *t* days after the launch of a new product the daily demand for the product will be increasing at a rate of

$$100 - 16t - 0.06t^2$$

units per day, for 1 < *t* < 20. Given that daily demand is 1500 units when *t* = 4, find a general expression for daily demand as a continuous function of *t*.

A9.12 The fluorescent tubes used to light an underground car park are left on all day and all night. The average proportion of tubes which fail between *A* and *B* hours after installation is given by

$$P = \int_A^B 0.0005\exp(-0.0005t)\,dt.$$

Integration

Find the average percentage of tubes which would fail within 1 year of installation.

The supplier of tubes claims to have a new tube which has an average proportion of failures between A and B hours given by

$$PN = \int_{A}^{B} 0.0001\exp(-0.0001t)\,dt.$$

Calculate the proportion of failures which will be expected within 1 year of installation with this new tube. If the new tube cost 20% more than the old one, is it worth changing over to this new product?

227

10

The application of mathematics

10.1 Mathematical style

Whether you have read through all the first nine chapters, or skipped a few of them, you will already have seen some examples of mathematics applied to business problems. However, this book is meant to prepare you to understand applications of mathematics in any of the numerate areas of management. There are no hard and fast boundaries between them, but the main areas that we have in mind are finance, economics, operational research, statistics and various aspects of operations management. In all of these areas, mathematical models are used in decision making, so the practitioner must be able to think and write in mathematical terms. However, you should remember that in a management environment it will usually be necessary to translate detailed mathematical reasoning into something closer to everyday language, so you should try to become 'bilingual' – able to translate to and from mathematics as required.

If you have studied the worked examples in this book, you should have some idea of the style in which a mathematical argument should be presented. The following points are particularly important:

1. Tailor the style to suit the level of mathematical skill of the reader. What is appropriate in this textbook might be quite out of place in a report for circulation in your company or for outside publication.
2. If there is a standard notation for a topic, keep to this – but do not be afraid to use your own notation if there is no agreed standard. Make sure that your notation will be clearly understood by the

reader and try to avoid unusual symbols unless there is a very good reason to use them. Many word processors now enable you to use all the mathematical symbols that we have introduced in this book, and also the Greek alphabet – which we have listed in the Appendix.

3. Remember that a mathematical argument should make sense and needs punctuation. For example, 'Hence $x = 6$' is a sentence and should end with a full stop if it is the end of the argument. Try to avoid starting a sentence with a mathematical symbol. Be particularly careful in the use of '$=$', which should not be used to link expressions which are not equal to each other.

4. Remember that the main reasons for using mathematical notation are to be compact and to avoid ambiguity. Only include enough detail to enable the reader to follow your argument. This would usually mean leaving out detailed arithmetic of the sort which we have shown in the worked examples.

5. Consult reports or other publications aimed at a readership similar to that which you are addressing in order to get an idea of the level of detail that is usually provided.

10.2   Tackling mathematical examination questions

So that a reasonable range of skills can be tested in a written paper lasting 2 or 3 hours, most individual questions on the material covered in this book would only involve one or two of the main topics that we have covered – unlike a real-life problem that might involve them all and take much longer to solve.

We recommend the following strategy for tackling an examination or test paper of this kind:

1. Read all the questions. Summarize the information that is given and write down what has to be found; then decide upon the best way to find it. Look for key words; for example, if the words 'rate of change' occur, this should set you thinking about the material in Chapters 7 and 8, where we discussed *differentiation*.

2. Select the questions where you can visualize in advance what techniques are required and how long it will take you to use those techniques. Do what you think are the easy questions first.

3. Having selected your questions, translate the words into mathematical notation so that the problem is formulated in mathematical terms.

4. If you are uncertain about any algebraic manipulation that is required for solving the problem, substitute numbers for symbols and check that your method gives arithmetically correct answers.
5. Always check any numerical results to see that they make sense in the context of the wording of the question. In effect, this means translating the mathematical results back into ordinary language.

10.3   Formulating real-life problems

Even if you do not feel competent to tackle a highly mathematical problem yourself, some preparatory work will need to be done before you hand it over to a specialist who has the necessary skills. To save time and facilitate communication with the specialist, a good first step is to identify the main features of the problem and try to express these in mathematical terms – as if you were setting the problem as an examination question, first in ordinary words and then in mathematics. Having formulated the problem, look for the key words in your formulation so that you can identify what sort of mathematical techniques will be needed to solve the problem.

10.4   Solving real-life problems

If you decide that the problem you have formulated looks simple enough to tackle yourself, then have a go at it. Besides the points we made about examination questions, there are some further considerations to bear in mind when you are tackling real-life problems:

1. Keep the mathematical models as simple as possible.
2. Determine how accurate the results should be. More accuracy will usually cost more money, so you must establish how much can be spent on solving the problem. Remember that graphical presentation will usually have the most impact, so decide whether the results can be expressed in terms of graphs alone.
3. Establish who needs to know the solution to the problem and what questions they will ask, so that you look at appropriate aspects of the problem.
4. Keep your final presentation of results as simple as possible, using graphs and words rather than mathematics wherever possible. Keep detailed justification of your results in reserve or put it in an appendix to the main report.

5. Be prepared to suggest the next step for further investigation.
6. Be prepared to consult an expert. In the long run this may cost less than committing your organization to future expenditure based upon results from an incorrect analysis. If you do decide on this, do not feel that you have wasted effort in formulating the problem because your experience will be needed in order to brief the expert.

Appendix
The Greek alphabet

A	α	alpha
B	β	beta
Γ	γ	gamma
Δ	δ	delta
E	ε	epsilon
Z	ζ	zeta
H	η	eta
Θ	θ	theta
I	ι	iota
K	κ	kappa
Λ	λ	lambda
M	μ	mu
N	ν	nu
Ξ	ξ	xi
O	o	omicron
Π	π	pi
P	ρ	rho
Σ	σ	sigma
T	τ	tau
Υ	υ	upsilon
Φ	ϕ	phi
X	χ	chi
Ψ	ψ	psi
Ω	ω	omega

Solutions to additional examples

Chapter 1

A1.1 (i) $9x$ (ii) $14a + 10$ (iii) $13u - 2v - uv$.

A1.2 (i) $3a^2 - 19ab - 14b^2$
(ii) $x^3 + 5x^2y + 7xy^2 + 2y^3$.

A1.3 (i) $4x + 5 = 20x + 15$; $-16x = 10$; $x = -10/16 = -5/8 = -0.625$.
(ii) $2x - 7 = 5$; $x = 12/2 = 6$.

A1.4 $$\frac{5(x+3) + 8(x-7)}{(x-7)(x+3)} = \frac{13x - 41}{(x-7)(x+3)}.$$

A1.5 (i) $2^2 \times 2^6 = 4 \times 64 = 256$ or $2^2 \times 2^6 = 2^{2+6} = 2^8 = 256$.

(ii), (iii) $\dfrac{2^8}{2^2} = \dfrac{256}{4} = 64$ or $\dfrac{2^8}{2^2} = 2^8 \times 2^{-2} = 2^6 = 64$.

(iv) $3^2.3^{1/2} = 9 \times 1.7321 = 15.5885 = 3^{2.5}$.
(v) $5^{1/3} = 5^{0.333} = 1.709\,976$.
(vi) $3^2 \times 3^{1/2} \times 5^{1/3} = 15.5885 \times 1.709\,976 = 26.656$.
Note that this result is only accurate to about three decimal places since the first term is only calculated to four decimal places.

A1.6 (i) 128.0000 (ii) -64.0000 (iii) 12.2500
(iv) 1.1225 (v) 18.5203 (vi) 0.1111.

A1.7 (i) a^2 (ii) a^6 (iii) $b^{2.5}$
(iv) $c^{1.5}$ (v) c^3 (vi) $c^{2.5}.d^{1/3}$.

A1.8 (i) $12(x + 1)$ (ii) $12x(1 + x)$
     (iii) $3y(x + 2)$ (iv) $3xy(x + 2)$
     (v) $12xy + 12x^2y = 12xy(1 + x)$ (vi) $7 + 5xy + 12x$.

A1.9 (i) $5a - 3b$ (ii) $3a^2 + 5ab + 2a$
     (iii) $a^2(5a + 4b)$ (iv) $3a^2 + 4a + 1$
     (v) $b^{3/2}$ (vi) $4a^4 + 5a^2 + 2a$.

A1.10 (i) 1.0 (ii) 46.0 (iii) 88.0
     (iv) 21.0 (v) 5.1962 (vi) 88.0.

A1.11 (i) $x^2 + 6x + 8$
     (ii) $x^2 + 4x + 4$
     (iii) $x^2 - 1$
     (iv) $(x + a)(x^2 + bx + cx + bc) = x^3 + (a + b + c)x^2$
                $+ (ab + bc + ac)x + abc$
     (v) $(x^2 + 2ax + a^2)(x + b) = x^3 + (2a + b)x^2 + (a^2 + 2ab)x + a^2b$
     (vi) $(x - 2)(x^2 - 4x + 4) = x^3 - 6x^2 + 12x - 8$.

A1.12 (i) $12a(a - 2b)$ (ii) $4x^2y^2(2y + 4x + 1)$
     (iii) $(a + b)(a + c)$ (iv) $(c - x)(2x - d)$
     (v) $(x - 3)(x - 5)$ (vi) $(6x - 5)(x + 1)$
     (vii) $-(5x - 1)(2x + 5)$ (viii) $(a + b)(5a - 9b)$
     (ix) $(7x - 3)(7x + 3)$ (x) $8(x - 2y)(x + 2y)$
     (xi) $(x + 4)^2$ (xii) $(2x + 1)^2$.

A1.13 $150 + 3.5q = 500$; $3.5q = 350$; $q = 100$.
       Hence 100 switches will give batch cost of £500.

A1.14   To break even $P(N) = 0$, so $25N - 60 = 0$; $25N = 60$; $N = 60/25 = 2.4$.
       But N must be an integer. Rounding down so that $N = 2$,
       $P(2) = 50 - 60 = -10$, representing a loss.
       Going to the next largest integer so that $N = 3$, $P(3) = 75 - 60 = 15$,
       representing a profit, so at least three sheds must be sold to avoid making
       a loss.

A1.15 $P = 100\,000$; $i = 0.07$; $n = 3$. $S_3 = 100\,000(1.07)^3 = 122\,504$ to
       nearest £1 or 122 500 to nearest £10.

Chapter 2

A2.1 (i) $\dfrac{(x + y)}{3} + \dfrac{(x^2 + y)}{4} = \dfrac{4(x + y) + 3(x^2 + y)}{3 \times 4} = \dfrac{3x^2 + 4x + 7y}{12}$.

     (ii) $\dfrac{x}{(x + a)} - \dfrac{y}{(x + b)} = \dfrac{x(x + b) - y(x + a)}{(x + a)(x + b)} = \dfrac{x^2 + bx - yx - ay}{(x + a)(x + b)}$.

(iii) Take $(x + 2)$ as a factor of the numerator, so that

$$x^2 + 6x + 8 = (x + 2)(x + a) = x^2 + (2 + a) + 2a.$$

Hence $a = 4$ and so

$$(x^2 + 6x + 8)/(x + 2) = (x + 4)(x + 2)/(x + 2) = x + 4.$$

(iv) $a^2 + b$.

(v) Take $(x + 1)$ as a factor of the numerator, so that

$$x^3 + 6x^2 + 11x + 6 = (x + 1)(ax^2 + bx + c)$$
$$= ax^3 + (a + b)x^2 + (b + c)x + c.$$

Equating coefficients of powers of x and the constant,

$$a = 1, \quad b = 5, \quad c = 6.$$

Hence

$$(x^3 + 6x^2 + 11x + 6)/(x + 1) = x^2 + 5x + 6,$$

which can be factorized as $(x + 2)(x + 3)$.

A2.2 (i) The roots are $x = -4$ and $x = -2$. Graph is U-shaped, like Figure 2.4.

(ii) Graph is U-shaped, like Figure 2.4.

(iii) The roots are $x = -1, x = +1, x = 1.5$. Graph is similar to Figure 2.5.

A2.3 (i) Expand the brackets:

$$x^2 + 3x - 5x - 15 = 20,$$
$$x^2 - 2x - 35 = 0.$$

Solve this quadratic equation using the standard formula with $a = 1$, $b = 2$, and $c = -35$.

$$x = \frac{-(-2) \pm \sqrt{(-2)^2 - 4 \times 1 \times (-35)}}{2 \times 1}$$

$$= \frac{2 \pm \sqrt{144}}{2} = \frac{2 \pm 12}{2}.$$

Thus the solution is $x = 7$ or $x = -5$.

Check: For $x = 7$: $(7 + 3)(7 - 5) = 20$ correct.

For $x = -5$: $(-5 + 3)(-5 - 5) = 20$ correct.

(ii) Expanding left-hand side of $x(10x - 21) - 10 = 0$ gives
$10x^2 - 21x - 10 = 0$.

Use $a = 10, b = -21, c = -10$ in standard formula.

$$x = \frac{-(-21) \pm \sqrt{(-21)^2 + 4 \times 10 \times (-10)}}{2 \times 10}$$

$$= \frac{21 \pm \sqrt{841}}{20} \quad \text{and} \quad \sqrt{841} = 29.$$

The solution is $\quad x = 5/2 \quad$ or $\quad x = -2/5$;
in decimal form, $\quad x = 2.5 \quad$ or $\quad x = -0.4$.

(iii) $x^2(4x^2 - 1) - 72(x^2 - 2) = 0$.
Substitute $y = x^2$ to give

$$y(4y - 1) - 72(y - 2) = 0.$$

Now solve for y.
Expand the brackets:

$$4y^2 - y - 72y + 144 = 0,$$

$$4y^2 - 73y + 144 = 0.$$

Use $a = 4, b = -73, c = 144$. This gives the solution for y as $y = 16$ or $y = 9/4$.
Since the problem was originally posed in terms of x and we later introduced $y = x^2$, we must now transform the y solution back into solutions for the original variable, x.
Note that if $y = x^2$, then $x = \pm\sqrt{y}$.

For $y = 16$, $\quad x = \pm\sqrt{16}$, so $x = +4$ or $x = -4$.
For $y = 9/4$, $\quad x = \pm\sqrt{9/4}$, so $x = +3/2$ or $x = -3/2$.

There are four solutions or roots of the original equation, which is of degree 4 in x. These solutions are: $x = +4, x = -4, x = +3/2, x = -3/2$.

(iv) $\quad \dfrac{5}{(x - 5)} - \dfrac{3}{(x - 3)} - \dfrac{2}{(x + 2)} = 0$.

First simplify the fractions.
The LCD is $(x - 5)(x - 3)(x + 2)$.

$$\frac{5(x - 3)(x + 2) - 3(x - 5)(x + 2) - 2(x - 5)(x - 3)}{(x - 5)(x - 3)(x + 2)} = 0.$$

Multiply both sides by $(x - 5)(x - 3)(x + 2)$ to remove the fraction.

$$5(x - 3)(x + 2) - 3(x - 5)(x + 2) - 2(x - 5)(x - 3) = 0.$$

Expand the brackets and collect up the terms.

$$5(x^2 - x - 6) - 3(x^2 - 3x - 10) - 2(x^2 - 8x + 15) = 0,$$
$$5x^2 - 5x - 30 - 3x^2 + 9x + 30 - 2x^2 + 16x - 30 = 0.$$

This reduces to $20x = 30$, and so $x = 3/2 = 1.5$.

A2.4 (i) Substitute $x = -1$ into the left-hand side of the equation and show that the result is zero. Hence $(x + 1)$ is a factor of $2x^3 + 7x^2 + 8x + 3$.

(ii) $2x^3 + 7x^2 + 8x + 3 = (x + 1)(ax^2 + bx + c)$
$$= ax^3 + (a + b)x^2 + (b + c)x + c.$$

Equating coefficients of the powers of x and the constant,

$$a = 2, \quad b = 5, \quad c = 3.$$

As a result, we now have the equation factorized into

$$(x + 1)(2x^2 + 5x + 3) = 0.$$

Factorize the quadratic expression

$$2x^2 + 5x + 3 = (2x + 3)(x + 1).$$

The cubic equation can now be written as

$$2x^3 + 7x^2 + 8x + 3 = (x + 1)(2x + 3)(x + 1) = 0.$$

For the left-hand side of the equation to be zero, one of the terms in brackets must be zero.

Either $(x + 1) = 0$ or $(2x + 3) = 0$,
so that $x = -1$ or $x = -3/2$.
The roots are $x = -1$ and $x = -3/2 = -1.5$.

Because the factor $(x + 1)$ appears twice in the equation, the root $x = -1$ is called a *repeated root*. The graph of the curve $y = 2x^3 + 7x^2 + 8x + 3$ is shown below in Fig. A1.

It can be seen that the curve touches the x-axis when $x = -1$ but does not cross it. The maximum and minimum points have been found by the methods of calculus, which are explained later in Chapter 8.

A2.5 (i) Divide by x to give: $3x^2 - 5x - 12 = 0$.

Factorize: $(3x + 4)(x - 3) = 0$.
Either $(3x + 4) = 0$ or $(x - 3) = 0$.
Thus $x = -4/3$ or $x = 3$.

(ii) $10x^2 + 5x - 6x - 3 = 0$, so that $10x^2 - x - 3 = 0$.

Factorize: $(2x + 1)(5x - 3) = 0$.
Hence $(2x + 1) = 0$ or $(5x - 3) = 0$
and so $x = -1/2$ or $x = 3/5$.

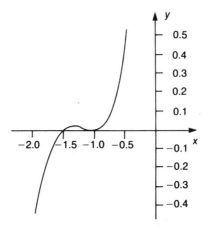

Figure A1 Graph of $y = 2x^3 + 7x^2 + 8x + 3$.

(iii) Take the 72 across to the left-hand side, then the equation becomes
$18x^2 - 30x - 72 = 0$.
Divide by 6: $3x^2 - 5x - 12 = 0$.
The solution is now the same as that for A2.4(i).

(iv) First try to find a factor of the cubic expression. Try $x = -1$ as a solution. Divide by $(x + 1)$ to obtain the equation

$$(x + 1)(3x^2 - 5x - 12) = 0.$$

Factorize the quadratic equation; this has been done in A2.5(i) above. The roots are then

$$x = -1, \quad x = -4/3, \quad x = 3.$$

Chapter 3

A3.1 (i) A $x + y = 6$
       B $x - y = 2.$
       B − A $-2y = -4$
                      $y = 2.$
       From B $x - 2 = 2$
                      $x = 4.$
       Check in A $4 + 2 = 6.$
(ii) $x = 1.5714, y = 1.0714.$
(iii) Solve the simultaneous equations

       A $2x + 3y + z = 6$
       B $3x + 5y - 4z = 2$
       C $5x - 2y + 3z = 7.$

$B' = B - A \times 3/2$ $0.50y - 5.50z = -7.00$
$C' = C - A \times 5/2$ $-9.50y + 0.50z = -8.00.$
$C'' = C' - B' \times (-9.5)/0.5$ $-104.00z = -141.00$
                                  $z = 1.3558.$

From C' $-9.50y = -8.6779$
                                  $y = 0.9135.$

From C $5x = 4.7596$
                                  $x = 0.9519.$

Check: Substituting for x, y and z in equation A gives the right-hand side $= 6.0001$.

Substituting for x, y and z in equation B gives the right-hand side $= 2.0001$.

The result is correct to three decimal places.

(iv) Working to four decimal places,

$$x = 7.0000, \quad y = 12.0002, \quad z = 4.0001.$$

(v) Working to four decimal places,

$$x = 2.2541, \quad y = 0.4045, \quad z = 2.3497.$$

(vi) Solve the set of simultaneous equations

A $2.1x + 3.0y + 1.5z = 6.3$
B $3.2x + 1.7y + 3.0z = 7.3$
C $1.6x + 1.9y - 2.3z = 4.2.$
$B' = B - A \times 3.2/2.1$ $-2.8714y + 0.7143z = -2.3$
$C' = C - A \times 1.6/2.1$ $0.3857y + 3.4429z = 0.6.$

Here the leading terms in equations B' and C' have opposite signs; hence a multiple of B' can be *added* to C' in order to eliminate y.

$C'' = C' + B' \times 0.3857/2.8714$ $3.5388z = 0.2911$
                                          $z = 0.0822.$

From C' $0.3857y = 0.3168$
                                  $y = 0.8215.$

From C $1.6x = 2.8284$
                                  $x = 1.7678.$

The solution is $x = 1.7678, y = 0.3168, z = 0.0822$. Substituting these values into equations A and B gives the right-hand side values of 6.3 and 7.3 respectively correct to three decimal places.

A3.2   Solve the pair of simultaneous equations

A $x^2 + y^2 = 4x + 3$
B $x - 3y = 1.$

From equation B we have $x = 1 + 3y$.

Now eliminate x in equation A by substituting the value $1 + 3y$ wherever an x appears.

$$(1 + 3y)^2 + y^2 = 4(1 + 3y) + 3.$$

Expand the brackets and collect up the terms.

$$1 + 6y + 9y^2 + y^2 = 4 + 12y + 3$$
$$1 + 6y + 10y^2 = 7 + 12y$$
$$10y^2 - 6y - 6 = 0.$$

There is a common factor of 2 in all of the coefficients which can be removed by dividing through by 2 to make the coefficients smaller and hence the arithmetic easier.

$$5y^2 - 3y - 3 = 0.$$

Use the standard quadratic form

$$ay^2 + by + c = 0.$$

Comparing the coefficients gives $a = 5, b = -3, c = -3$.
Substitute these values into Standard Form 2.5 for the solution for a quadratic equation.

$$y = \frac{-(-3) \pm \sqrt{(-3)^2 - 4 \times 5 \times (-3)}}{2 \times 5} = \frac{3 \pm \sqrt{69}}{10} = \frac{3 \pm 8.3066}{10}.$$

This gives the solutions $y = 1.1307, y = -0.5307$.
We now return to the equation $x = 1 + 3y$ to evaluate x.
When $y = 1.1307, x = 4.3921$.
When $y = -0.5307, x = -0.5921$.
Check the result by substituting the solution into equation A and ensuring that the left-hand side is equal to the right-hand side.

A3.3   The graph of the straight-line equation

$$y = \frac{6x}{80} + \frac{17}{80} = 0.075x + 0.2125$$

is drawn on the same graph as the curve

$$y = 3x/(2x^2 + 5).$$

Figure A2 below shows that the lines cross when $x = 0.441, y = 0.246$ and when $x = 2.691, y = 0.414$. These two points are the solutions to the pair of equations specified.

240

Solutions to additional examples

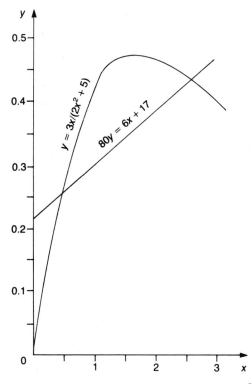

Figure A2   Graphs of $80y = 6x + 17$ and $y = 3x/(2x^2 + 5)$.

A3.4   Call the number of type A product x, the number of type B product y and the number of type C product z. The problem then reduces to finding the solution to the set of simultaneous equations:

$5x + 7y + 8z = 695$

$3x + 4y + 7z = 510$

$2x + 3y + 4z = 320$.

The solution is to produce 25 type A product, 30 type B product and 45 type C product.

A3.5   Let the number of type A boats be x, the number of type B boats be y and the number of type C boats be z. The values of x, y and z can be determined by solving the equations:

$4x + 10y + 10z = 162$

$x + 7y + 12z = 110$

$4x + 8y + 8z = 140$.

241

The elimination of x can be made easier in this example by multiplying the second equation throughout by 4 thus making the first term identical for all three equations.

The number of boats produced is 13 type A, 7 type B and 4 type C in order to use all of the available labour time.

The cost of building all the boats can be found in several ways. Basically the problem reduces to finding the total labour costs and total material costs.

The total labour used is $162 + 110 + 140 = 412$ hours.

At a cost of £50 per hour the total labour cost is £50 × 412 = £20 600.

The material cost is £400 × 13 + £1100 × 7 + £2000 × 4 = £20 900.

The total cost is then £20 600 + £20 900 = £41 500 for all of the boats.

A3.6 The problem reduces to that of solving the set of three simultaneous equations:

Machine time $2x + 3y + 4.5z = 55$

Manpower $9x + 5y + 12z = 139$

Material $7x + 6y + 8z = 108.$

The solution is to produce 2 batches of type A product, 5 batches of type B product and 8 batches of type C product.

A3.7 Let the number of skirts produced be x, the number of blouses be y and the number of jackets be z. The values of x, y and z are found by solving the set of equations:

$$0.5x + y + 2.0z = 96$$
$$2.0x + 3.0y + 5.0z = 268$$
$$x + 1.5y + 1.5z = 104.$$

The solution is to make 20 skirts, 26 blouses and 30 jackets in order to utilize completely all of the available time.

A3.8 Call the number of type X machines x, the number of type Y machines y and the number of type Z machines z. The problem then becomes that of solving the three equations:

$$5.3x + 2.1y + 4.7z = 196$$
$$7.2x + 8.3y + 0.6z = 177$$
$$3.5y + 4.5z = 107.$$

The solution is $x = 17.3173$ type X, $y = 4.8571$ type Y and $z = 20.0019$ type Z.

Rounding down the number of each type of machine gives $x = 17$ of type X, $y = 4$ of type Y and $z = 20$ of type Z.

Substitute these values into each of the equations in turn in order to determine the slack time.

For fitters the slack is $196 - 5.3 \times 17 - 2.1 \times 4 - 4.7 \times 20 = 3.5$ hours.

For electricians the slack is

$$177 - 7.2 \times 17 - 8.3 \times 4 - 0.6 \times 20 = 9.4 \text{ hours.}$$

For carpenters the slack is $107 - 3.5 \times 4 - 4.5 \times 20 = 3.0$ hours.

Chapter 4

A4.1 (i) There is a common difference $d = 35$, so the sequence is an AP. The first term is $a_1 = 100$ so formula (4.5) gives:

$$S_n = n\left[a_1 + \frac{(n-1)d}{2}\right] = n\left[100 + 35\frac{(n-1)}{2}\right].$$

Putting $n = 3$, $S_3 = 3[100 + 35] = 405$, which agrees with $100 + 135 + 170$.

(ii) There is a common difference of -22, so the sequence is an AP. The first term is 200, so formula (4.5) gives:

$$S_n = n\left[a_1 + \frac{(n-1)d}{2}\right] = n\left[200 - 22\frac{(n-1)}{2}\right].$$

Putting $n = 3$, $S_3 = 3[200 - 22] = 534$, which agrees with $200 + 178 + 156$.

A4.2 (i) There is a common ratio of $r = 1.2$, so the sequence is a GP. The first term is $a = 100$. We use formula (4.15) because $r > 1$, and so:

$$S_n = \frac{a(r^n - 1)}{(r - 1)} = \frac{100(1.2^n - 1)}{0.2} = 500(1.2^n - 1).$$

Putting $n = 3$, $S_3 = 500(1.2^3 - 1) = 364$, which agrees with $100 + 120 + 144$.

(ii) There is a common ratio of $r = 0.8$, so the sequence is a GP. The first term is $a = 500$. We use formula (4.14) because $r < 1$, and so:

$$S_n = \frac{a(1 - r^n)}{(1 - r)} = \frac{500(1 - 0.8^n)}{0.2} = 2500(1 - 0.8^n).$$

Putting $n = 3$, $S_3 = 2500(1 - 0.8^3) = 1220$, which agrees with $500 + 400 + 320$.

A4.3 The first thing to do is to lay out a table showing how many units are held in the store in each month. In some months it is useful to distinguish between the original 27 units and the 24 which are delivered later – these appear in the columns headed 'Old' and 'New' respectively in the table below. We also distinguish between delivery in April ('Plan A') and delivery in July ('Plan B').

	Plan A			Plan B		
	Old	New	Total	Old	New	Total
Jan.	27	—	27	27	—	27
Feb.	23	—	23	23	—	23
Mar.	19	—	19	19	—	19
Apr.	15	—	15	15	—	15
May	11	24	35	11	—	11
June			31	7	—	7
July			26	2	—	2
Aug.			21	−3	24	21
Sept.			16			16
Oct.			11			11
Nov.			6			6
Dec.			1			1
		Sum =	231		Sum =	159

Since each unit costs £20 for each month held in store, the total storage cost under each plan will be the sum of the figures in the 'Total' column for that plan multiplied by £20. The most straightforward method is to add the totals directly, but to check the results we may note that they form arithmetic progressions.

Plan A: From January to April we have an AP of four terms with common difference −4, first term 27, last term 15, so by formula (4.6) the sum is

no. of terms × average of first and last terms

$$= 4\frac{(27 + 15)}{2} = 4 \times 21 = 84.$$

May and June form a separate series for which the sum is 35 + 31 = 66.

July to December forms another AP of six terms with common difference −5, first term 26, last term 1, so its sum is

$$6\frac{(26 + 1)}{2} = 6 \times 13.5 = 81.$$

The sum for the whole year is therefore $84 + 66 + 81 = 231$, as shown in the table.
The cost will be £20 × 231 = £4620.

Plan B: From January to June the totals form an AP of six terms with common difference -4, first term 27, last term 7, so the sum is

$$6\frac{(27 + 7)}{2} = 6 \times 17 = 102.$$

July must be treated on its own, contributing two unit months.

August to December forms another AP of five terms with common difference -5, first term 21, last term 1, so its sum is

$$5\frac{(21 + 1)}{2} = 5 \times 11 = 55.$$

The sum for the whole year is therefore $102 + 2 + 55 = 159$, as shown in the table.
The cost will be £20 × 159 = £3180, which is £1440 less than that for Plan A, so it would be sensible to adopt Plan B. This example illustrates the general principle that storage costs are increased by ordering stock before it is absolutely necessary.

A4.4 The basic equation for compound interest tells us that

$$A_n = P(1 + i)^n.$$

We know that $n = 4$ and, working in units of £1000, $P = 3$ and $A_4 = 5$, so

$$5 = 3(1 + i)^4.$$

The problem is to find i, so we rearrange the last equation to read

$$(1 + i)^4 = 5/3.$$

Then we take the fourth root of each side:

$$1 + i = (5/3)^{1/4} = 1.1362 \quad \text{to four decimal places.}$$

Hence the company would just get its £5000 in 4 years if the interest rate were 13.62% p.a. To allow for possible price increases, it would be prudent to try to obtain a rate higher than 13.62%.

A4.5 This is a problem about *present values*. Although the management offer totals £2.0 million as opposed to the £1.7 million offered by the engineering company, it is not all available immediately. To make a valid comparison of the bids, we must therefore find the present value of each of the proposed annual payments, that is the amount of money that we would need to invest now in order to produce £0.25 million at the time of payment.

To do this, we start with the basic formula for compound interest, but instead of P for 'Principal' we write PV for 'Present Value', that is the sum of money which if invested now at interest rate i would yield A_n in n years:

$$A_n = PV(1 + i)^n.$$

Rearranging this gives

$$PV = \frac{A_n}{(1 + i)^n}.$$

Putting $i = 0.15$ and working in £m units we can then find the PV of each annual payment by putting $n = 1, 2, 3, 4$ and each $A_n = 0.25$.

1st Payment	$PV_1 = 0.25/1.15$	$= 0.217\,391$
2nd Payment	$PV_2 = 0.25/1.15^2$	$= 0.189\,036$
3rd Payment	$PV_3 = 0.25/1.15^3$	$= 0.164\,379$
4th Payment	$PV_4 = 0.25/1.15^4$	$= 0.142\,938$
	Total	$= 0.713\,744.$

Rather than evaluate each of the four PV terms and then sum them, we could note that they form a GP with a constant common ratio $r = 1/1.15$ (which is less than 1) and first term $a = 0.25/1.15$. Hence formula (4.14) gives the sum of the four PV terms:

$$S_4 = \frac{0.25[1 - (1/1.15)^4]}{1.15[1 - (1/1.15)]} = 0.713\,745,$$

which is actually correct to six decimal places, unlike the previous result which was based on summing the four terms that had each been rounded to six decimal places before they were summed. If more than four equal payments had been involved, the method based on formula (4.14) would become even more attractive than the direct method by reason of its speed and accuracy.

Whichever method is used for summing the four PV terms, when the £1m cash is included the management's offer is therefore worth £1.713\,745m as opposed to the engineering company's £1.700\,000m. Other things being equal, the difference of nearly £14\,000 should secure the management control of Knudsen.

[Note that if the interest rate rose to 16% p.a. the total PV of the management's offer would fall slightly short of the £1.7m (check this for yourself), so the final decision may rest on a judgment about likely interest rates.]

Chapter 5

A5.3 (i) $f(x) = 2\ln(x - 1) + \ln(x + 1) - 2\ln(x^2 - 1)$.
Substitute $(x^2 - 1) = (x - 1)(x + 1)$:

$$f(x) = 2\ln(x - 1) + \ln(x + 1) - 2\ln[(x - 1)(x + 1)]$$
$$= 2\ln(x - 1) + \ln(x + 1) - 2[\ln(x - 1) + \ln(x + 1)]$$
$$= 2\ln(x - 1) + \ln(x + 1) - 2\ln(x - 1) - 2\ln(x + 1)$$
$$f(x) = -\ln(x + 1).$$

(ii) $f(x, y) = 2\log_a(x - y) + 3\log_a(x + y) - 2\log_a(x^2 - y^2)$.

Substitute $(x^2 - y^2) = (x - y)(x + y)$.

$$f(x, y) = 2\log_a(x - y) + 3\log_a(x + y) - 2\log_a[(x - y)(x + y)]$$
$$= 2\log_a(x - y) + 3\log_a(x + y) - 2[\log_a(x - y) + \log_a(x + y)]$$
$$= \log_a(x + y).$$

A5.4   Take logs of both sides.

$$\log(0.56^{x - 1}) = \log(0.37^{2x + 1})$$
$$(x - 1)\log(0.56) = (2x + 1)\log(0.37).$$

The above equation holds no matter what base is chosen.
If the base e is used:

$$(x - 1)[-0.5798] = (2x + 1)[-0.9943]$$
$$-0.5798x + 0.5798 = -1.9885x - 0.9943$$
$$+1.4087x = -1.5741$$

The solution is $x = -1.1174.$

If the base 10 is used:

$$(x - 1)[-0.2518] = (2x + 1)[-0.4318]$$
$$-0.2518x + 0.2518 = -0.8636x - 0.4318$$
$$0.6118x = -0.6836$$

The solution is $x = -1.1174.$

A5.5 $(0.35)^{x + 1} = (0.52)^{x - 1}$

$$(x + 1)\log(0.35) = (x - 1)\log(0.52).$$

Use either the base 10 or the base e.
If the base e is used:

$$(x + 1)[-1.0498] = (x - 1)[-0.6539]$$
$$0.3959x = -1.7037$$

247

The solution is $x = -4.3036$.

If the base 10 is used:

$$(x + 1)[-0.4559] = (x - 1)[-0.2840]$$
$$0.1719x = -0.7399$$

The solution is $x = -4.3042$.

The discrepancy between the two solutions is due to rounding errors. If greater accuracy is needed more decimal places should be used.

A5.6 $P = be^{ct}$.

where $b = £100$ and $c = 0.02$ per month.

The growth function is

$$P = 100e^{0.02t}$$

(i)   When $t = 6$ months

$$P = 100e^{0.02 \times 6} = £112.75.$$

(ii)   When $t = 18$ months

$$P = 100e^{0.02 \times 18} = £143.33.$$

These values can be confirmed from the graph.

A5.7   (i)   After 5 years

$$y = 10\,000e^{-0.1 \times 5} = £6065.31.$$

After 10 years

$$y = 10\,000e^{-0.1 \times 10} = £3678.79.$$

(ii)   If the asset halves in value $P = £5000$.

$$5000 = 10\,000e^{-0.1t}$$
$$0.5 = e^{-0.1t}$$

To find t use the method employed in Example 5.10. Since the equation involves an exponential the base e is used in this case.

$$\ln(0.5) = \ln(e^{-0.1t})$$
$$-0.6931 = -0.1t$$
$$t = 6.9315 \text{ years.}$$

(iii)   At the time $t = 0$ the value was £10 000. After 10 years the value was £3678.79, and therefore the loss in value over the 10 year period is the difference £6321.21.

A5.8 Put $N = 3000$ into the formula for N.

$$3000 = \frac{10\,000}{[1 + 9e^{-0.03t}]}$$

$$1 + 9e^{-0.03t} = \frac{10\,000}{3000} = 3.3333$$

$$9e^{-0.03t} = 2.3333$$

$$e^{-0.03t} = 0.2593.$$

Since the variable, t, is in the exponent (power) and the exponential term, e, is involved, take the logarithm to the base e of both sides of the equation.

$$-0.03t = \ln(0.2593) = -1.3499$$

$$t = -1.3499/(-0.03) = 44.9976.$$

It will take 45 months for the daily volume of traffic to reach 3000 vehicles.

A5.9 (i) (a) $658.5740 = 659$ rounded up to the nearest whole number.
(b) $361.4331 = 362$ rounded up to the nearest whole number.
(ii) This reduces to finding the solution to the equation.

$$0.5 = e^{-0.1t}$$

giving

$$t = 6.9315 = 7 \text{ years}$$

to the nearest whole number for the workforce to reduce to 600 people.
(iii) Use the same method as part (ii) above.
It will take $t = 24.8491 = 25$ months to the nearest whole number for the workforce to reduce to 100 people.

A.5.10 First put the given values for M, p, Q, i and s into the equation.

$$\exp(-r/M) = piQ/(sM)$$

$$\exp(-r/20) = \frac{12 \times 0.01 \times 200}{25 \times 20} = 0.048.$$

Next take the logarithm to the base e of both sides of the equation.

$$\frac{-r}{20} = \ln(0.048) = -3.0366$$

$$r = 60.731$$

or 61 items to the nearest whole number.

A6.4 The input–output model can be written as $\mathbf{Tx} = \mathbf{d}$. To solve this for $\mathbf{x}$, we premultiply both sides by $\mathbf{T}^{-1}$ to give $\mathbf{x} = \mathbf{T}^{-1}\mathbf{d}$.
With the first $\mathbf{d}$ vector: $\mathbf{x}' = [16.285\ 15.040\ 10.707]$.
With the second $\mathbf{d}$ vector: $\mathbf{x}' = [21.578\ 21.428\ 14.937]$.
Notice that in each case we have shown the transpose of $\mathbf{x}$ in order to save space by writing the result as a row vector.

A6.5 To check that $\mathbf{C}$ is the inverse of $\mathbf{A}$, use Rule 6.16. The rule tells us that, in this case, if we premultiply or postmultiply $\mathbf{A}$ by $\mathbf{C}$ the result should be an identity matrix. This multiplication will be simplest if the scalar factor 1/32 is kept outside the main body of $\mathbf{C}$ so that the product first appears as 1/32 outside a matrix with each component on the main diagonal equal to 32 and all other components equal to zero. The rule for multiplication by a scalar can then be applied to simplify this to an identity matrix.

$$\mathbf{CA} \quad \text{or} \quad \mathbf{AC} = \frac{1}{32}\begin{bmatrix} 32 & 0 & 0 \\ 0 & 32 & 0 \\ 0 & 0 & 32 \end{bmatrix} = \begin{bmatrix} 1 & 0 & 0 \\ 0 & 1 & 0 \\ 0 & 0 & 1 \end{bmatrix}.$$

250

The matrix equation $\mathbf{Ab} = \mathbf{g}$ is solved by premultiplying each side by $\mathbf{A}^{-1}$ to give $\mathbf{b} = \mathbf{A}^{-1}\mathbf{g}$. Again, keep the factor 1/32 outside until the final stage of calculation. The numerical result is that

$$\mathbf{b}' = (1/32)[224 \quad 480 \quad -64]$$
$$= [7.0 \quad 15.0 \quad -2.0].$$

Chapter 7

A7.1 (i) $dy/dx = 2 \times 2x^1 = 4x$; when $x = 2$ the gradient is 8.
    (ii) $dy/dx = 2x - 0 = 2x$; when $x = 3$ the slope is 6.
    (iii) $dy/dx = 2 + 2x$; when $x = 1$ the slope is 4.
    (iv) $dy/dx = 2 \times 5x = 10x$; when $x = 1$, the slope is 10.

A7.2 (i) $dy/dx = 8 \times 5x^7 = 40x^7$.
    (ii) $y = 6x^{-2}; dy/dx = 6 \times (-2)x^{-3} = -12x^{-3}$.
    (iii) $dy/dx = \frac{3}{4} \times 2x^{-1/4} = 1.5x^{-1/4}$.
    (iv) $dy/dx = \frac{1}{2} \times 10x^{-1/2} - \frac{1}{3} \times 9x^{-2/3} = 5x^{-1/2} - 3x^{-2/3}$.
    (v) $df(x)/dx = 24x^3 + 9x^2 - 4x + 5$.
    (vi) Divide through by x^2 to simplify:

$$f(x) = 7x - 5 - 6x^{-1} + 4x^{-2}.$$

$$\frac{df(x)}{dx} = 7 - (-1) \times 6x^{-2} + (-2) \times 4x^{-3}$$
$$= 7x + 6x^{-2} - 8x^{-3}.$$

Hence

$$\frac{df(x)}{dx} = 7x + \frac{6}{x^2} - \frac{8}{x^3}.$$

A7.3 (i) $dy/dx = 2 \times 6e^{2x} = 12e^{2x}$.
    (ii) $dy/dx = 3 \times 1/x = 3/x$.
    (iii) $dy/dx = -4 + 3e^{-4x} = -12e^{-4x}$.
    (iv) $dy/dx = \frac{1}{2} \times 2e^{x/2} = e^{x/2}$.
    (v) $dy/dx = 12e^{2x} + 3/x$.
    (vi) $dy/dx = 4 \times 3/x = 12/x$.
    (vii) $dy/dx = 4 \times 1/x = 4/x$.

A7.4 (i) The rate at which D varies with t is given by

$$\frac{dD}{dt} = 50 - 0.16t.$$

(ii) Draw a graph of cumulative demand against time and see where the decrease in D starts. This graph is shown in Figure A3 below.

From the graph it can be seen that D starts to decrease around 312 days, and thus the model is only valid for times of less than 312 days.

If a more accurate value for the point at which this cumulative demand starts to fall is required, the methods of Chapter 8 must be used. This alternative approach is developed in the next chapter.

(iii) There were 7500 items initially and the stock has dropped to 100 items. This means that 7400 items have been demanded. We now need to find the values of t for which $D = 7400$. This means solving the equation

$$7400 = 50t - 0.08t^2.$$

This gives the solutions $t = 240.6930$ and $t = 384.3070$.

Since the model is only valid for values of time less than 312 days only the solution $t = 240.693$ is feasible. Rounding to the nearest day, the answer is therefore 241 days.

Chapter 8

A8.1 (i) $y = 5(2x^3 + 1)^8$.

Use the 'function of a function rule'.

$$\frac{dy}{dx} = 8 \times 5(2x^3 + 1)^7 (6x^2) = 240x^2(2x^3 + 1)^7.$$

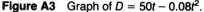

Figure A3 Graph of $D = 50t - 0.08t^2$.

(ii) $y = 3(x^2 + 1)^{-3/2}$.

$$\frac{dy}{dx} = \frac{-3}{2} \times 3(x^2 + 1)^{-5/2}(2x) = \frac{-9x}{(x^2 + 1)^{5/2}}.$$

A8.2 (i) $y = (1 + x^2)^{1/2}$.

$$\frac{dy}{dx} = \frac{1}{2} \times (1 + x^2)^{-1/2}(2x) = x(1 + x^2)^{-1/2}.$$

$$\frac{d^2y}{dx^2} = \frac{d}{dx}\left[\frac{dy}{dx}\right] = 1.(1 + x^2)^{-1/2} + x\left[\frac{-1}{2}(1 + x^2)^{-3/2}(2x)\right]$$

$$= (1 + x^2)^{-1/2} - x^2(1 + x^2)^{-3/2}.$$

This can be simplified to

$$\frac{d^2y}{dx^2} = \frac{1}{(1 + x^2)^{3/2}}.$$

(ii) $y = 2x^2(1 + x)^4$.

Use the 'product rule' with $u = 2x^2$ and $v = (1 + x)^4$.

$$\frac{dy}{dx} = 4x(1 + x)^4 + 2x^2 \times 4(1 + x)^3$$

$$= 4x(1 + x)^4 + 8x^2(1 + x)^3.$$

$$\frac{d^2y}{dx^2} = 4(1 + x)^4 + 16x(1 + x)^3 + 16x(1 + x)^3 + 8x^2 \times 3(1 + x)^2$$

$$= 4(1 + x)^4 + 32(1 + x)^3 + 24x^2(1 + x)^2$$
$$= 4(1 + x)^2[(1 + x)^2 + 8x(1 + x) + 6x^2]$$
$$= 4(1 + x)^2[1 + 10x + 15x^2].$$

(iii) $y = 3xe^{4x}$.

Use the 'product rule' with $u = 3x$ and $v = e^{4x}$.

$$\frac{dy}{dx} = 3e^{4x} + 3x[4e^{4x}]$$

$$= 3e^{4x} + 12xe^{4x}$$
$$= [3 + 12x]e^{4x}.$$

Use the 'product rule' again with $u = (3 + 12x)$ and $v = e^{4x}$.

$$\frac{d^2y}{dx^2} = \frac{d}{dx}\left[\frac{dy}{dx}\right] = 12e^{4x} + (3 + 12x)4e^{4x}$$

$$= e^{4x}[12 + 12 + 48x]$$

$$= 24e^{4x}(1 + 2x).$$

A8.3 $y = 3x^{1/2}(1 + x^2)^{-2}.$

Use the 'product rule' with $u = 3x^{1/2}$ and $v = (1 + x^2)^{-2}$.

$$\frac{dy}{dx} = \frac{1}{2} \times 3x^{-1/2}(1 + x^2)^{-2} + 3x^{1/2} \times (-2)(1 + x^2)^{-3} \times (2x)$$

$$= \frac{3}{2}x^{1/2}(1 + x^2)^{-2} - 12x^{3/2}(1 + x^2)^{-3}$$

$$\frac{dy}{dx} = \frac{3}{2x^{1/2}(1 + x^2)^2} - \frac{12x^{3/2}}{(1 + x^2)^3}.$$

A8.4 (i) A minimum at $(3, -6)$.
(ii) A maximum at $(-2, 21)$; a minimum at $(2, -11)$.
(iii) A point of inflexion at $(1, 0)$.

A8.5 (i) The stationary points are the points where $dTC/dq = 0$. That is, the solution to the equation

$$\frac{dTC}{dq} = 3q^2 - 24q + 21 = 0.$$

Solve this equation either by factorizing or using the standard form for the solution of a quadratic equation.
The solutions are $q = 7$ and $q = 1$ with the corresponding total cost values of $TC = 7$ and $TC = 115$ respectively.
Next determine the nature of the stationary point by examining the sign of the second derivative

$$\frac{d^2TC}{dq^2} = 6q - 24.$$

When $q = 7$, the second derivative is positive indicating that the point $q = 7$, $TC = 7$ is a minimum.
When $q = 1$, the second derivative is negative indicating that the point $q = 1$, $TC = 115$ is a maximum.

(ii) The marginal cost is defined as $MC = dTC/dt$. We have already found this in part (i).

$$MC = 3q^2 - 24q + 21.$$

To find the value of q which minimizes this differentiate with respect to q and solve the equation

$$\frac{dMC}{dq} = 6q - 24 = 0.$$

When $q = 4$ the marginal cost is a minimum.
(The sign of $d^2 MC/dq^2 = 6$ is positive.)

(iii) The average cost per can is given by TC/q, that is the total cost divided by the number of cans produced.
When $q = 7$, $TC = 7$ and the average cost is $7/7 = 1$ per can.
When $q = 4$, $TC = 61$ and the average cost is $61/4 = 15.25$ per can.

Clearly the average cost is lower when the total cost, TC, is lowest. (To find the lowest possible average cost it would be necessary to minimize the function TC/q.)

A8.6 To find the value of q which will minimize C we need to solve the equation $dC/dQ = 0$.

$$C = kMQ^{-1} + pM + 0.5piQ$$

where Q is the only variable.

$$\frac{dC}{dQ} = -kMQ^{-2} + 0.5pi.$$

Solve this equation

$$\frac{-kM}{Q^2} + 0.5pi = 0.$$

The solution is

$$Q = \sqrt{[2kM/(pi)]}.$$

Substitute the given values for k, M, and i to obtain the solution $Q = 40.8248$ or 41 to the nearest whole number. When $Q = 41$, then $C = 244.899$. When $Q = 40.8248$, d^2C/dQ^2 is positive, and hence the point is a minimum.

A8.7 (i) When $t = 10$ weeks

$$S(10) = \frac{300\,000}{1 + 500\exp(-0.3 \times 10)} = 11\,585.904.$$

Similarly, $S(52) = 299\,974.82$.

(ii) The rate of change is dS/dt.

$$S = 300\,000[1 + 500e^{-0.3t}]^{-1}$$

$$\frac{dS}{dt} = 300\,000(-1)[1 + 500e^{-0.3t}]^{-2} \times [500(-0.3)e^{-0.3t}]$$

$$= \frac{300\,000 \times 150e^{-0.3t}}{[1 + 500e^{-0.3t}]^2}.$$

When $t = 52$ weeks, then $dS/dt = 7.5534$ per week or 8 per week to the nearest whole number. If the increase per week in cumulative sales is only 8 per week 52 weeks after the launch and dS/dt is getting smaller as time goes on, then after 52 weeks there will be little further increase in the cumulative sales.

A8.8 The net benefit is

$$N = B - C = -90 + 25t - 1.5t^2.$$

N will be a maximum when $dN/dt = 0$.

$$\frac{dN}{dt} = 25 - 3t.$$

Thus $dN/dt = 0$ when $t = 25/3 = 8.33$ hours per year. When $t = 8.33$, then $N = 14.166$ in units of £1000.

A8.9 $\quad A = 3000[1 + 25e^{-0.2t}]^{-1}$

$$\frac{dA}{dt} = 3000(-1)[1 + 25e^{-0.2t}]^{-2} \times [25(-0.2)e^{-0.2t}]$$

$$= \frac{15\,000e^{-0.2t}}{[1 + 25e^{-0.2t}]^2}.$$

(i) When $t = 10$ days, then $dA/dt = 105.65 = 106$ to the nearest whole number. When $t = 21$ days, $dA/dt = 118.99 = 119$ to the nearest whole number. When $t = 35$ days, $dA/dt = 13.08 = 13$ to the nearest whole number.

(ii) The rate of increase in the cumulative total of applications has reached a peak somewhere between 10 and 35 days and is slowing down as t increases. With 100 posts left to fill after 35 days and applications increasing at a rate of 13 per day after 35 days it is unlikely that the original advertisement will attract sufficient applicants to fill the posts.

Solutions to additional examples

Chapter 9

A9.1

$$\int_{-1}^{1} 2x \, dx = \left[\frac{2x^2}{2} \right]_{-1}^{1} = \left[x^2 \right]_{-1}^{1}$$

$$= 1^2 - (-1)^2$$

$$= 0.$$

The area represented by this integral is shaded on the graph in Figure A4. The area consists of two parts of equal size, one below the x-axis and the other above the x-axis. The area above is positive while that below is negative, so the sum of the two areas is zero, as shown by the integration process.

A9.2

$$\int_{-1}^{1} 2x^2 \, dx = \left[2 \times \frac{x^3}{3} \right]_{-1}^{1}$$

$$= 2 \times \frac{1^3}{3} - 2 \times \frac{(-1)^3}{3} = \frac{4}{3}.$$

The graph is shown in Figure A5.

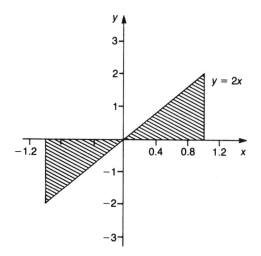

Figure A4 Graph of $y = 2x$. Shaded area is $\int_{-1}^{1} 2x \, dx$.

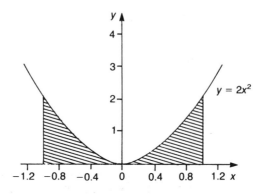

Figure A5   Graph of $y = 2x^2$. Shaded area is $\int_{-1}^{1} 2xu22\ dx$.

Use Rule 9.1 and remember the rules for multiplying negative terms. Here the area between the curve and the x-axis is in two equal-sized parts, above the x-axis to either side of the origin. Since the two parts are both above the x-axis they are both positive and the result could have been found by doubling the integral from $x = 0$ to $x = 1$.

A9.3   The graph of the curve $y = 2x^3$ is similar to that described above for A9.1.

$$\int_{-1}^{1} 2x^3\,dx = \left[2 \times \frac{x^4}{4}\right]_{-1}^{1} = \left[2 \times \frac{1^4}{4}\right] - \left[2 \times \frac{(-1)^4}{4}\right]$$

$$= \frac{2}{4} - \frac{2}{4} = 0.$$

The remarks about positive and negative areas in the solution to A9.1 also apply here.

A9.4   The graph of the curve $y = 1/x^2$ is shown in Figure A6.
   The first step in the integration procedure is to remove the fraction in x^2 by rewriting the term as x^{-2}. Then Rule 9.1 is used.

$$\int_{0.1}^{1} \frac{1}{x^2}\,dx = \int_{0.1}^{1} x^{-2}\,dx = \left[\frac{x^{-2+1}}{-1}\right]_{0.1}^{1}$$

$$= -1 + (0.1)^{-1} = 9.$$

Examine the graph in Figure A6. As the value of x approaches zero the value of y approaches infinity (any number divided by zero is equal to infinity). Although some variables in the management field are very large,

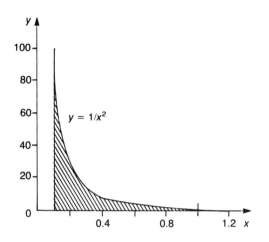

Figure A6 Graph of $y = 1/x^2$. Shaded area is $\int_{0.1}^{1} 1 x^2 \, dx$.

in practice they cannot be infinite. Hence the integral from $x = 0$ to $x = 1.0$ could not arise in practice in this environment.

A9.5

$$y = \int (3x^2 + 2x + 3) \, dx = \frac{3x^3}{3} + \frac{2x^2}{2} + 3x + C$$

$$= x^3 + x^2 + 3x + C.$$

Since $y = 6$ when $x = 1$,

$$6 = 1^3 + 1^2 + 3 \times 1 + C$$

and $C = 1$, the function is

$$y = x^3 + x^2 + 3x + 1.$$

A9.6 (i)

$$\int_0^1 e^{2x} \, dx = \left[\frac{e^{2x}}{2} \right]_0^1 = \frac{e^2}{2} - \frac{e^0}{2} = \frac{e^2}{2} - \frac{1}{2} \quad \text{since } e^0 = 1.$$

$$= \frac{1}{2}(e^2 - 1) = 3.1945.$$

(ii)

$$\int_0^1 e^{-2x} \, dx = \left[\frac{-e^{-2x}}{2} \right]_0^1 = \frac{-e^{-2}}{2} - \left(\frac{-e^0}{2} \right)$$

$$= \frac{1}{2}(1 - e^{-2}) = 0.4323.$$

The Essence of Mathematics for Business

(iii) $\int_1^\infty e^{-2x}\,dx = \left[\dfrac{-e^{-2x}}{2}\right]_1^\infty = \dfrac{-e^{-\infty}}{2} - \left(-\dfrac{e^{-2}}{2}\right)$

$$= \dfrac{e^{-2}}{2} = 0.0677 \quad \text{since } e^{-\infty} = 0.$$

The principles to be used here are similar to those described in Example 9.10.

A9.7 (i) $\int_{0.1}^1 \dfrac{1}{x}\,dx = \left[\ln(x)\right]_{0.1}^1$

$$= 0 - (-2.3026) = 2.3026.$$

(ii) $\int_1^{20} \dfrac{1}{x}\,dx = \left[\ln(x)\right]_1^{20} = 2.9957 - 0 = 2.9957.$

(iii) $\int_{-2}^2 (x^2 + e^{3x} + 2)\,dx = \left[\dfrac{x^3}{3} + \dfrac{e^{3x}}{3} + 2x\right]_{-2}^2$

$$= \left(\dfrac{8}{3} + \dfrac{1}{3} \times 403.4288 + 4\right)$$

$$- \left(-\dfrac{8}{3} + \dfrac{1}{3} \times 0.0025 - 4\right)$$

$$= 147.8105.$$

(iv) $\int \left(\dfrac{1}{x} + \dfrac{e^{x/2}}{2}\right)dx = \ln(x) + e^{x/2} + C.$

A9.8 The average number of future years expected is

$$\dfrac{1}{p(x)} \cdot \int_x^{20} p(t)\,dt$$

where x is the present age which in this case is $x = 8$ years. We have

$p(x) = 1 - 0.025x - 0.001\,25x^2$

$= 1 - 0.025 \times 8 - 0.001\,25 \times 8^2 = 0.72.$

Now we need to find the value of the integral

$$\int_8^{20} p(t) \cdot dt = \int_8^{20} (1 - 0.025t - 0.001\,25t^2) \cdot dt$$

$$= \left[t - 0.025 \times \frac{t^2}{2} - 0.001\,25\,\frac{t^3}{3} \right]_8^{20}$$

$$= 11.6667 - 6.9867$$

$$= 4.6800.$$

The expected number of years can now be found by substituting into

$$\frac{1}{p(x)} \cdot \int_x^{20} p(t) \cdot dt = \frac{4.68}{0.72} = 6.5 \text{ years.}$$

A machine which is now aged 8 years can be expected to work for 6.5 more years.

It is worth noting here that although the question looks difficult at first sight this is not really so. By thinking in terms of words initially and then working each component out in turn the answer can be found relatively easily.

A9.9   First evaluate the integral in terms of t and then substitute the specified values of t into the formula for H to find the cost of holding the land for the specified periods of time.

$$H = \int_0^t 8e^{-0.2x}\,dx = \left[8\frac{e^{-0.2x}}{-0.2} \right]_0^t = \left[-40e^{-0.2x} \right]_0^t$$

$$= -40e^{-0.2t} + 40.$$

When $t = 3$ years, then $H = 18.0475$.
When $t = 5$ years, then $H = 25.2848$.
When $t = 10$ years, then $H = 34.5866$.

A9.10 $$TC = \int (2x^2 - 16x + 11)\,dx = \frac{2x^3}{3} - \frac{16x^2}{2} + 11x + C.$$

To find C put $TC = 50$ and $x = 0$ into the above formula for TC. This results in the formula for the total cost

$$TC = \frac{2x^3}{3} - 8x^2 + 11x + 50.$$

A9.11 Call the daily demand for the product D. The rate of increase is

$$\frac{dD}{dt} = 100 - 16t - 0.06t^2.$$

We want to find the formula for D. Integrate dD/dt with respect to t.

$$D = \int (100 - 16t - 0.06t^2)\,dt$$

$$= 100t - \frac{16t^2}{2} - \frac{0.06t^3}{3} + C.$$

To find the value of C substitute $t = 4$ and $D = 1500$ in the formula for D. This gives the formula for D as

$$D = 100t - 8t^2 - 0.02t^3 + 1229.28.$$

A9.12 First evaluate the integral in terms of the limits of integration, A and B.

$$P = \int_A^B 0.0005\exp(-0.0005t)\,dt.$$

$$= -e^{-0.0005B} + e^{-0.0005A},$$

where P is the average proportion of tubes failing between $t = A$ and $t = B$ hours. We want to find the average proportion failing between $t = 0$ and $t = 24 \times 365 = 8760$ hours, that is $A = 0$ and $B = 8760$ hours. Putting these values for A and B into the formula above for P gives

$$P = 0.9875.$$

In other words, on average 98.75% of these fluorescent tubes will fail within 1 year of installation.

Now consider the new tubes. Use the same procedure to find PN, the average proportion of failures for the new tube.

$$PN = \int_A^B 0.0001\exp(-0.0001t)\,dt.$$

$$= -e^{-0.0001B} + e^{-0.0001A}.$$

Put $A = 0$ and $B = 8760$ in the formula for PN to obtain

$$PN = 0.5836.$$

In other words, an average 58.36% of the new tubes would fail within one year of installation, a great improvement on the 98.75% with the old tubes. Even paying 20% more for the new tubes, ignoring labour costs and so on, it makes economic sense to change to the new tubes.

Index